IMAGES
of America

GLENWOOD

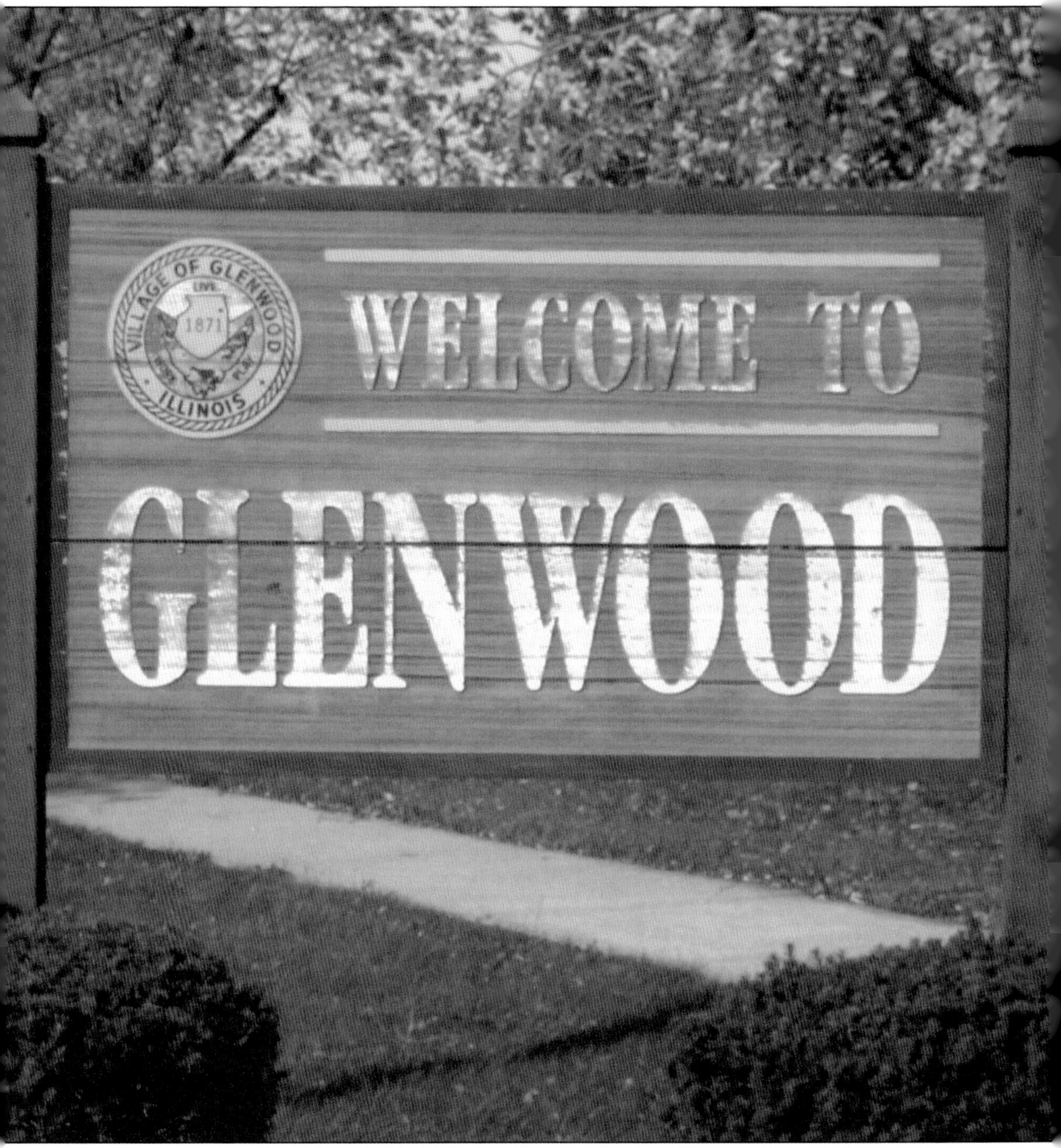

Glenwood is a village in Cook County, Illinois. It is partly surrounded by Cook County Forest Preserves. The population was 9,000 at the 2000 census. (Photograph by the author.)

On the Cover: In this c. 1945 photograph is Voelker's Service Station, which was located at 151 Glenwood Avenue. (Courtesy of the Glenwood Historical Society.)

IMAGES
of America

GLENWOOD

Ken Bult

ARCADIA
PUBLISHING

ISBN 978-0-7385-8323-5

Published by Arcadia Publishing
Charleston, South Carolina

Printed in the United States of America

Library of Congress Control Number: 2011920927

For all general information, please contact Arcadia Publishing:
Telephone 843-853-2070
Fax 843-853-0044
E-mail sales@arcadiapublishing.com
For customer service and orders:
Toll-Free 1-888-313-2665

Visit us on the Internet at www.arcadiapublishing.com

For my girls, Taylor and Kaylee

Contents

Acknowledgments 6

Introduction 7

1. Old Glenwood 9
2. Brookwood School 43
3. The Glenwood School for Boys and Girls 69
4. Mount Glenwood Cemetery 121

ACKNOWLEDGMENTS

As much as I tried my hardest to make this book free of errors, I apologize in advance for any that may have slipped in despite my efforts. That being said, I would like to offer my thanks to the following people, without whose help this project would have been impossible: Layle Irwin of the Glenwood Historical Society; Sergio Rodriquez and Crystal Phillips from the Glenwood School for Boys and Girls; Dr. Pamela Hollich and Debbie Young of Brookwood School District No. 167; Tammecia Smith from Mount Glenwood Memory Gardens; Jeff Ruetsche at Arcadia Publishing; Darlene Uhter, friend, neighbor, and my former school bus driver; my mother, Kay Bult; and my wife and research assistant, Carol.

The following sources have been used: L. Aumund Andre's 1987 *Glenwood: Boys and Dogs Have Right of Way: The First Hundred Years of Glenwood School for Boys* published by Glenwood Press; www.majortaylorassociation.org/biography.htm; and www.mtglenwood.com/history.htm.

INTRODUCTION

The village of Glenwood is about 23 miles south of Chicago and was originally founded as Hickory Bend. Surrounded by forest preserves, some of which are named for early settlers, it is a quiet community with tree-lined streets. The Glenwood Shoreline is an ancient one that represented the edge of Lake Chicago. It is named after Glenwood—not the other way around. The shoreline was formed when the lake, which was higher during the last Ice Age, receded and left behind a sand ridge. This ridge can be seen clearly in Glenwood and along the Glenwood-Dyer Road into Indiana. According to the US Census Bureau, the village has a total area of 2.7 square miles.

In 1838, Job Campbell and John Barton were the first white men to settle in the area. Campbell and O.R. Axtell founded Hickory Bend in 1846 in the part of town that is now known as Old Glenwood. This was, of course, long before the subdivisions of Glenwood Forest, Glenwood Manor, Glenwood Estates, and Brookwood Point were even conceived. The name was changed from Hickory Bend to Glenwood in 1871. On March 5, 1871, a post office was established, with Henry K. Axtell as postmaster. It was Job Campbell and Flores Young that requested the village be surveyed and its name changed to Glenwood. Campbell and Young Streets still run down either side of the railroad tracks.

Other early settlers who came to Hickory Bend included Caleb Sweet, Claus Jurgensen, Joseph Kinsley, William Wilkie, Henry Kaiser, James Hemingway, Richard Hemingway, Fremont Holbrook, Clark Holbrook, Thomas Dyer, Julius Wadsworth, John Finn, Sheldon James, and Samuel Peck.

Glenwood has come a long way from the days when it was known as Hickory Bend, in large part due to the arrival of the railroad. The Chicago, Danville and Vincennes Railroad (later the Chicago and Eastern Illinois Railroad) decided to lay tracks through Hickory Bend and along the lines from Chicago to Momence. The railroad incorporated on February 16, 1865, and began its work laying tracks south from Dolton, Illinois, on May 21, 1869. By the time the main line was completed in 1872, Hickory Bend had changed its name to Glenwood. Service started October 10, 1869, between Momence and Chicago.

In 1847, an inn was one of the first buildings constructed in Hickory Bend. This inn would later become Hottinger's Garden and then the Fireside Chalet.

Glenwood was a stop on the Underground Railroad. Escaped slaves and their conductors would stop at the inn before moving on, often by way of the nearby railroad.

Hickory Bend children attended a log cabin school built in 1850. It was about one and a half miles east of the village. In 1895, the Brookwood School District was formed, and the first brick school was constructed at the meeting of Glenwood-Lansing and Glenwood-Dyer Roads where they merge into Main Street. That building is still standing.

The first birth and death recorded in the Hickory Bend settlement were of Thomas and Mary Borrows's infant daughter, who was both born and died in 1855.

By 1880, Glenwood was becoming a busy community. In addition to two inns, there was also a saloon and a general store. In 1889, Milton George donated 300 acres of farmland known as Rural Glen to what would one day become the Glenwood School for Boys and Girls. North of town is the Mount Glenwood Memory Gardens, a cemetery that has traditionally been African American and where several prominent people are buried.

A Metra SouthEast Service commuter rail station on Main Street at the old Chicago and Eastern Illinois Railroad tracks is in the planning stage right now. Come visit Glenwood, a town with a rich past and a promising future.

One

OLD GLENWOOD

Old Glenwood roughly includes the area west from Cottage Grove Avenue to the Glenwood School for Boys and Girls entrance, excluding the Glenwood Forest and Glenwood Estates subdivisions. Glenwood-Dyer Road forms the southern border, and Sweet and Jurgensen Woods served as the northern edge of town. It was not that long ago that this was all of Glenwood. With the arrival of developers, Old Glenwood became surrounded by subdivisions. The population jumped from 900 in the early 1960s to 9,000 with the 2000 census, peaking out at just over 10,000 in 1980. Hottinger's Garden is long gone, replaced by Nugent Square. Jurgensen's General Store at the corner of Young and Main Streets is now the popular restaurant Gabe's Place, but the village hall is still located in Old Glenwood. The original brick Brookwood School is still standing in Old Glenwood, as is the 1940s version of St. John Church, even though the congregation itself has moved to a new location just east of Cottage Grove Avenue near Glenwood Lansing Road.

Early Glenwood depended heavily on the railroad, and the tracks still run right through the center of town. Several well-maintained older homes still line Main Street between Campbell Street and Wabash Avenue. The Little Brown Church is now white but still looks much the same nonetheless. Sanfratello's has been at 127 West Main Street for so long now (opening in 1969) that it is hard to remember when it was not there. Starting in a converted house in the early days of the restaurant, one might find oneself eating pizza in a former bedroom. Sanfratello's has expanded from a place that could seat 20 to one that can hold 300, and all without taking away from the character of Main Street in Old Glenwood. Glenwood Oaks, located at 106 North Main Street, was known as Glenwood Gardens in 1925. It later went on to become Gasper's Spa in 1937 and Poor Richards in 1954. Today, it is the Glenwood Oaks and is still serving fine dining in Old Glenwood, right next door to the Glenwood Woods Forest Preserve.

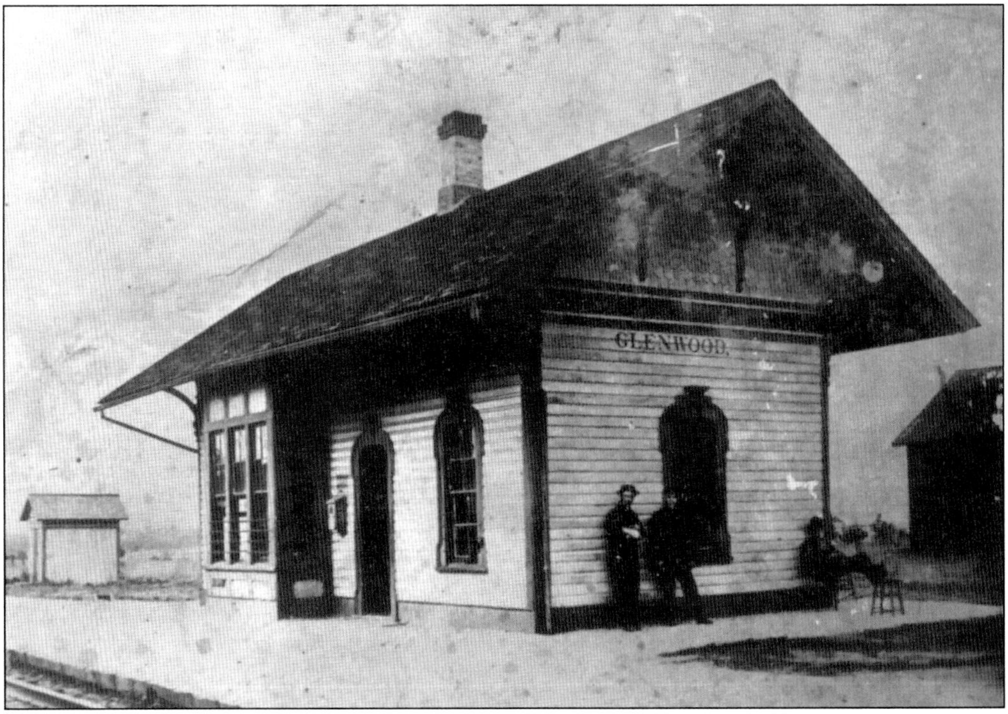

The Chicago, Danville and Vincennes Railroad decided to lay tracks through Hickory Bend and along the lines from Chicago to Momence. The railroad incorporated on February 16, 1865, and began its work, laying tracks south from Dolton, on May 21, 1869. By the time the main line was completed in 1872, Hickory Bend changed its name to Glenwood. Service had started October 10, 1869, between Momence and Chicago. (Courtesy of the Glenwood Historical Society.)

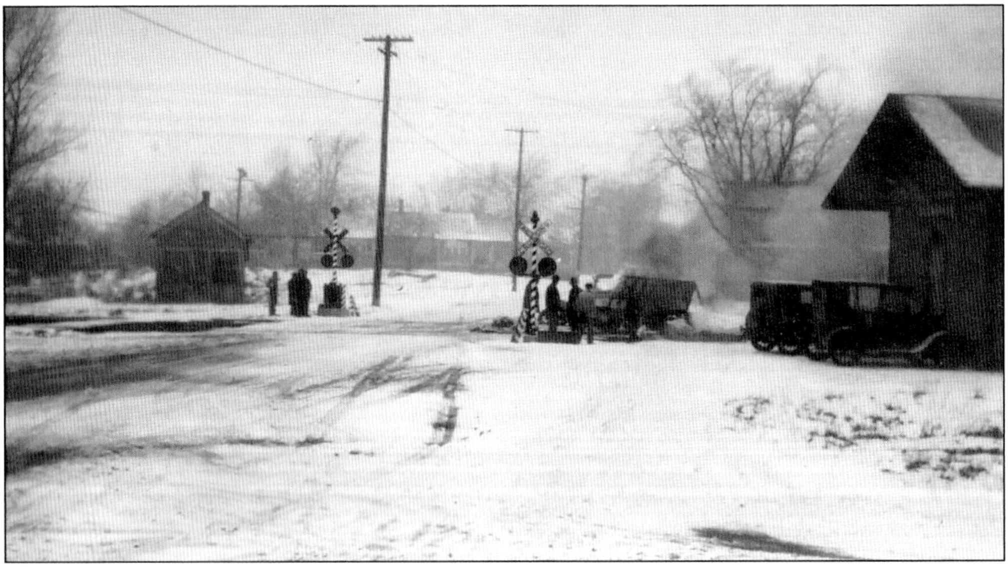

Here is an early photograph of the Chicago and Eastern Illinois Railroad crossing in Glenwood near Campbell Street. (Courtesy of the Glenwood Historical Society.)

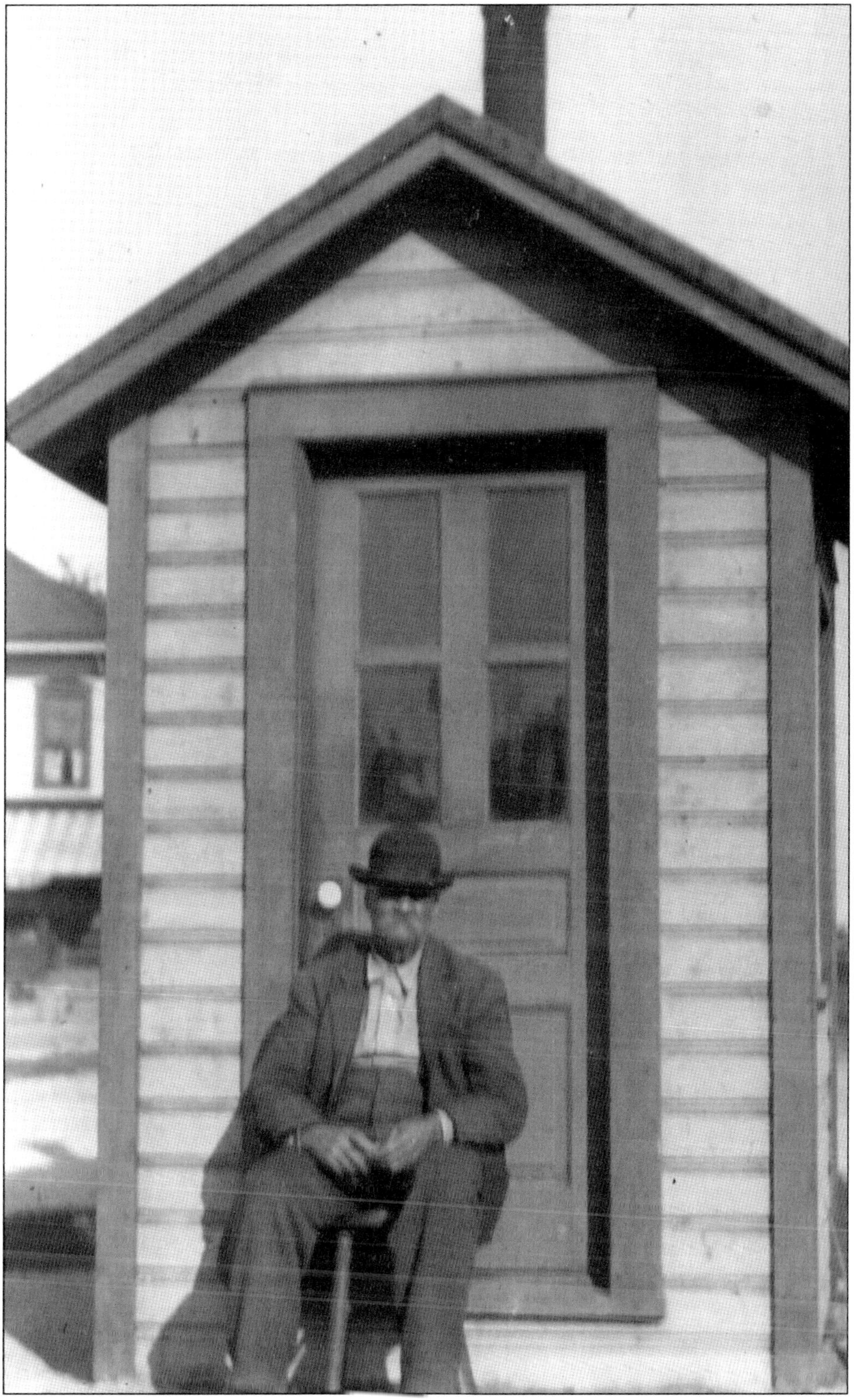

Flagman G.W. Pearson is pictured on duty at the Chicago and Eastern Illinois Railroad crossing in Glenwood. (Courtesy of the Glenwood Historical Society.)

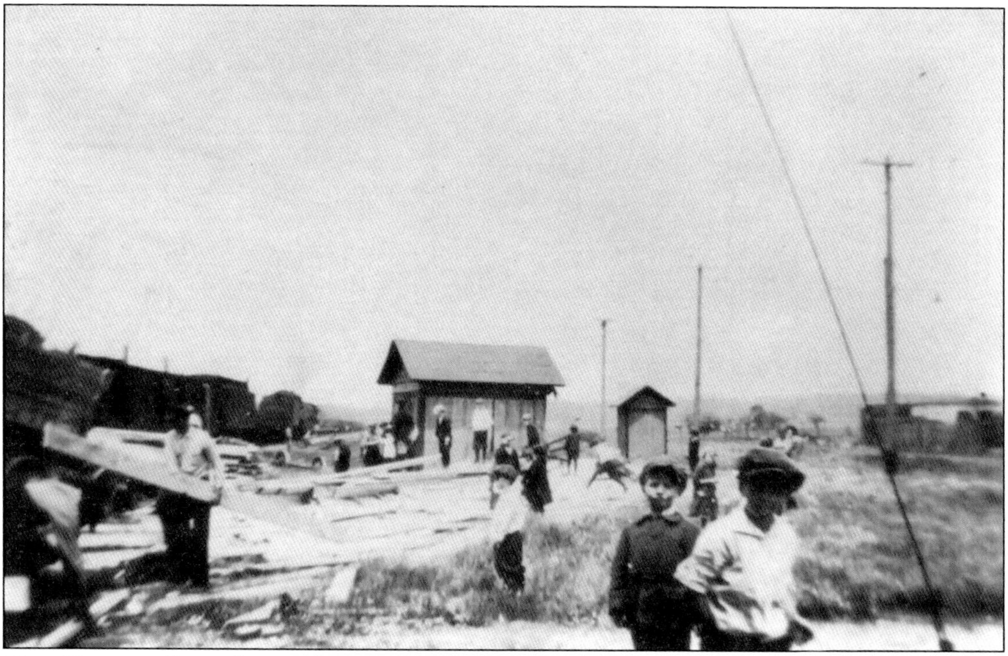

The Chicago, Danville and Vincennes Railroad became the Chicago and Nashville, and then in 1877, it became the Chicago and Eastern Illinois Railway. (Courtesy of the Glenwood Historical Society.)

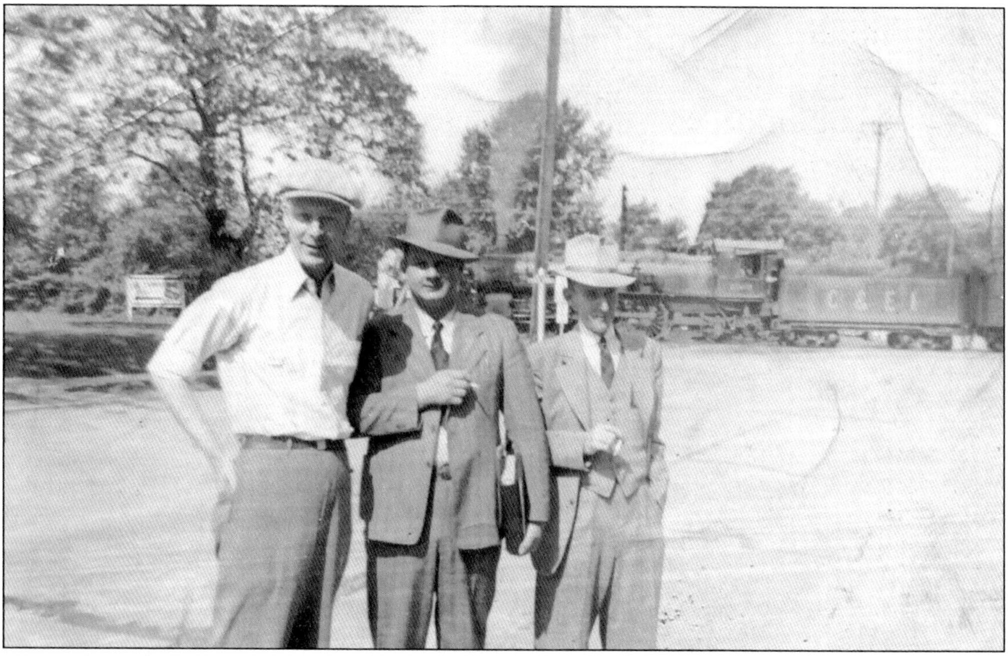

Posing for a photograph on Main Street in front of Jurgensen's store are, from left to right, Nate Jurgensen, Coke Nelson, and Bill Davis. One can see a Chicago and Eastern Illinois Railroad train running through town in the background. (Courtesy of the Glenwood Historical Society.)

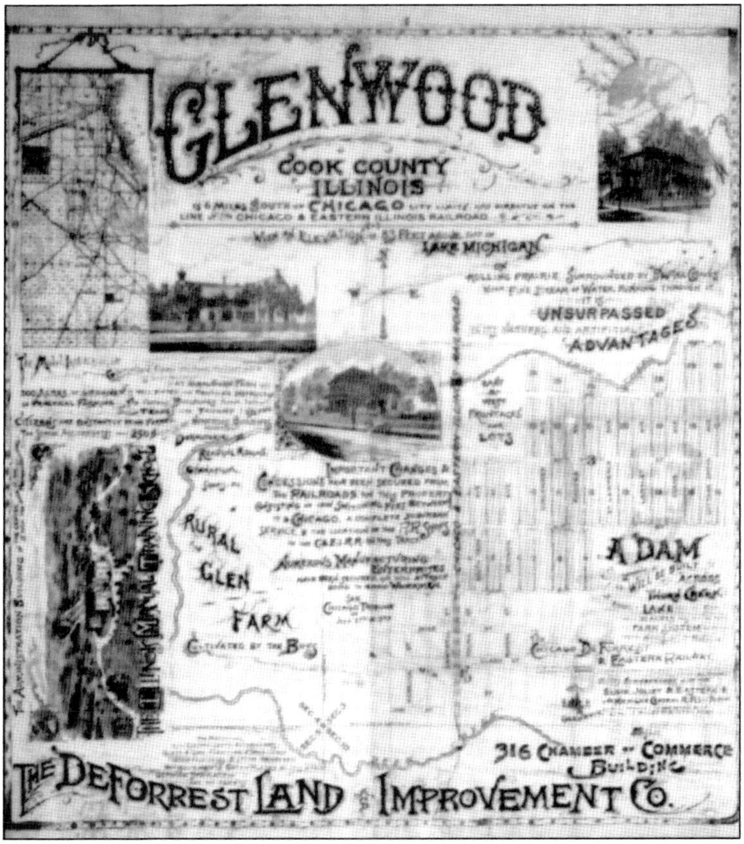

Rolling prairie is surrounded by beautiful groves with a fine stream of water running through. It is unsurpassed in its natural and man-made advantages. (Courtesy of the Glenwood School for Boys and Girls.)

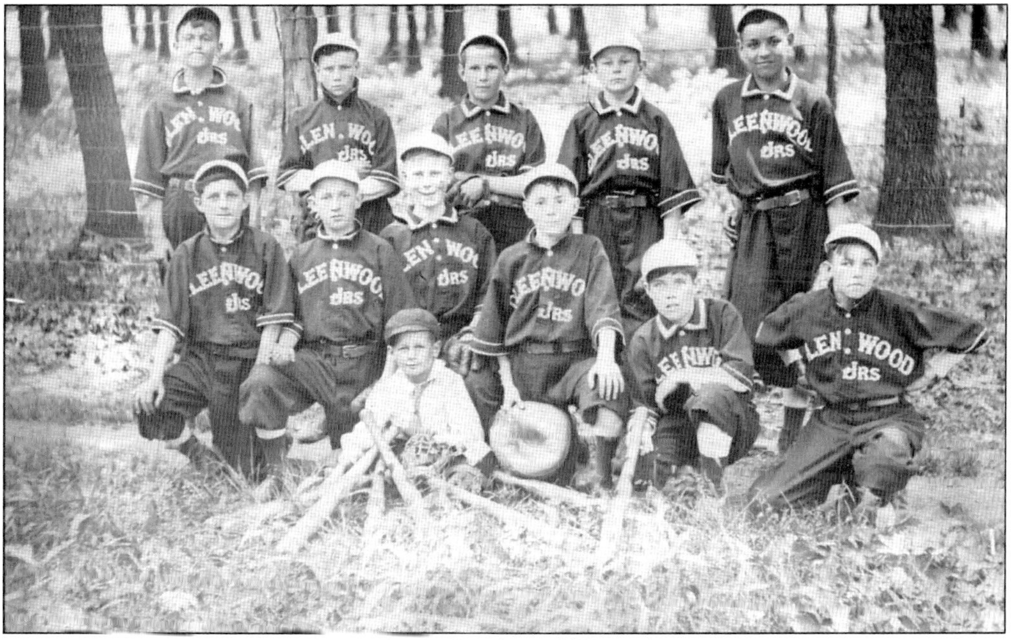

The Glenwood Nine are ready to play ball. About 500 residents incorporated Glenwood as a village in 1903. (Courtesy of the Glenwood Historical Society.)

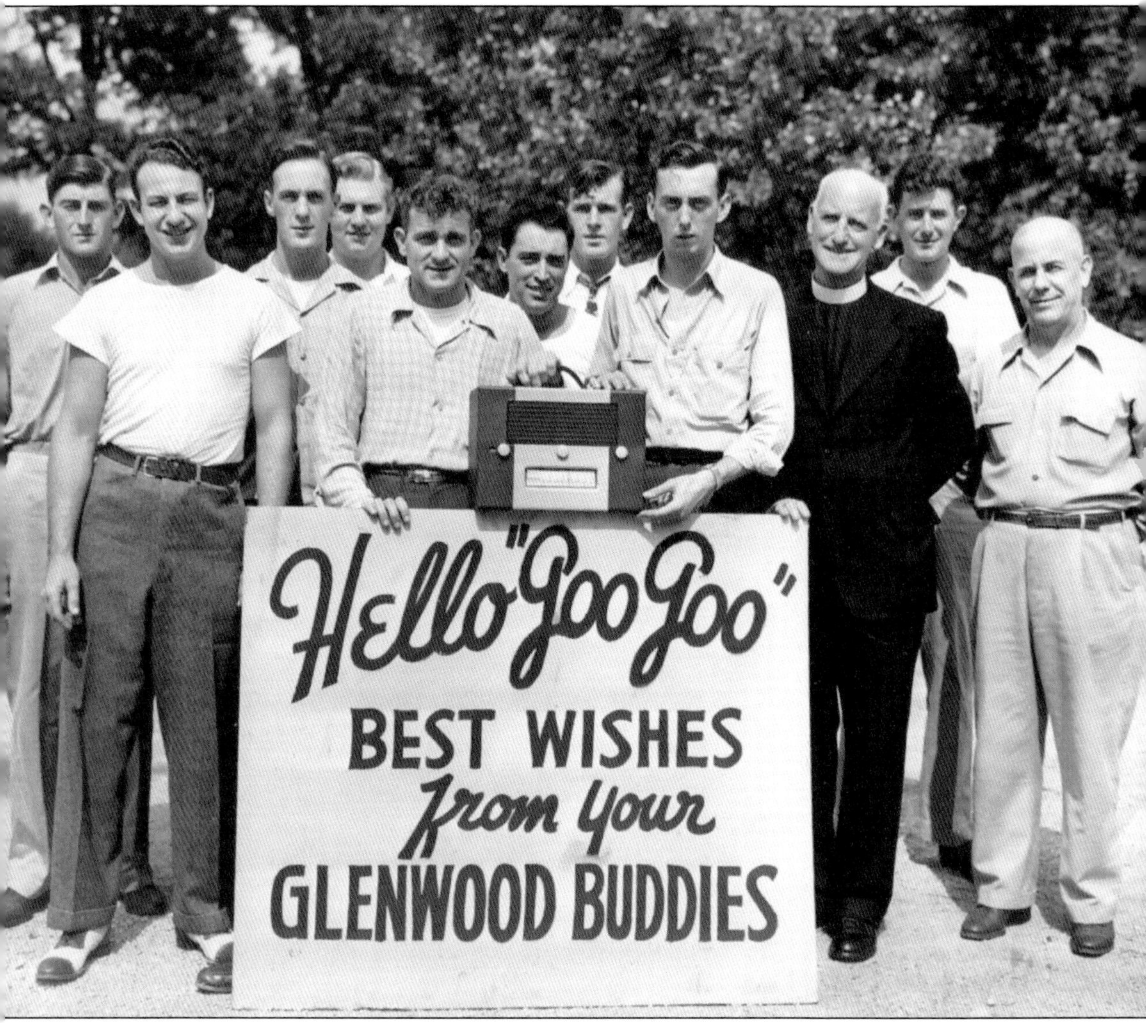

Goo Goo Zentara was wounded in World War II. His buddies from Glenwood sent him this greeting. Those gathered in this photograph are, from left to right, Wilard Housman, Bill Voelker, Bill Catto, Hank Veldhuizen, Neil Bakker, Frank Gregory, Nick Gorkowski, Sonny Randolph, Father Burke, Mort Shine, and Coy Baumgardner. (Courtesy of the Glenwood Historical Society.)

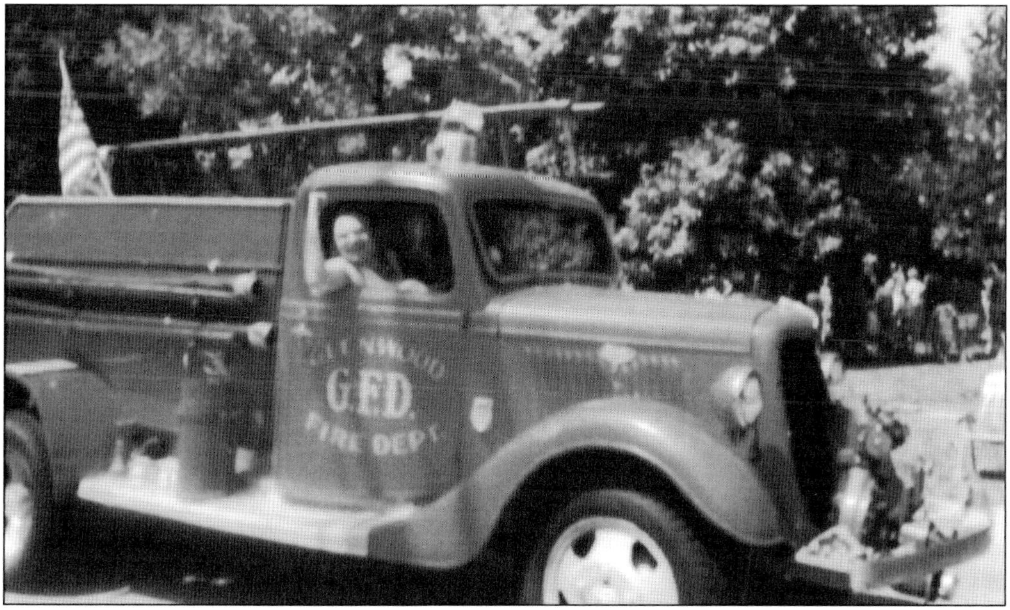

This 1936 Ford, now owned by the Glenwood Historical Society, was bought in Joliet, Illinois, in 1940 for $800. (Courtesy of the Glenwood Historical Society.)

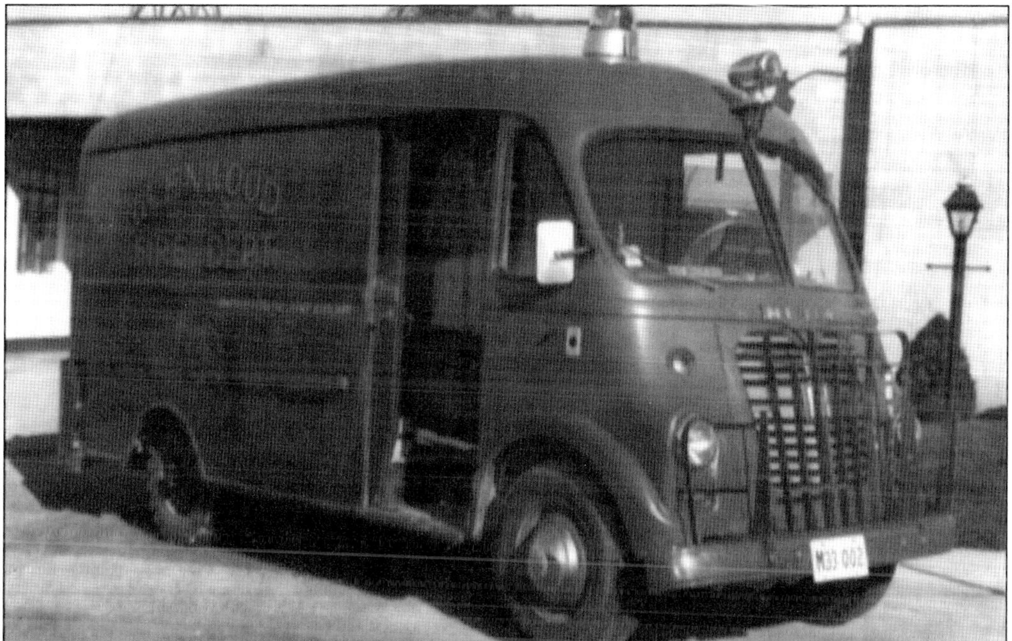

The Glenwood Volunteer Fire Department supply truck was used in the 1950s and into the 1960s. On November 28, 1960, the Glenwood Volunteer Fire Department, along with fire departments from five other south Cook County communities, responded to 15 East Main Street to fight a fire in the one-story brick store at that location. The estimated damage was $70,000. (Courtesy of the Glenwood Historical Society.)

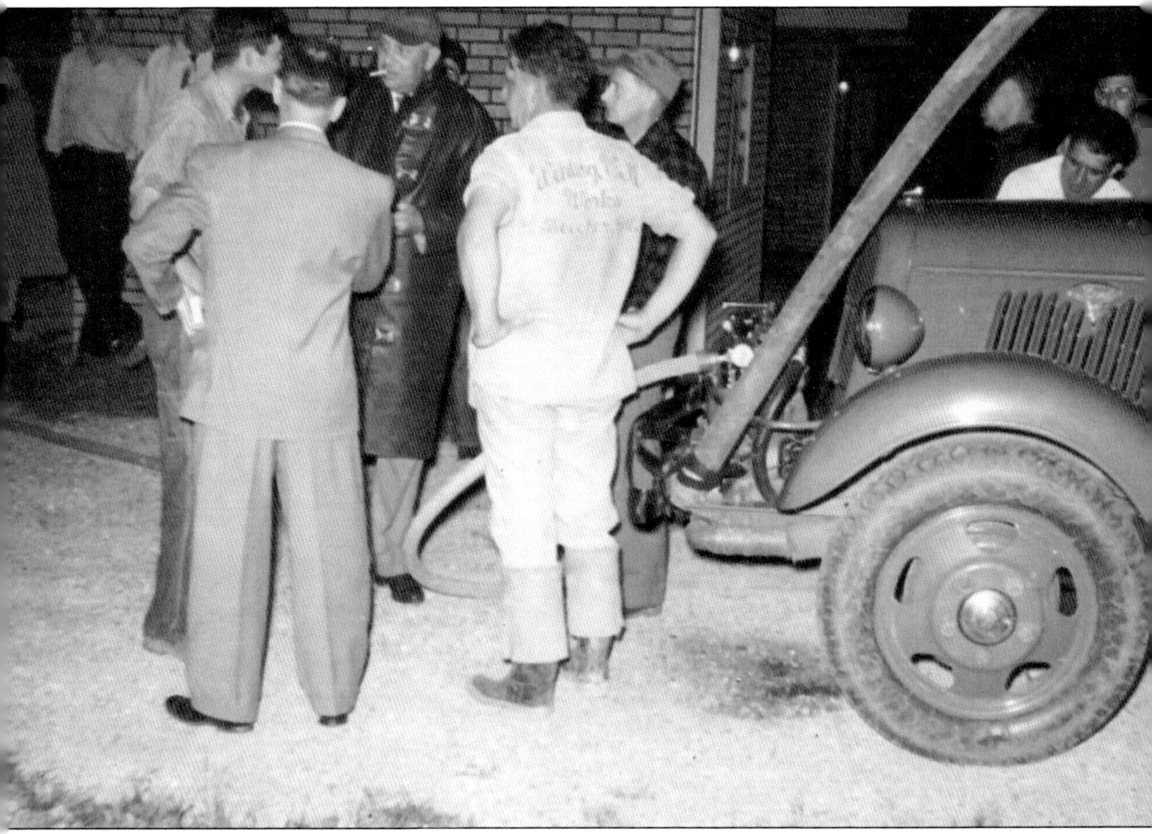

Ralph Strand (center, with the cigarette) is pictured taking care of business during his tenure as Glenwood's police chief. (Courtesy of the Glenwood Historical Society.)

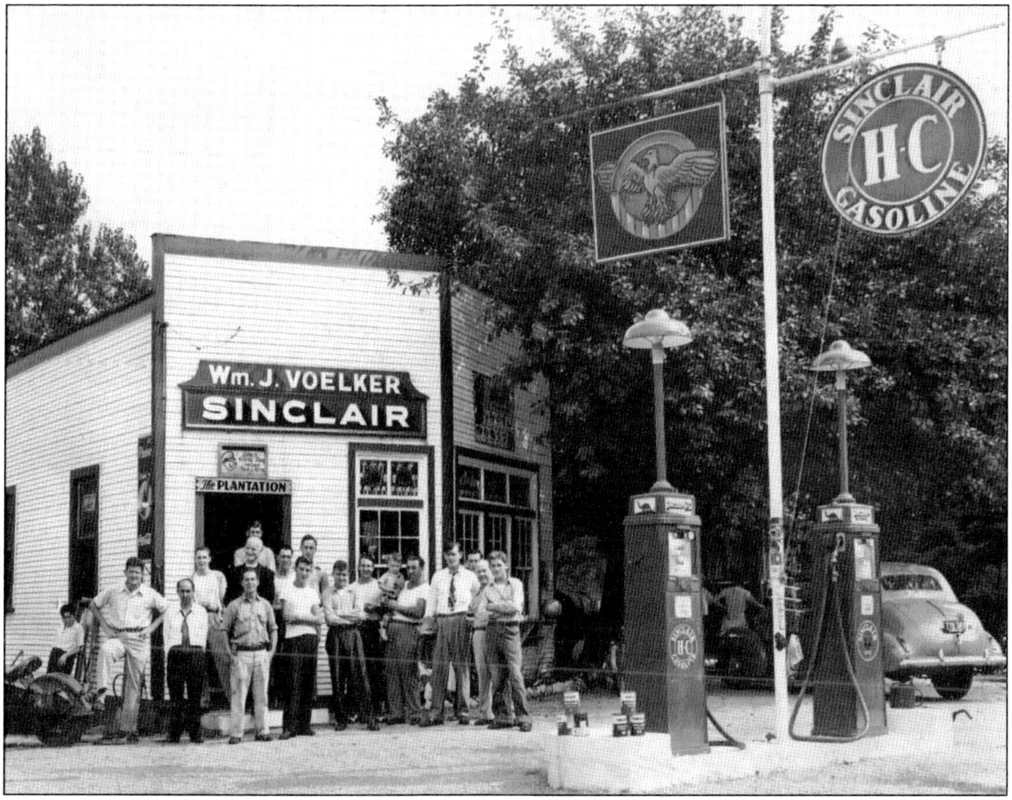

Voelker's Service Station is still standing and drawing a crowd. This building now houses the Station Bar and Grill at 151 Glenwood Avenue. (Courtesy of the Glenwood Historical Society.)

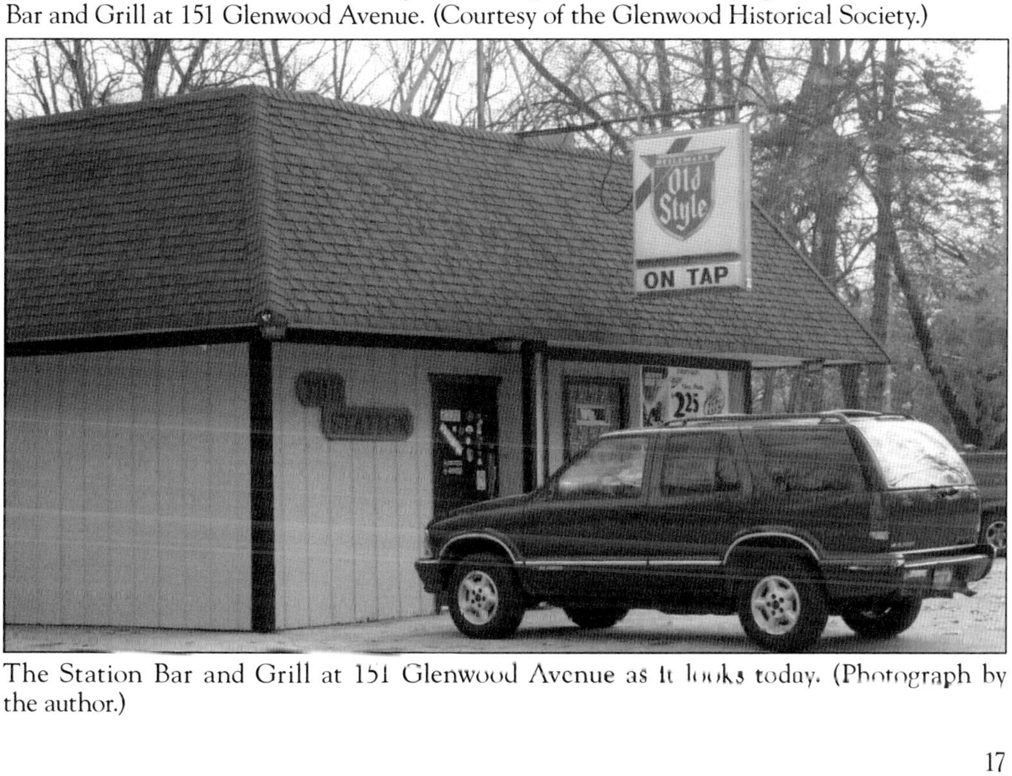

The Station Bar and Grill at 151 Glenwood Avenue as it looks today. (Photograph by the author.)

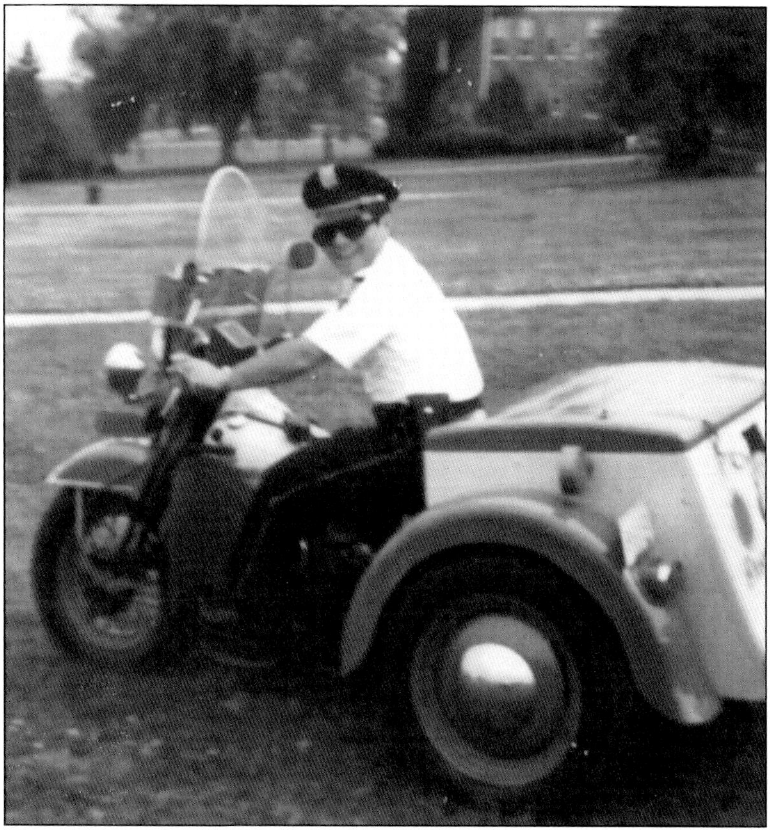

Through the 1960s and 1970s, speeders in Glenwood were on the lookout for motorcycle officer Bill Richoto. (Courtesy of the Glenwood Historical Society.)

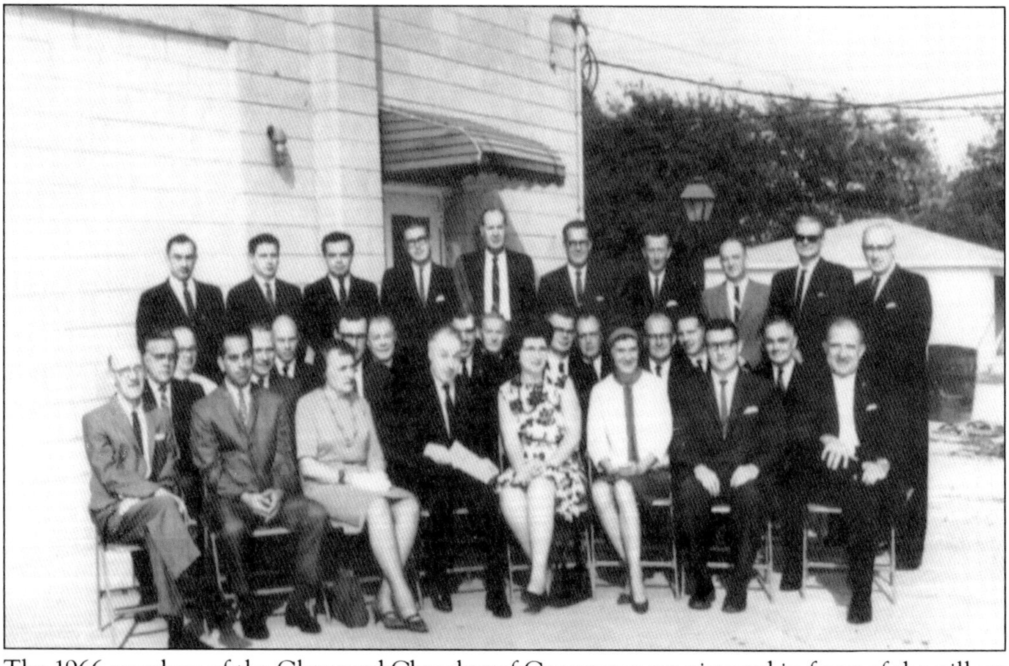

The 1966 members of the Glenwood Chamber of Commerce are pictured in front of the village hall on Rebecca Street. (Courtesy of the Glenwood Historical Society.)

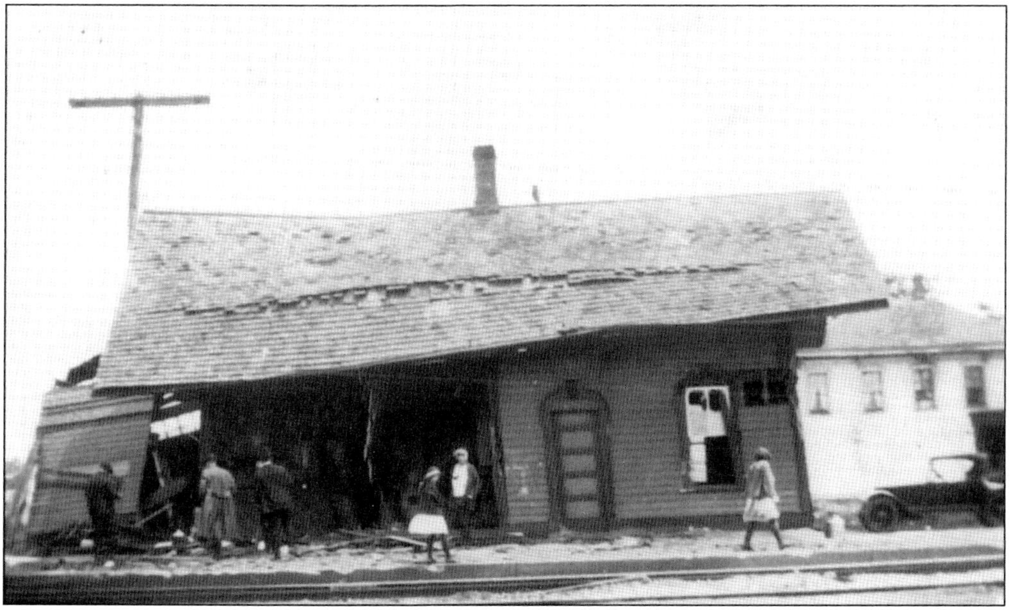

On June 13, 1904, twenty people were killed and approximately twenty-five were injured in a train collision on the Chicago and Eastern Illinois Railroad at Glenwood. (Courtesy of the Glenwood Historical Society.)

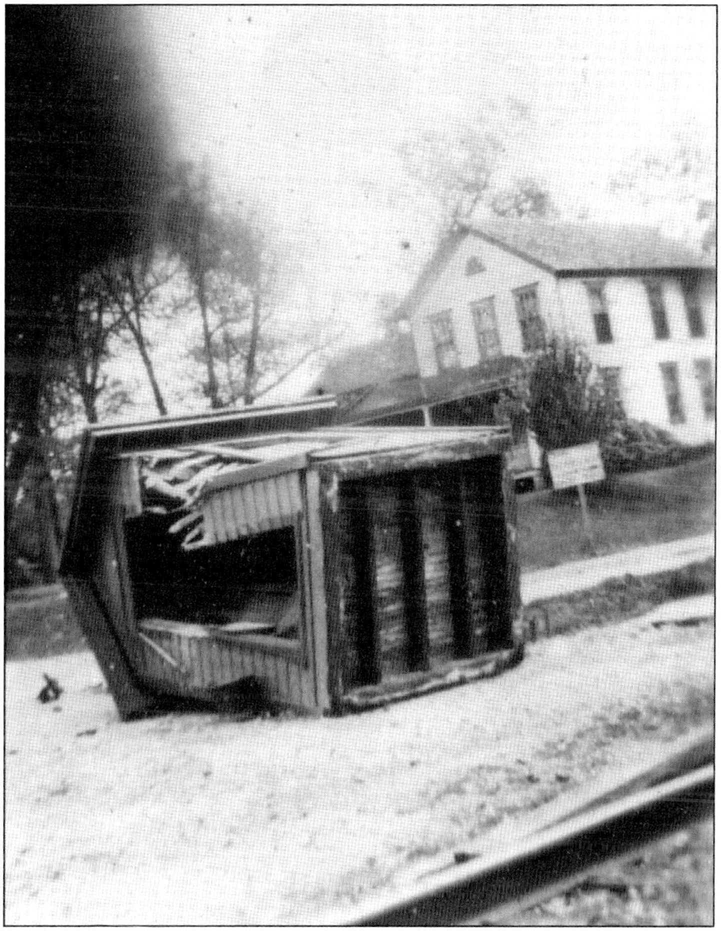

The collision was between a northbound picnic train and a southbound freight train. A misplaced switch caused the picnic train to head onto the southbound track. (Courtesy of the Glenwood Historical Society.)

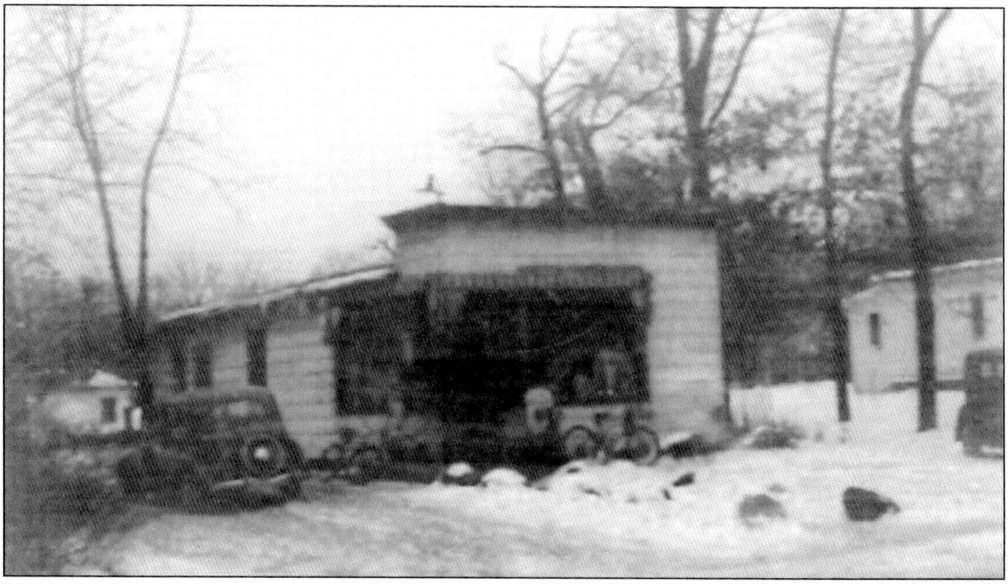

Pictured is 67 Main Street as it once looked. (Courtesy of the Glenwood Historical Society.)

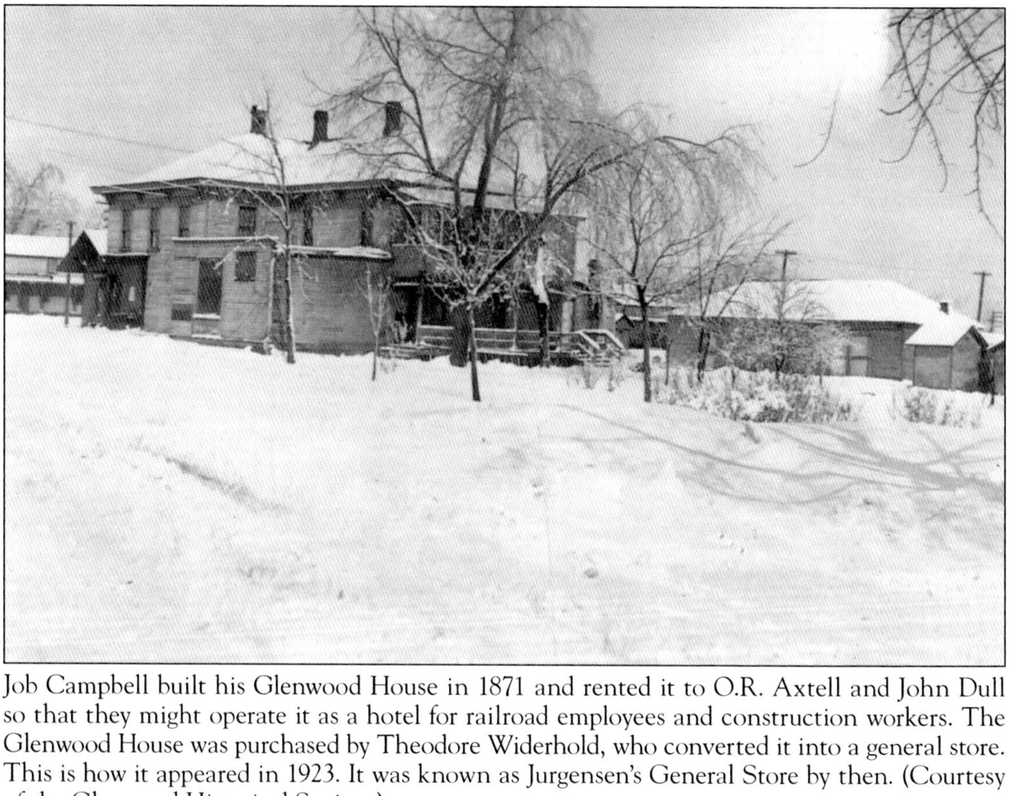

Job Campbell built his Glenwood House in 1871 and rented it to O.R. Axtell and John Dull so that they might operate it as a hotel for railroad employees and construction workers. The Glenwood House was purchased by Theodore Widerhold, who converted it into a general store. This is how it appeared in 1923. It was known as Jurgensen's General Store by then. (Courtesy of the Glenwood Historical Society.)

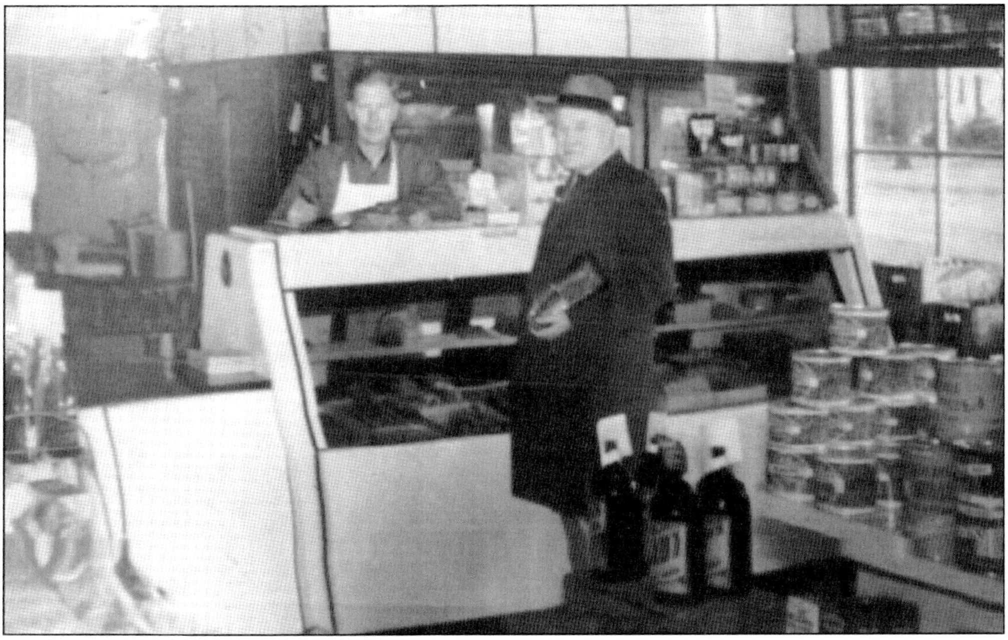

The inside of Jurgensen's General Store is captured in this photograph, with Jurgensen behind the counter. Notice the large bottles of Dad's Root Beer for sale. There was also plenty of penny candy to be bought. (Courtesy of the Glenwood Historical Society.)

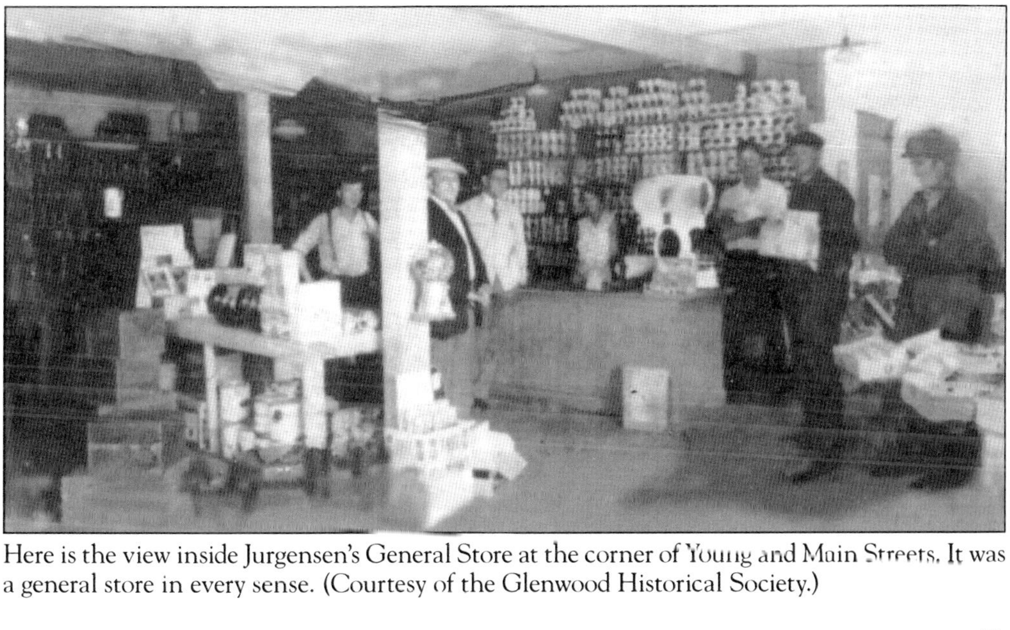

Here is the view inside Jurgensen's General Store at the corner of Young and Main Streets. It was a general store in every sense. (Courtesy of the Glenwood Historical Society.)

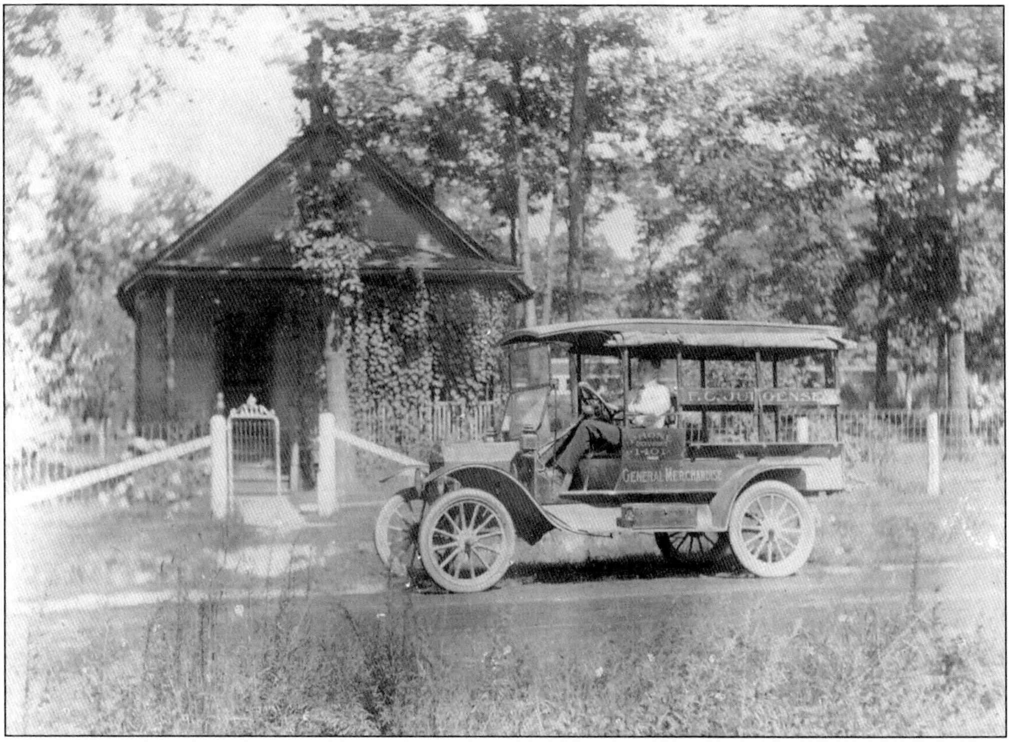

Jurgensen's truck makes deliveries to the people of Glenwood. Jurgensen Woods, located just outside of town, is a remnant of the woodlands and prairie ecosystems that at one time existed on the sandy plains of glacial Lake Chicago. (Courtesy of the Glenwood Historical Society.)

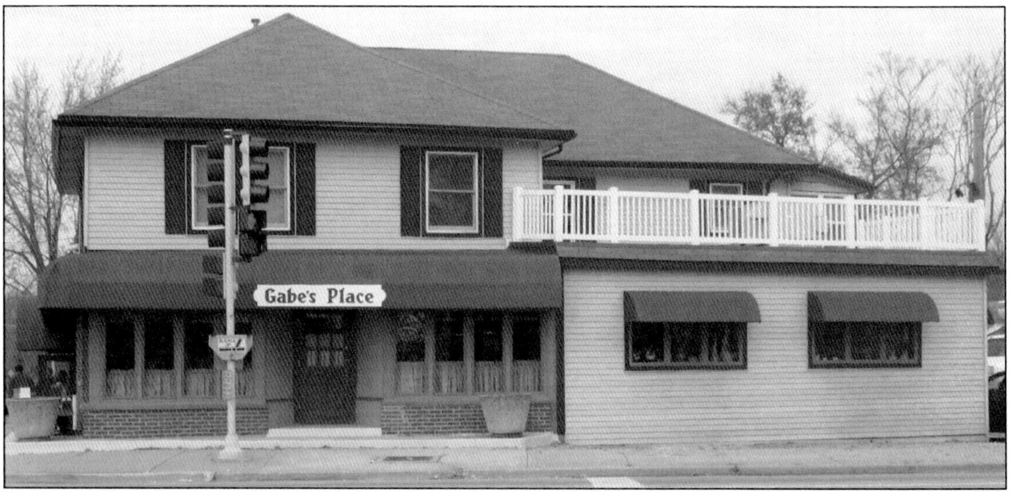

The building at 9 East Main Street, where Jurgensen's General Store was once located, is now home to the popular restaurant Gabe's Place. Be prepared to wait for a table on Sunday mornings. (Photograph by the author.)

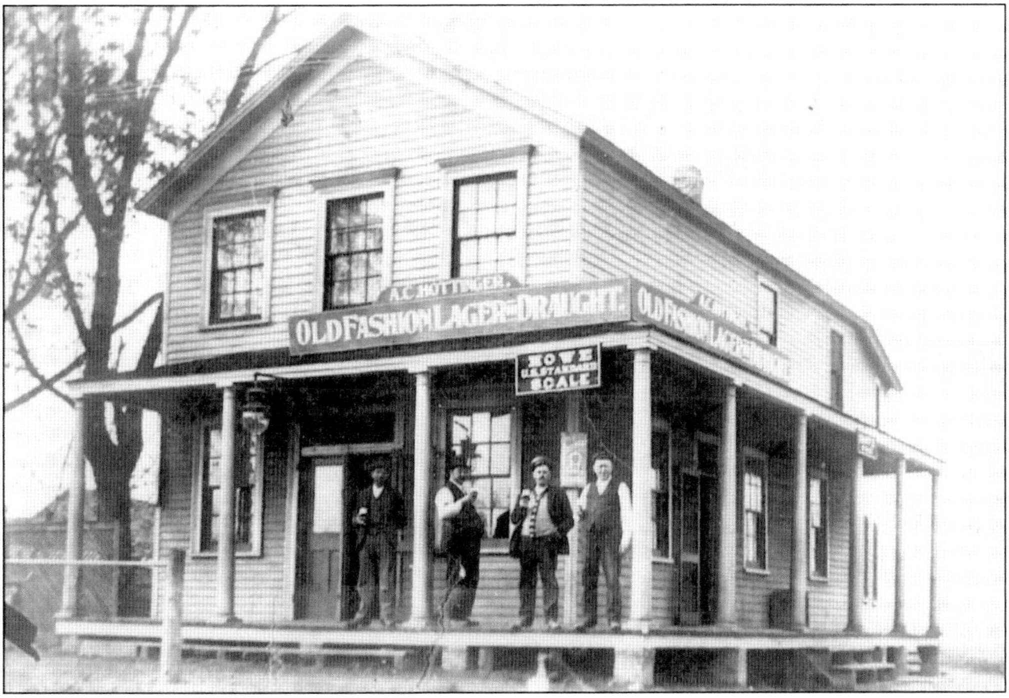

Hottinger's was originally built as a weigh station for local farmers who would bring their goods to be weighed before loading them on the train to be shipped to market. (Courtesy of the Glenwood Historical Society.)

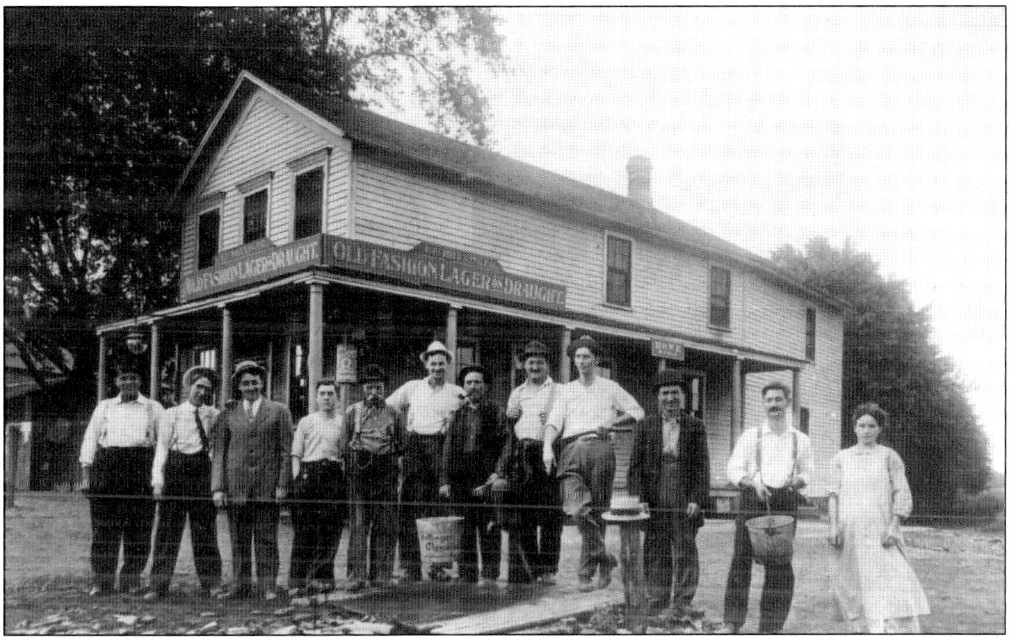

Hottinger's was built in 1847, when Glenwood was still called Hickory Bend. It was located on Main Street, also known as Glenwood-Dyer Road, just west of the railroad tracks. The building also served as a drugstore and a hotel for railroad employees. (Courtesy of the Glenwood Historical Society.)

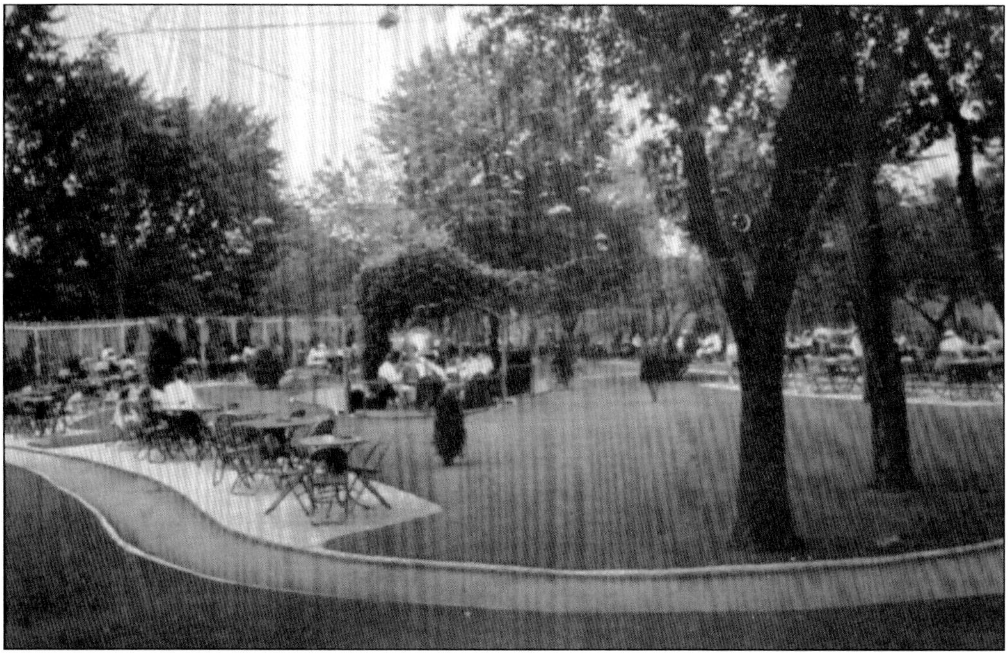

Hottinger's Garden became famous when the Hottinger family built the outdoor garden. Known for its lush lawn and vines imported from the Netherlands, people would travel from miles away and stand in line for hours to enjoy the outdoor dining and dancing. (Courtesy of the Glenwood Historical Society.)

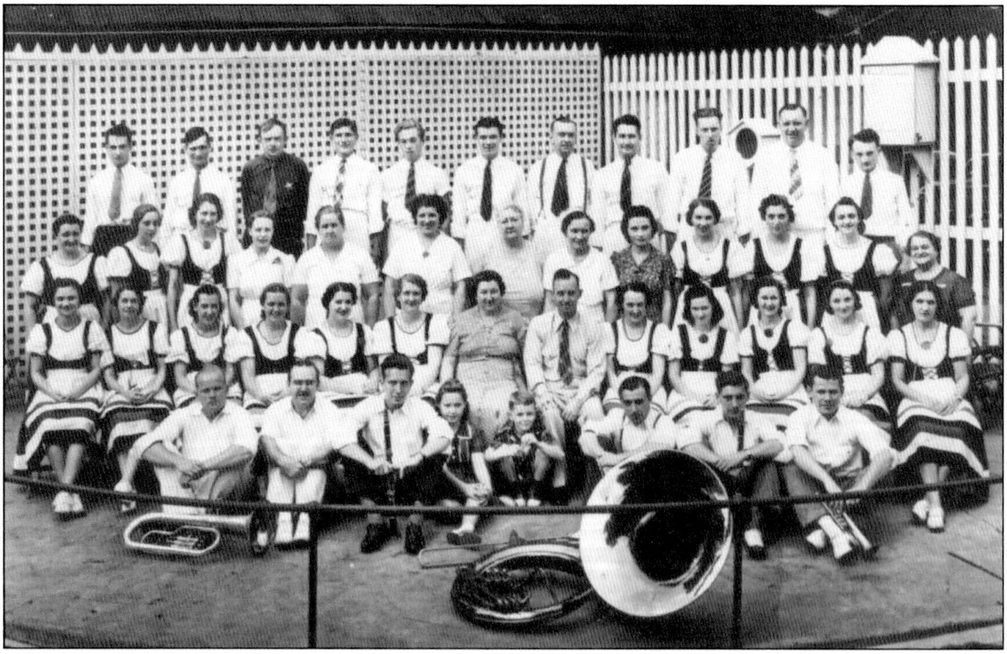

The Hottinger's Garden staff of 1940, band and all, waits to serve up an evening of fun and relaxation. (Courtesy of the Glenwood Historical Society.)

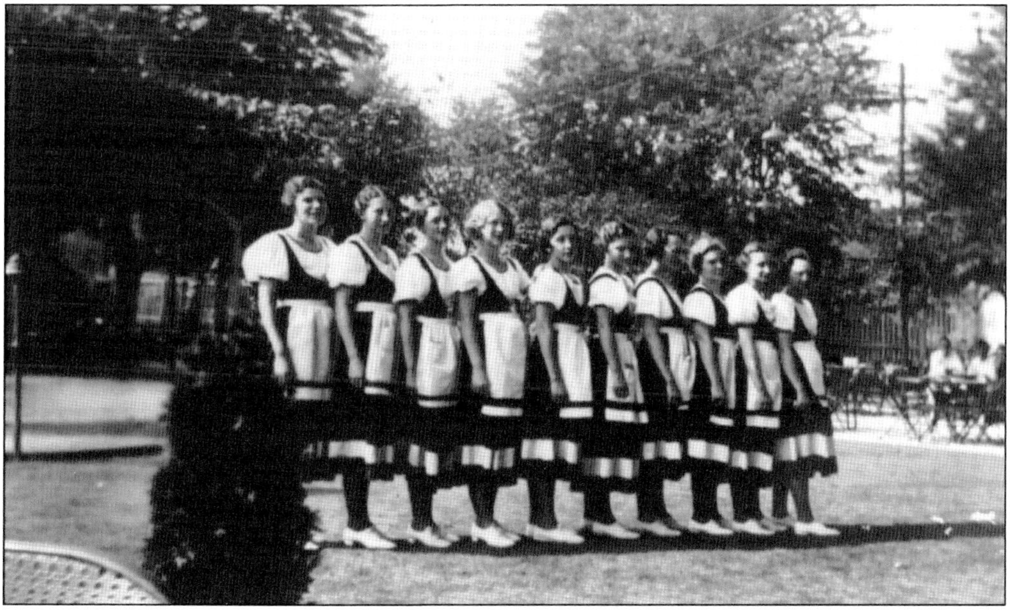

Hottinger waitresses pose in uniform for this charming photograph. (Courtesy of the Glenwood Historical Society.)

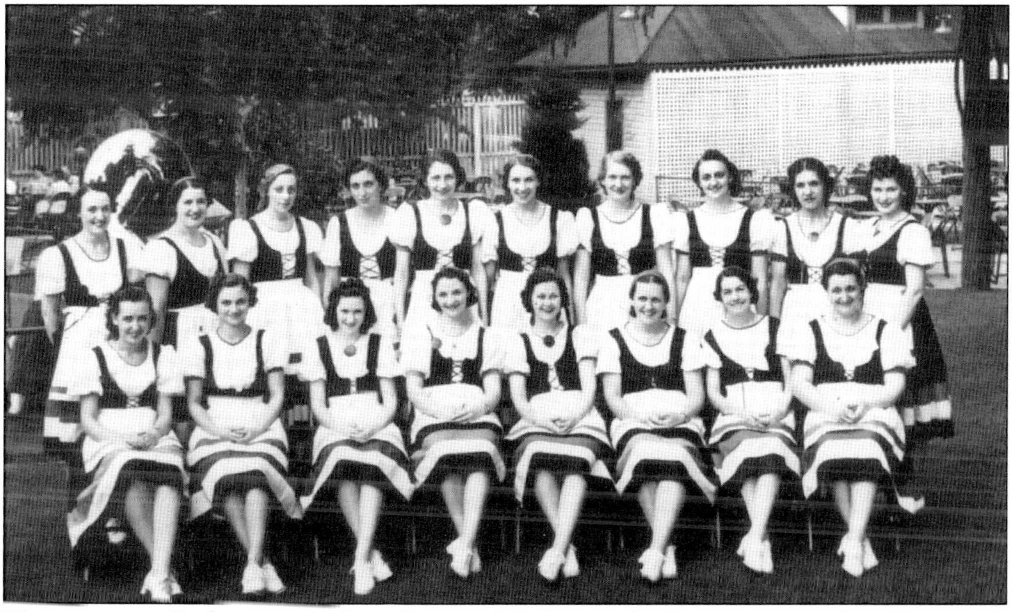

The waitress staff takes time out for a photograph before another busy summer night at Hottinger's Garden. (Courtesy of the Glenwood Historical Society.)

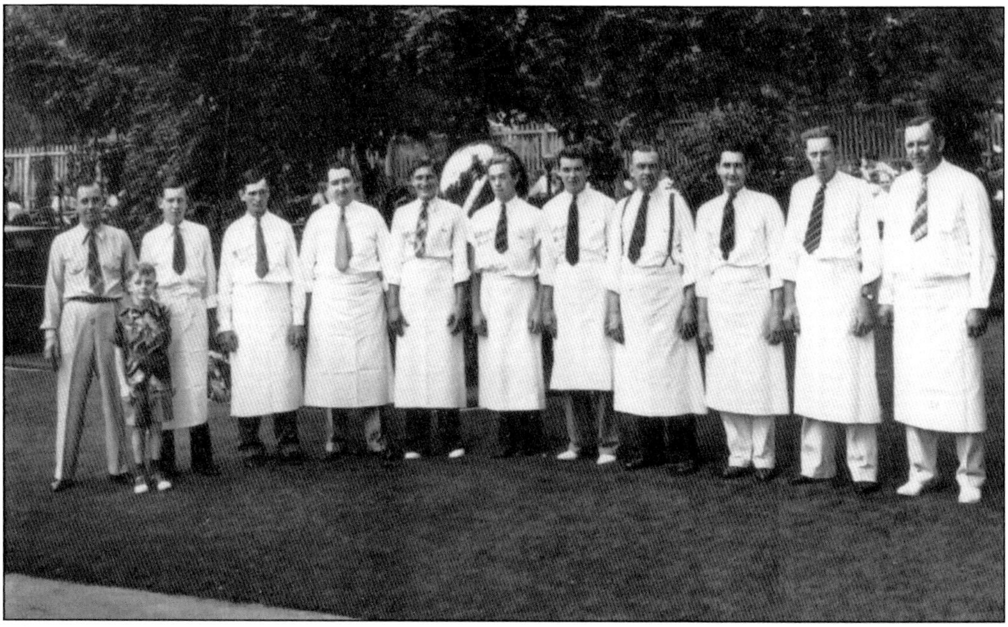

The Hottinger's Garden bartender crew waits to serve thirsty customers in 1940. (Courtesy of the Glenwood Historical Society.)

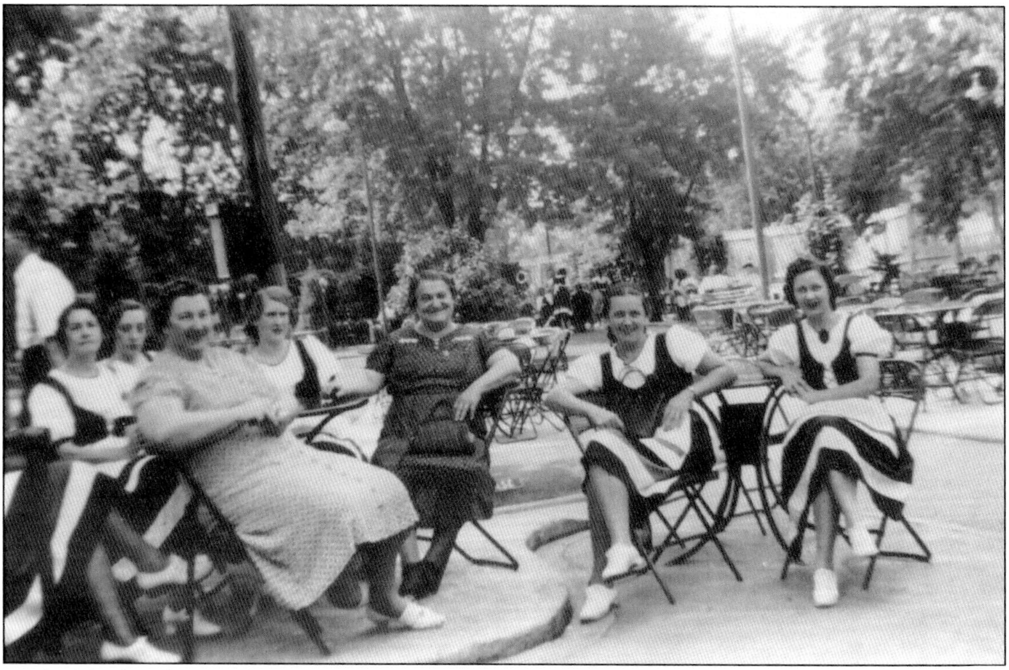

Looks like break time for some of the staff at Hottinger's Garden. (Courtesy of the Glenwood Historical Society.)

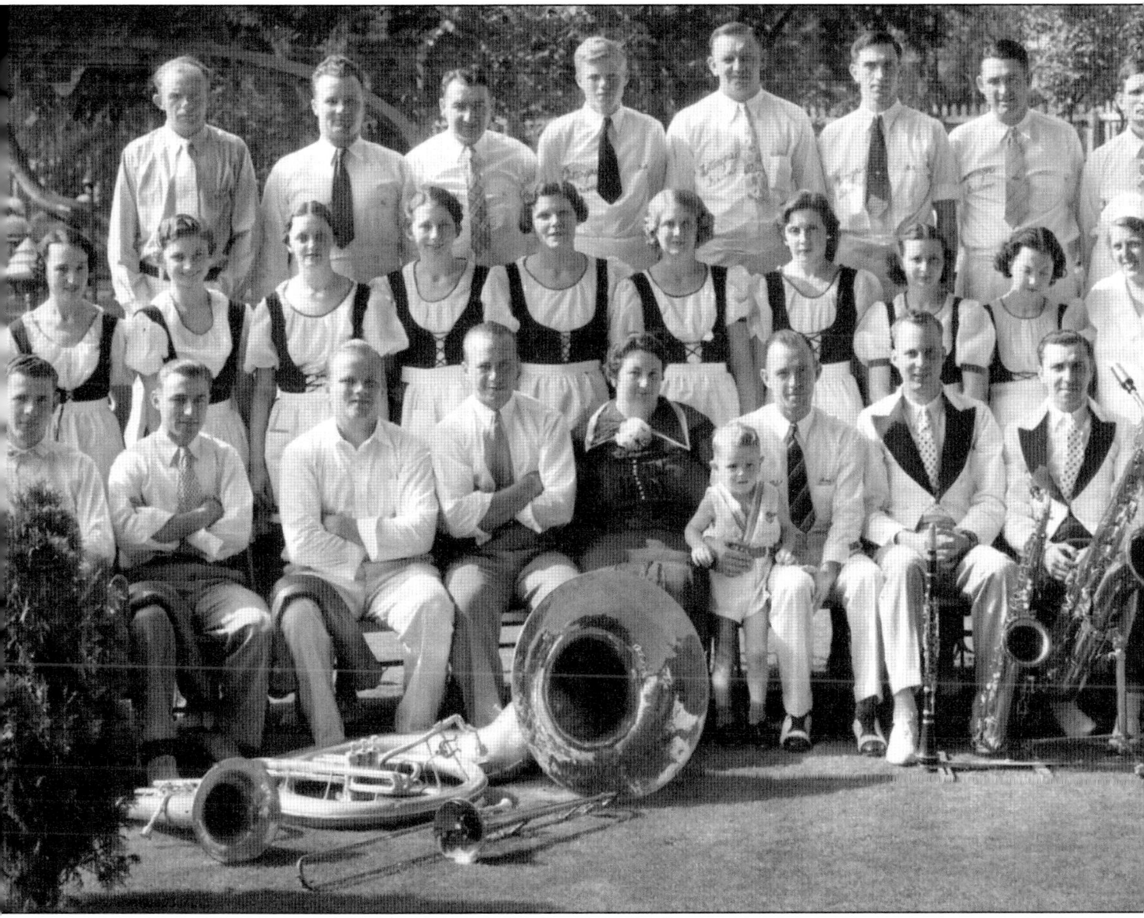

The Hottinger's Garden staff is ready for business in 1936. (Courtesy of the Glenwood Historical Society.)

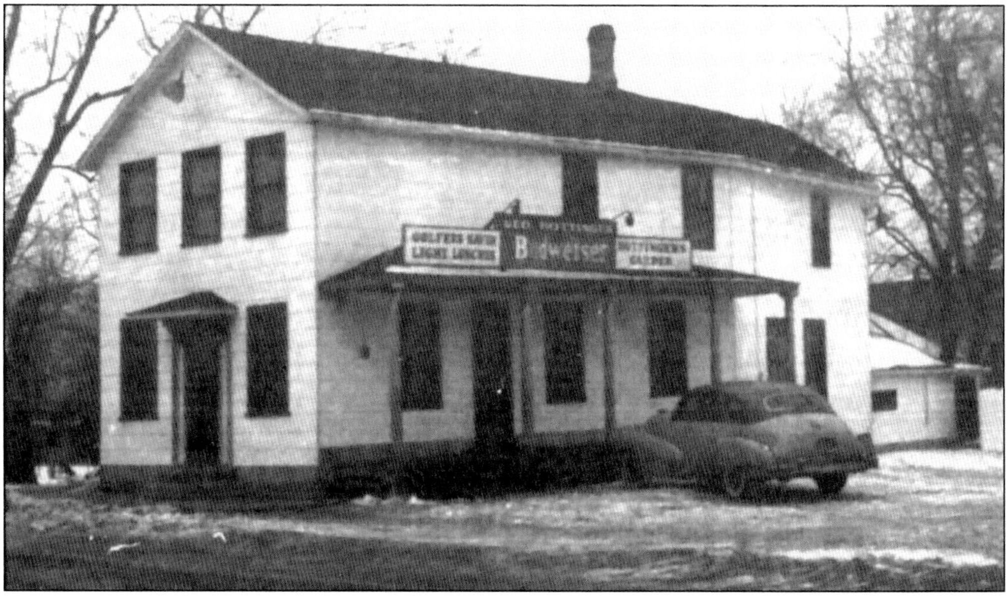

Seen here is Hottinger's Garden as it looked in the 1950s. (Courtesy of the Glenwood Historical Society.)

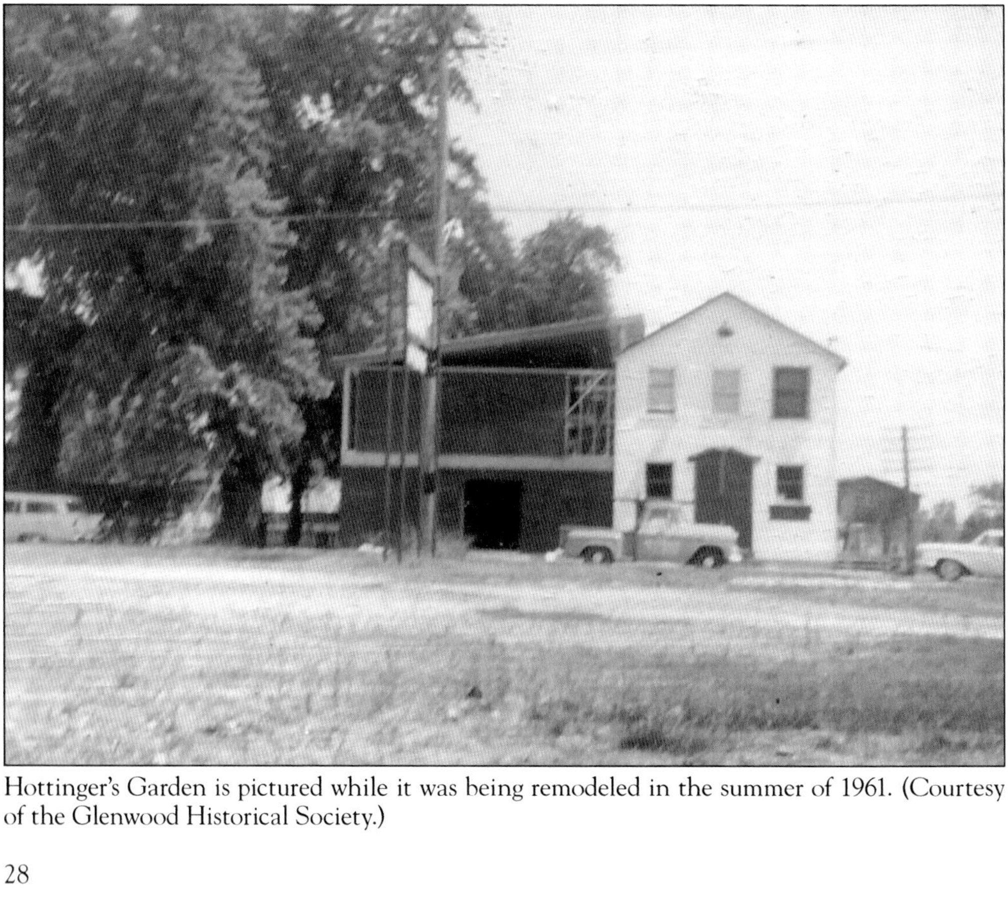

Hottinger's Garden is pictured while it was being remodeled in the summer of 1961. (Courtesy of the Glenwood Historical Society.)

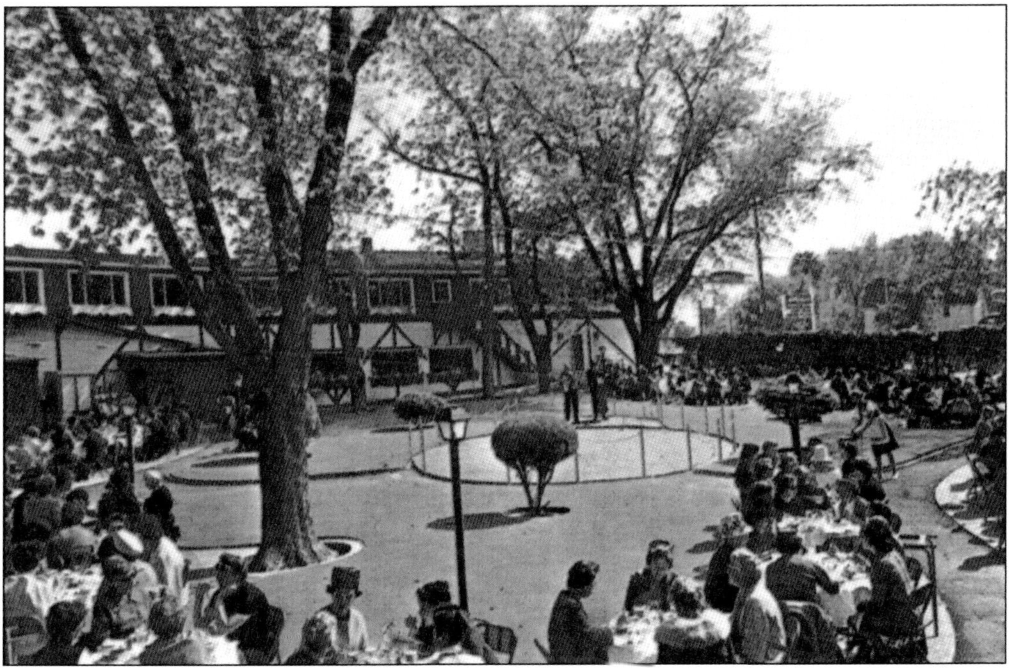

A picture postcard of Hottinger's Garden shows the atmosphere enjoyed by a lunchtime crowd. (Courtesy of the Glenwood Historical Society.)

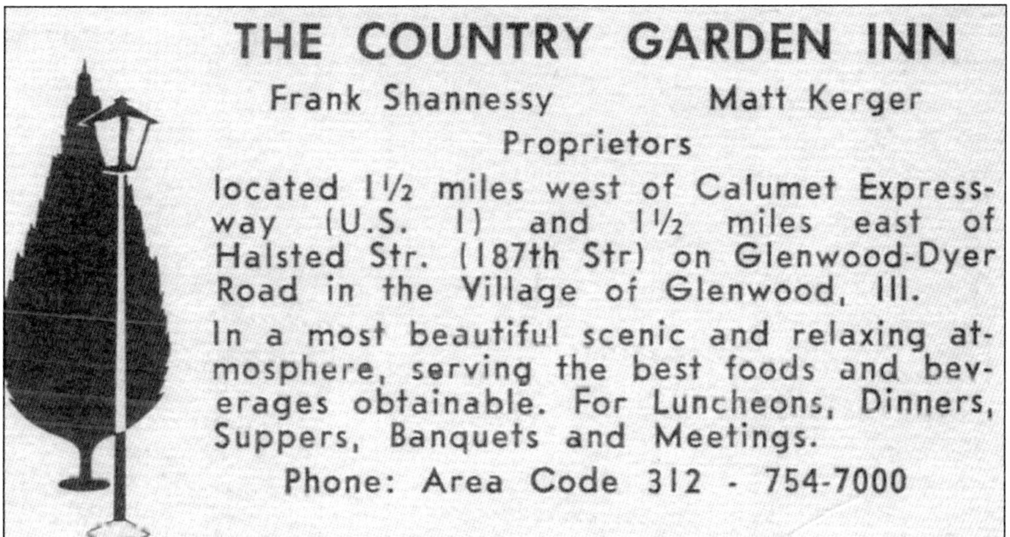

Information from the back of this postcard makes it sound like a wonderful place to visit. (Courtesy of the Glenwood Historical Society.)

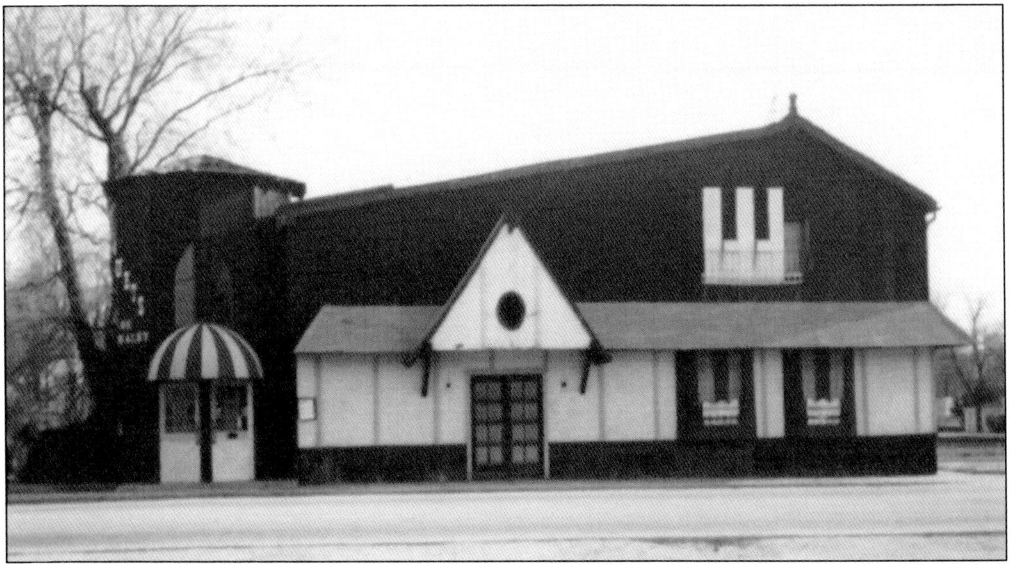

Hottinger's Garden later became the Fireside Chalet, which had a restaurant, lounge, and banquet facilities. Pictured here is the north entrance. (Courtesy of the Glenwood Historical Society.)

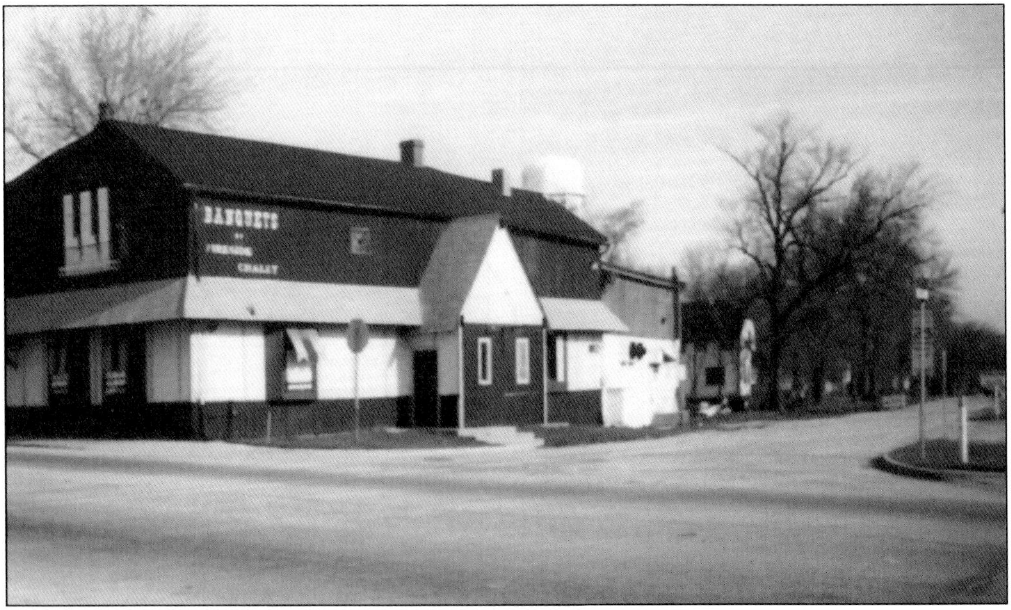

Pictured is the corner of Main and Campbell Streets in the 1980s, as it looked when the Fireside Chalet was still standing. (Courtesy of the Glenwood Historical Society.)

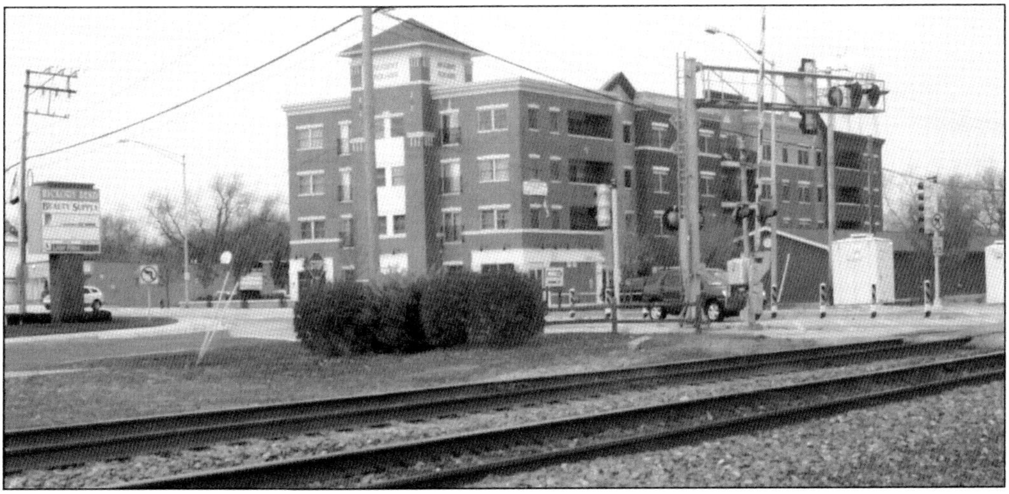

Nugent Square is now located at the corner of Main and Campbell Streets. (Photograph by the author.)

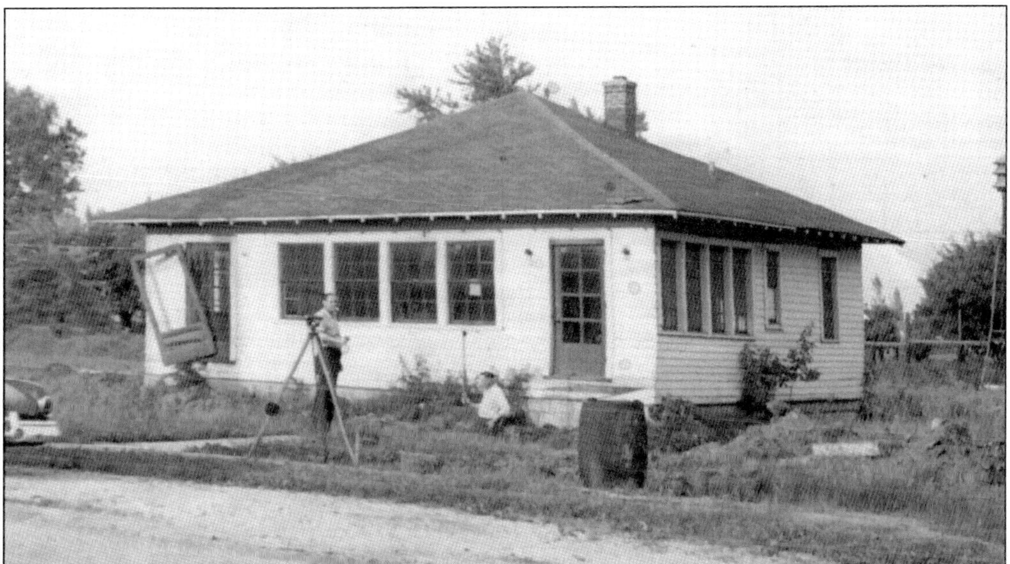

The Doll House, originally located on Merrill Street, was moved to the village hall site in 1941, where it was used for municipal functions until 1950. It is now located at 34 North Rebecca Street. (Courtesy of the Glenwood Historical Society.)

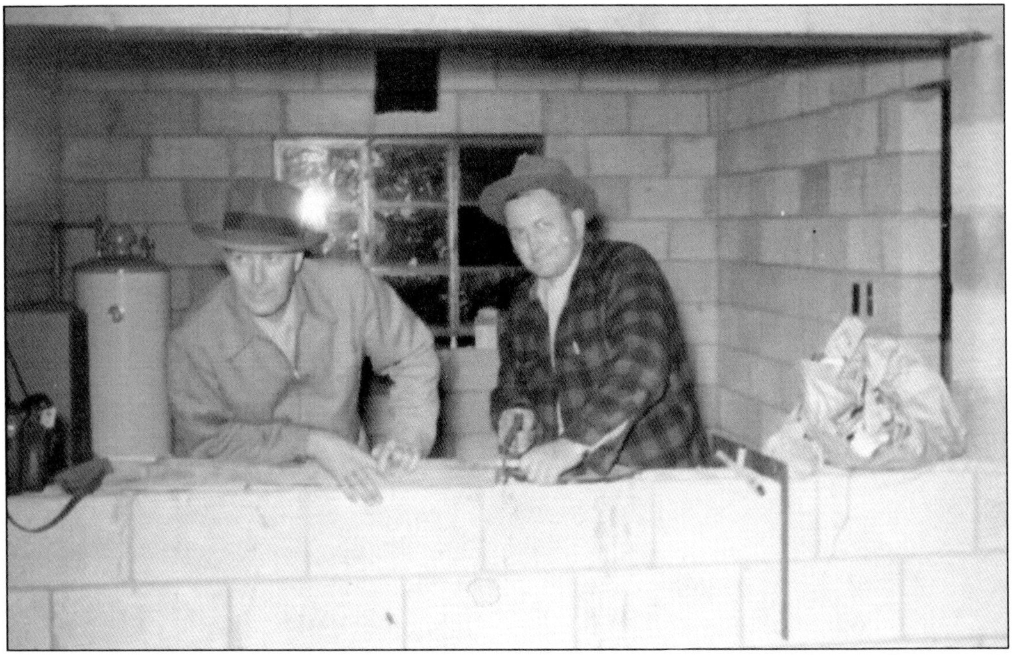

Nate Jurgensen (left) and Bud Hatfield work on the kitchen of the new village hall on North Rebecca Street in 1950. (Courtesy of the Glenwood Historical Society.)

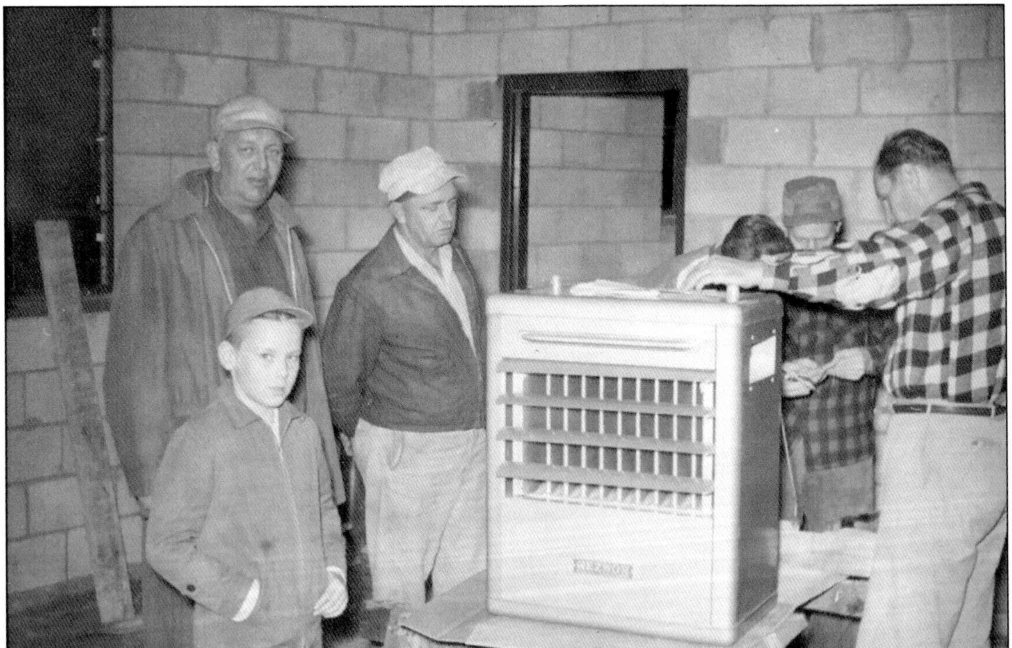

Ralph Strand (the adult on the far left) stands next to John Gieber as a heater is installed in the new village hall. (Courtesy of the Glenwood Historical Society.)

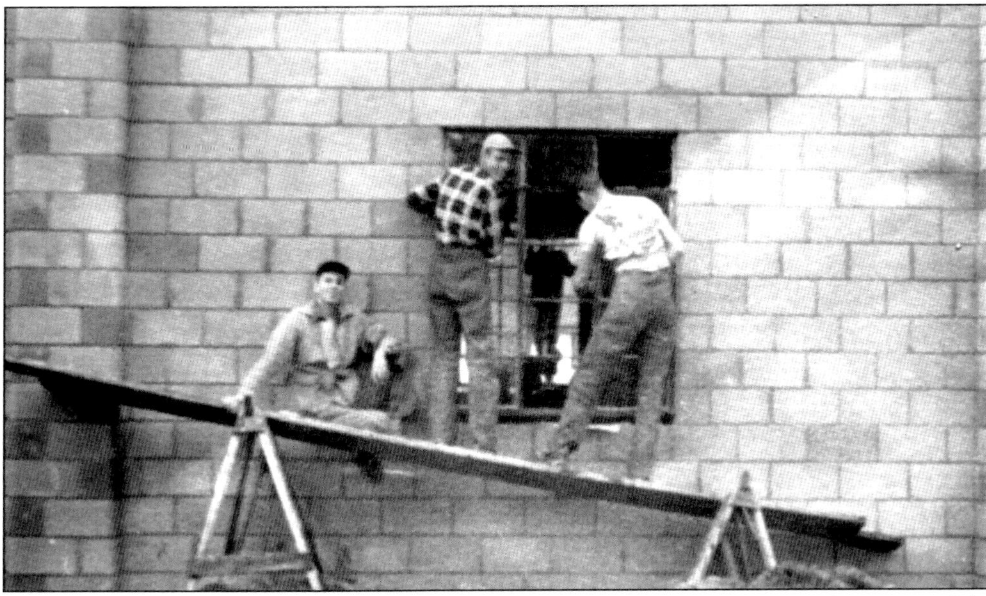

These three men are working on a two-man job at the new village hall in 1950. (Courtesy of the Glenwood Historical Society.)

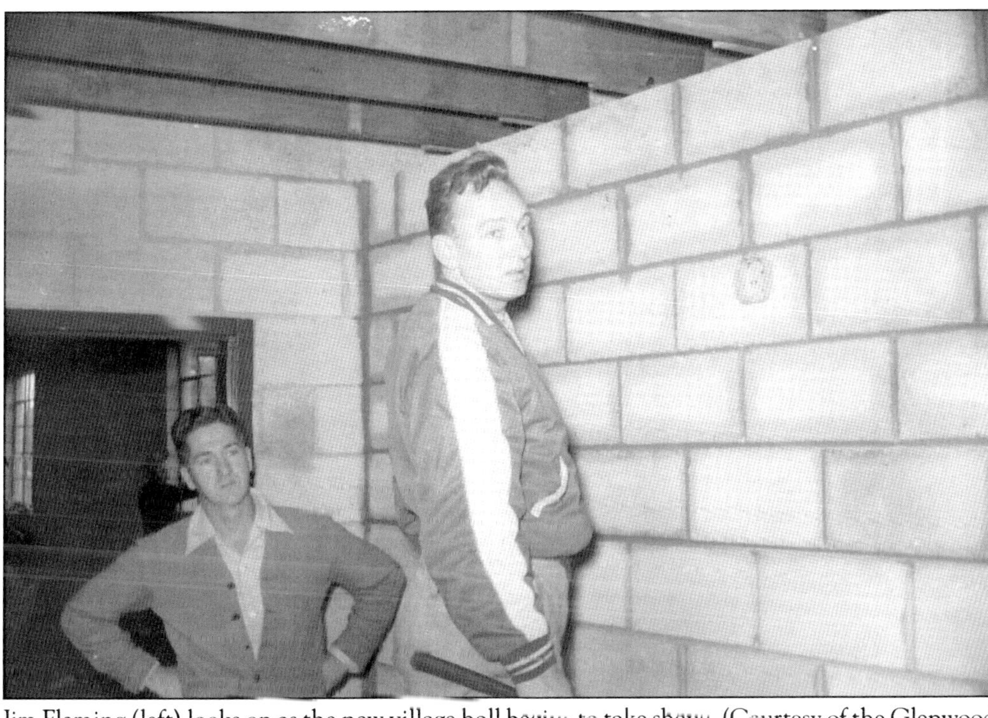

Jim Fleming (left) looks on as the new village hall begins to take shape. (Courtesy of the Glenwood Historical Society.)

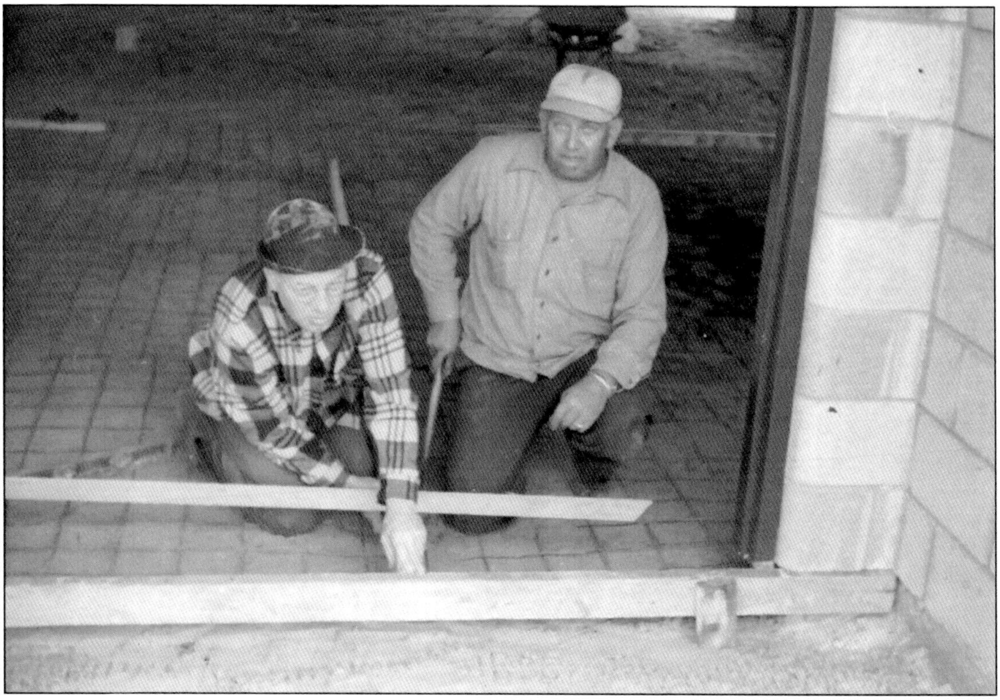

Ralph Strand (right) and a friend do some low work on the new village hall in 1950. (Courtesy of the Glenwood Historical Society.)

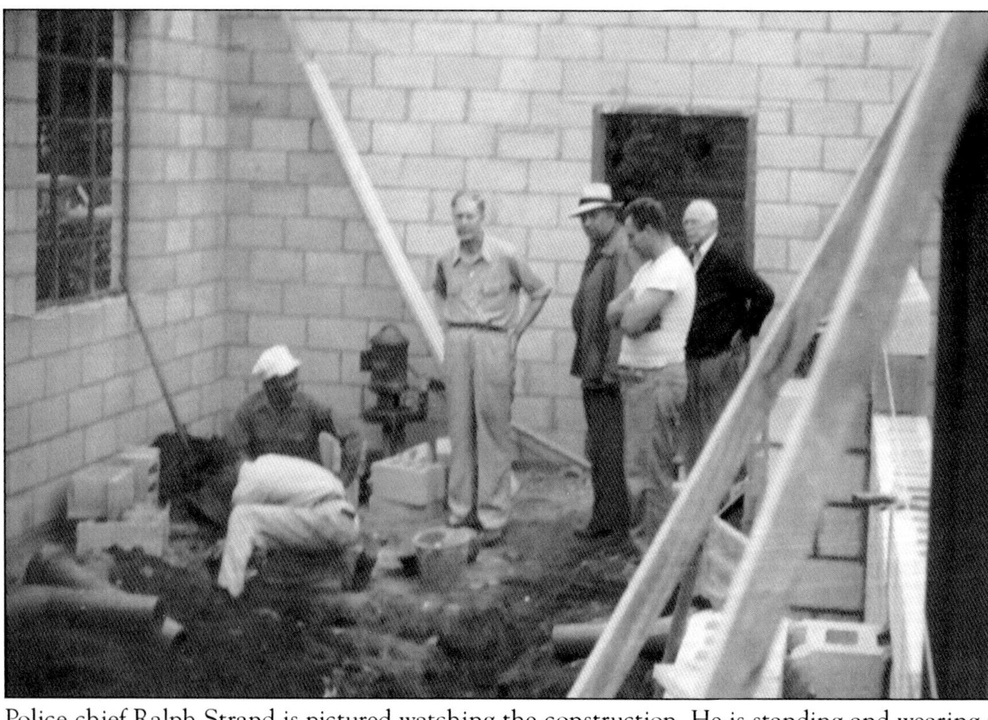

Police chief Ralph Strand is pictured watching the construction. He is standing and wearing a white hat. (Courtesy of the Glenwood Historical Society.)

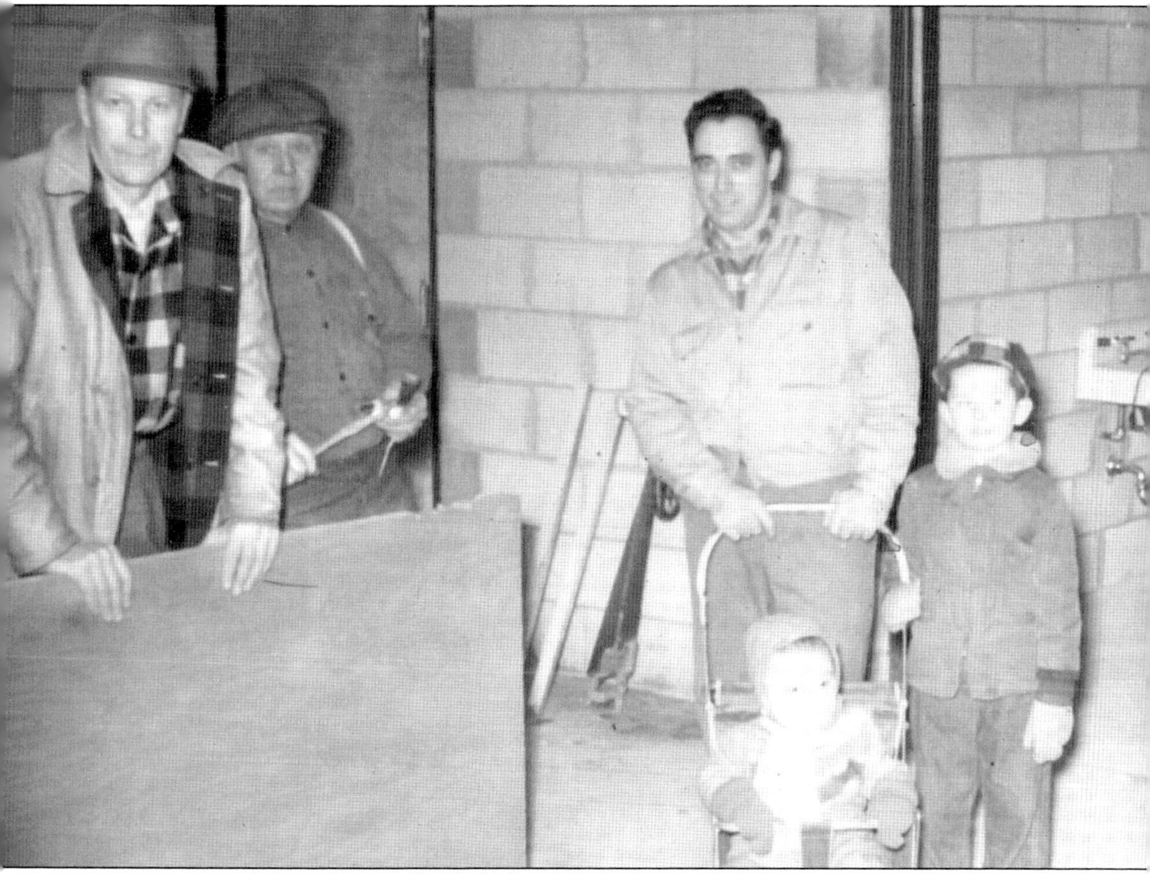

Fred Gregory (adult at right) and his children stop by to check on the progress for the new village hall. (Courtesy of the Glenwood Historical Society.)

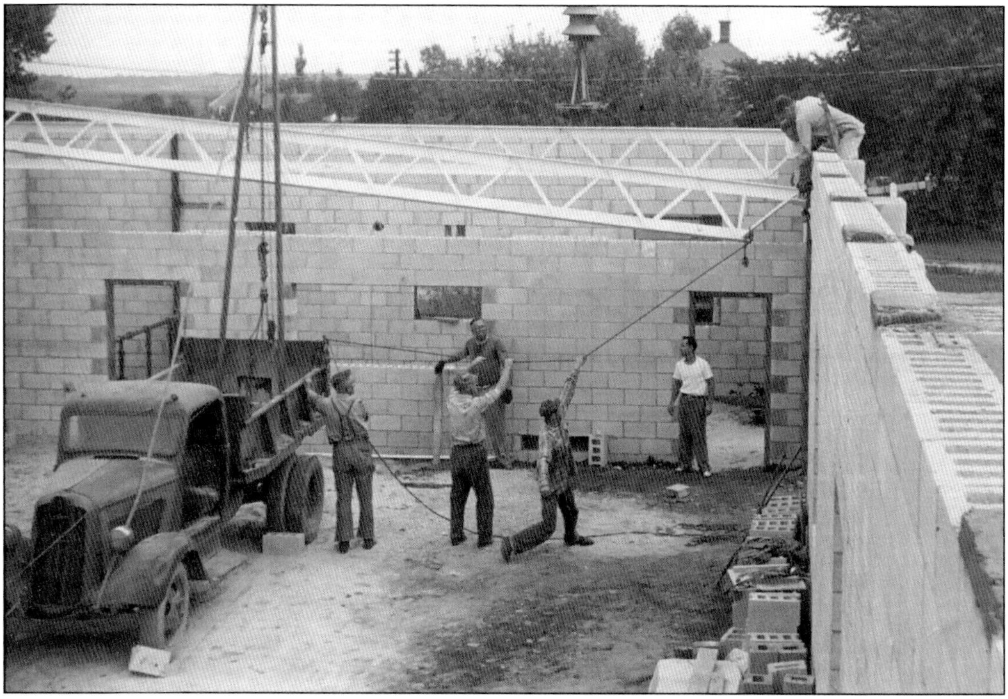

These men are getting ready to install the roof on the new village hall in 1950. (Courtesy of the Glenwood Historical Society.)

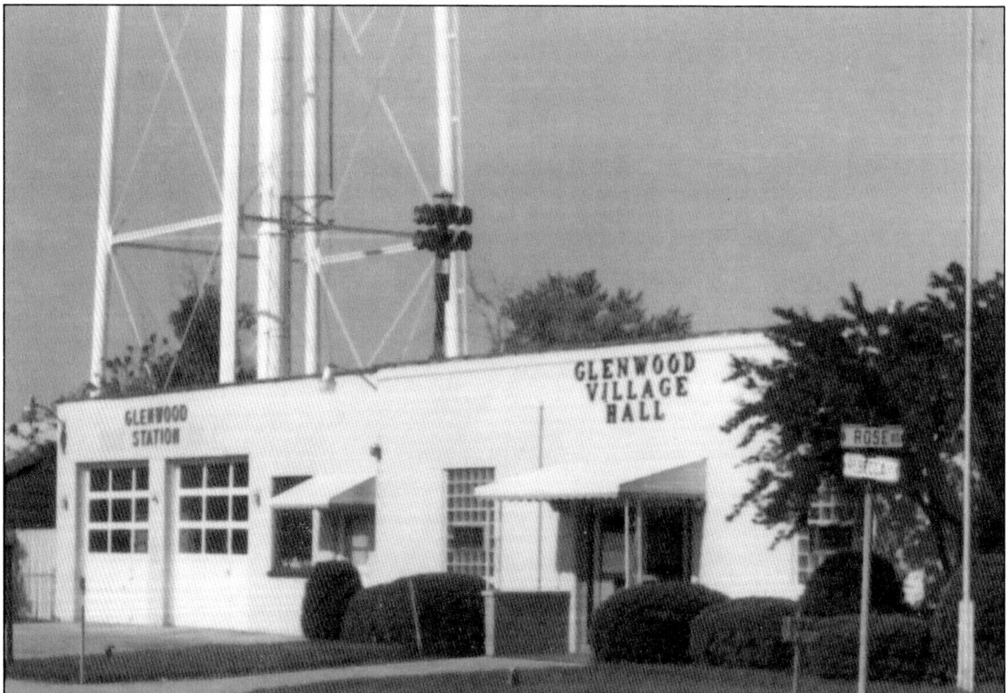

The Glenwood Village Hall is pictured as it looked in the 1960s. It was used for a variety of village social functions as well. (Courtesy of the Glenwood Historical Society.)

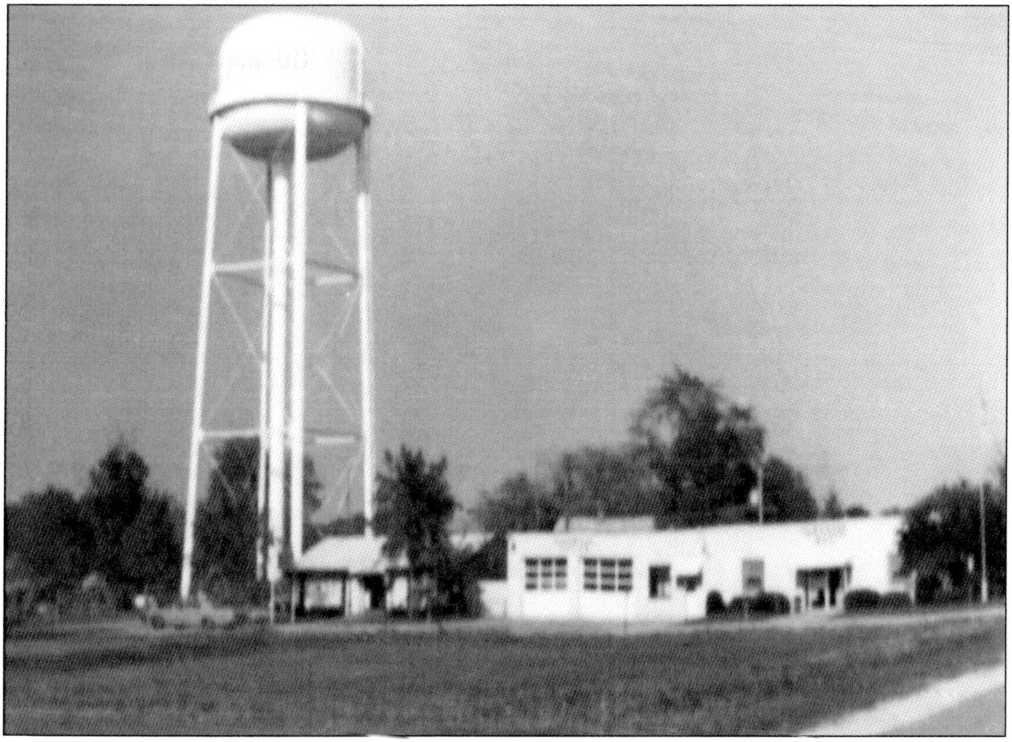

Seen here are the village hall and water tower at the corner of Rose and Rebecca Streets. (Courtesy of the Glenwood Historical Society.)

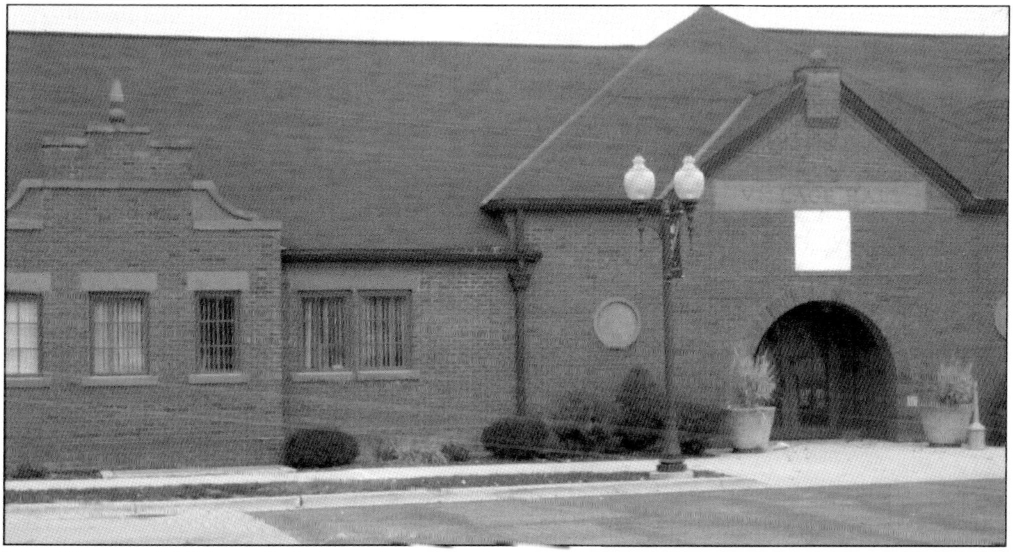

The Glenwood Village Hall (seen here as it looks today) was built in 2000 on the site of the previous village hall. (Photograph by the author.)

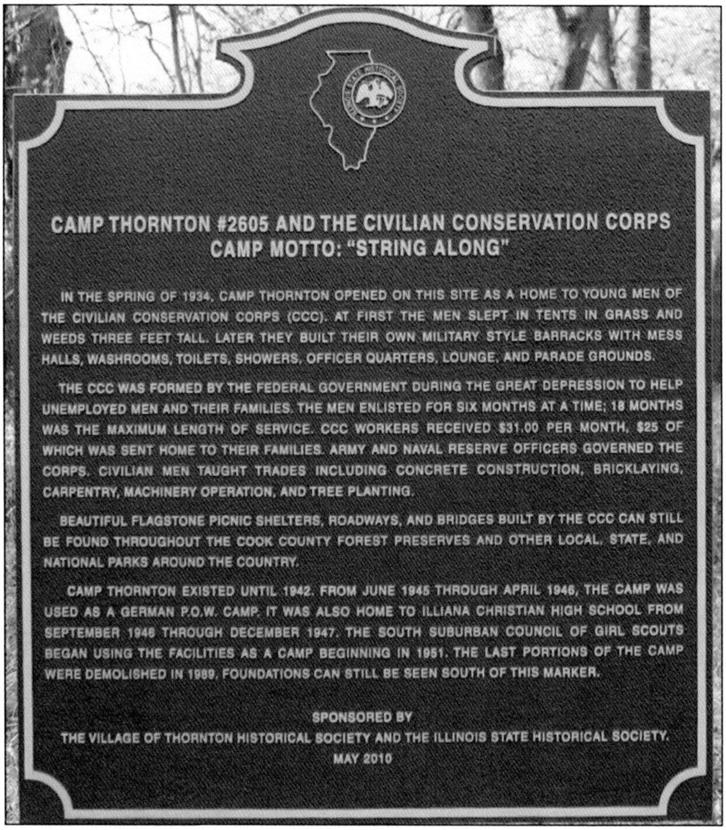

This historical marker just outside of town commemorates the Civilian Conservation Corps (CCC) camp that once stood on this site. During World War II, it was used as a German prisoner-of-war camp and was later the site of Illiana Christian High School from September 1946 through December 1947. The German prisoners held here were put to work in the nearby onion fields of South Holland, Illinois. (Photograph by the author.)

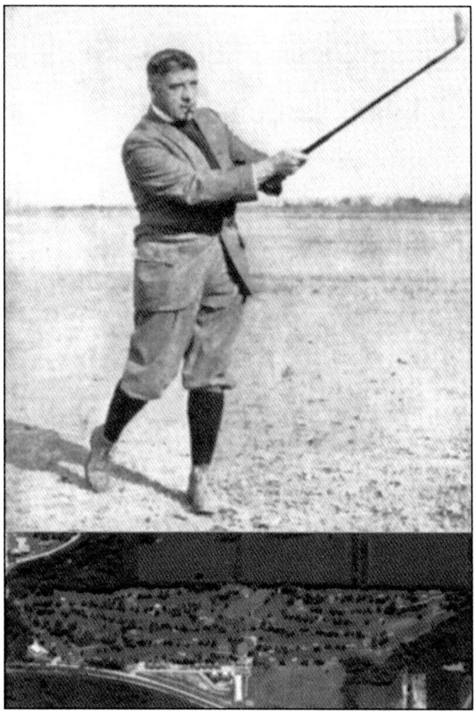

The Glenwoodie Golf Course, located at 19301 State Street, was designed by Harry Collis (pictured) and Jack Daray and opened in 1926. An estimated 33,000 rounds are played annually at this 18-hole public course. It was allegedly one of Al Capone's numerous golf hangouts. (Private collection.)

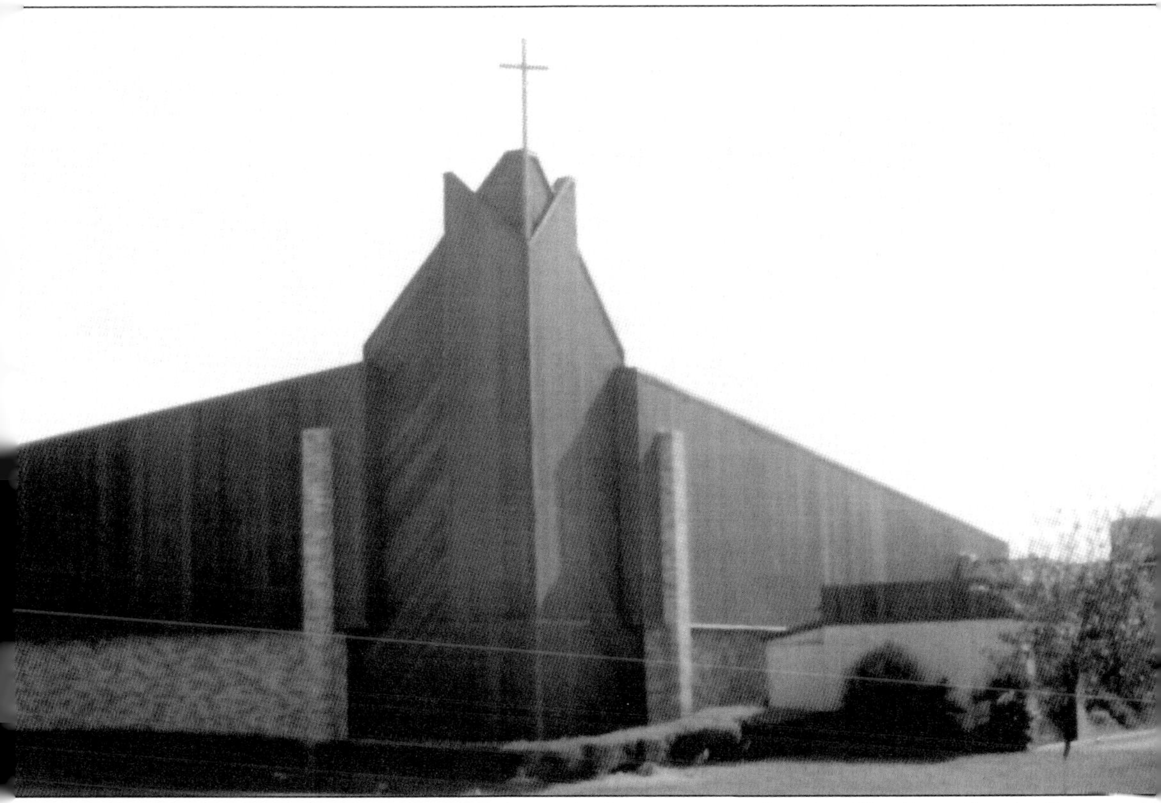

In 1884, the first St. John Catholic Church was built as a mission church of St. Kevin Parish. On January 6, 1885, Margaret Joan O'Connor received the first recorded baptism in the new church. The dedication of a new brick church located at 220 East Main Street took place on May 27, 1941. The most recent church (above), located on Cottage Grove Avenue, was dedicated April 17, 1977. (Photograph by the author.)

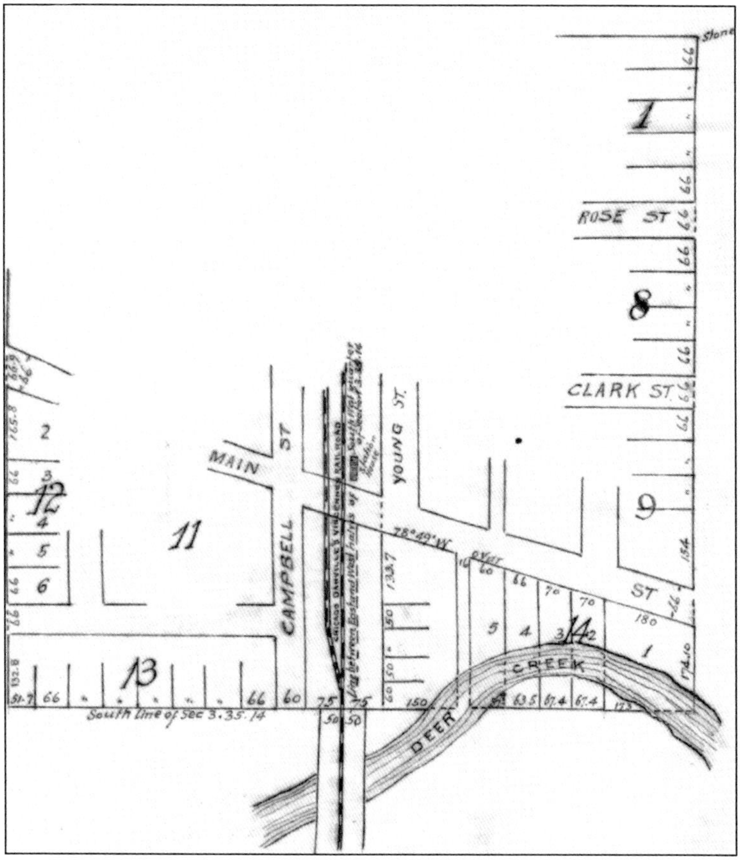

This map was titled "Glenwood, Cook Co., Ill." In 1870, Joseph Young and Job Campbell had some land subdivided that is still laid out in much the same way. They also picked out interesting names for a couple of the streets: Campbell and Young. (Private collection.)

23 Note: Recorded August 26, 1874, as Doc. 187299, in book 8 of plats, page 58, is a map entitled "Glenwood, Cook Co., Ill."

George E. Dolton, surveyor, certifies June 14, 1870, that under the direction of Joseph E. Young and Job Campbell, he did survey, subdivide and lay out in blocks, lots, streets and alleys a portion of the South West quarter of Section 3, in T. 35 N., of R. 14, E. of the "3d P. M." to be known as the village of Glenwood; "that the annexed" plat is a true and correct representation of said survey by him made and that the distances are correctly given on said plat in feet and inches and the courses in degrees and minutes.

Said map is in part as follows:

Here is the legal description of the Glenwood map shown in the image above. It was certified by surveyor George E. Dolton on June 14, 1870. (Private collection.)

This map shows Job Campbell's first addition. According to the 1850 census, Job and Rebecca Campbell's real estate property was valued at $1,600. (Private collection.)

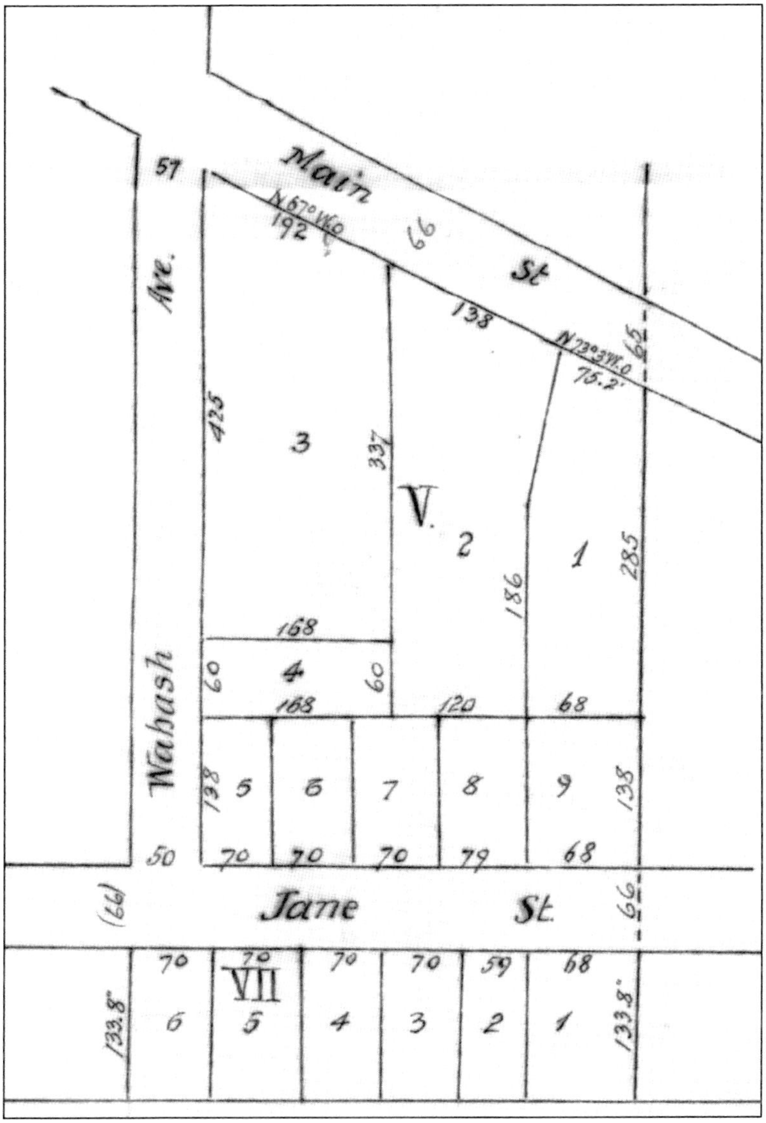

"Campbell's 1st Addition
24 "to
"Glenwood being the West
"half of the S. W. ¼ of the
"S. W. ¼ Sec. 3, T. 35
"N. R. XIV, East 3rd Prl.Medn."
Doc. 162603.

Plat, entitled as in the margin recorded December 18, 1877, in book 13 of plats, page 32.

Surveyor's certificate dated December 14, 1877.

Acknowledged by Job Campbell as owner December 14, 1877.

This legal description of the map shown above acknowledges Job Campbell as owner of the land south of Main Street and east of Wabash Street. Campbell's wife inspired the name for Rebecca Street. (Private collection.)

"(L. S.)" "Thos. H. Campbell,

"Auditor."

69 On page 27 of said book entitled: "Swamp Land Record" was the following: "A transcript of swamp and overflowed lands inuring to the State of Illinois under the act of Congress approved Sept. 28, 1850, lying in the county of Cook, in the Chicago Land District" and describing, among other property N. 1/2 of Section 17 in T. 35 R. 15, E.

"Auditor's office, Springfield, Illinois.

"I, Thomas H. Campbell, auditor of public accounts of the "state of Illinois, certify that the foregoing is a true and correct "transcript of swamp and overflowed lands lying in the county of Cook "as appears by the transcript of such swamp and overflowed lands furnished by the commissioners of the General Land office to the governor "of this state and filed in this office.

"In testimony whereof I have hereunto subscribed my name and affixed "the seal of said office this 23d day of March, 1855.

"Thos H. Campbell,

"(L. S.)" "Auditor."

70 Note: In book 2 of Supervisor's Records on page 294 in the office of the county clerk of Cook county prior to October 9, 1871, under date of March 9, 1859, the following resolution was entered.

"Resolved that a swamp land commissioner be appointed and that he "proceed to advertise and sell such of said lands as have been appraised "by this board or so much thereof as may be necessary and apply the pro- "ceeds towards the drainage of the same as required by law."

(The swamp lands in T. 35 R. 15, having been appraised at $5.00 per acre as appeared on page 280 of same record.) A. H. Dalton being declared elected as such commissioner.

Passed.

This legal document concerning swampland located in Glenwood was certified by auditor Thomas Campbell in 1855. (Private collection.)

Two

Brookwood School

Back when Glenwood was still called Hickory Bend, the children of the community attended a log cabin school that was built in 1850 about one and a half miles east of the village. In 1882, a two-room frame school was built on the site of today's Brookwood Junior High School at 201 Glenwood-Lansing Road. In 1895, the Brookwood School District was formed, and the first brick school was constructed. Additions to the school were completed in 1928, 1950, and 1958. That building and all of its additions are still standing today.

In 1990, the Brookwood School District Administration and Diagnostic Building was completed right next door to Brookwood Middle School at 201 Glenwood-Dyer Road. Until the 1960s, all of Glenwood's public schoolchildren went to the same school. Those of a certain age will no doubt remember the third-floor fire escape's tubes. With the building boom of the 1960s, subdivisions Glenwood Forest, Glenwood Manor, Glenwood Estates, and Brookwood Point were built, and it became clear that more classrooms were needed. Longwood School was built on former farmland that had once belonged to the Glenwood School for Boys. It had kindergarten through fifth-grade classes for children living in the Glenwood Manor development. The junior high was constructed right across the street from the 1895 building and next to the Glenwood Forest development. It opened its doors in the fall of 1967, but students still went across the street for the cafeteria, public basketball games, and the band room. For many years, all basketball games and anything requiring a stage still took place in the old gym. Development of the Brookwood Point subdivision eventually required building the Hickory Bend Elementary School within that development. Today, Brookwood School District No. 167 includes four schools, all within the town limits: Hickory Bend and Longwood Elementary Schools, Brookwood Middle School, and Brookwood Junior High School.

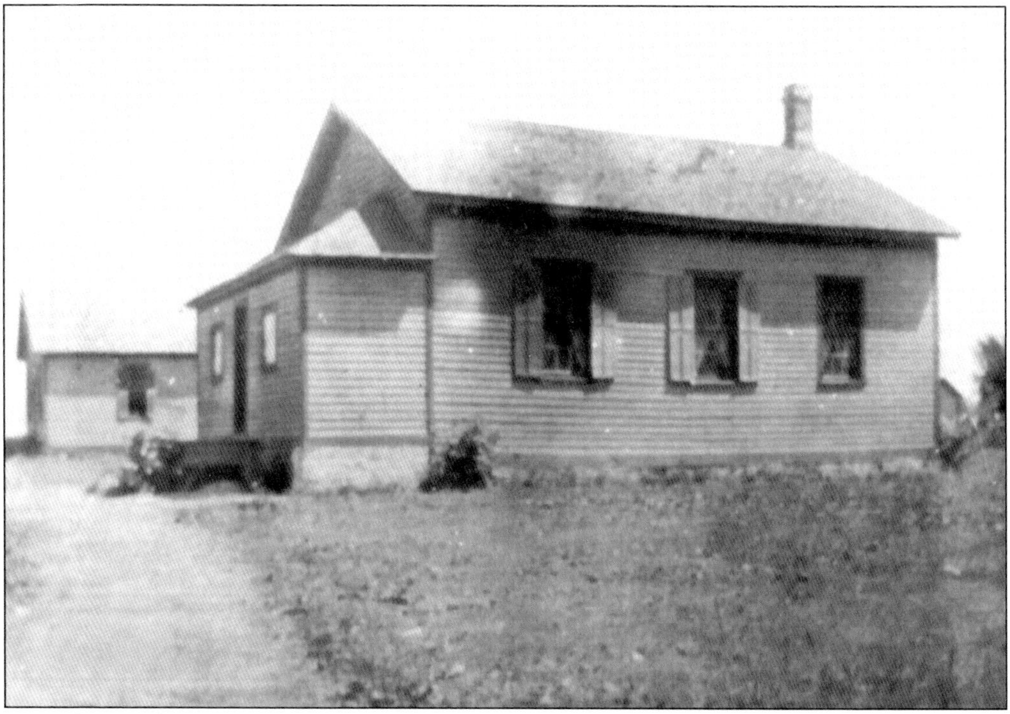

According to the records, the only schoolhouse up until this time was a little log cabin that was one and a half miles east of the village, but in 1882, a two-room frame school was built on the site of today's Brookwood Junior High School. (Courtesy of the Glenwood Historical Society.)

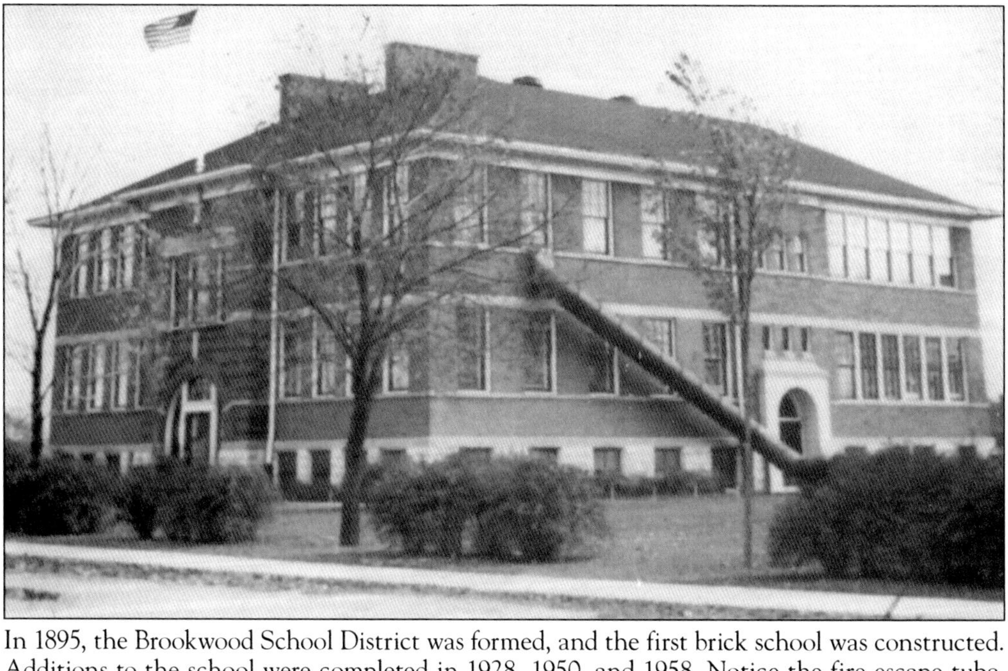

In 1895, the Brookwood School District was formed, and the first brick school was constructed. Additions to the school were completed in 1928, 1950, and 1958. Notice the fire escape tube. Contrary to old rumors, there is no record of anyone ever being trapped on the way down because of their size. (Courtesy of the Glenwood Historical Society.)

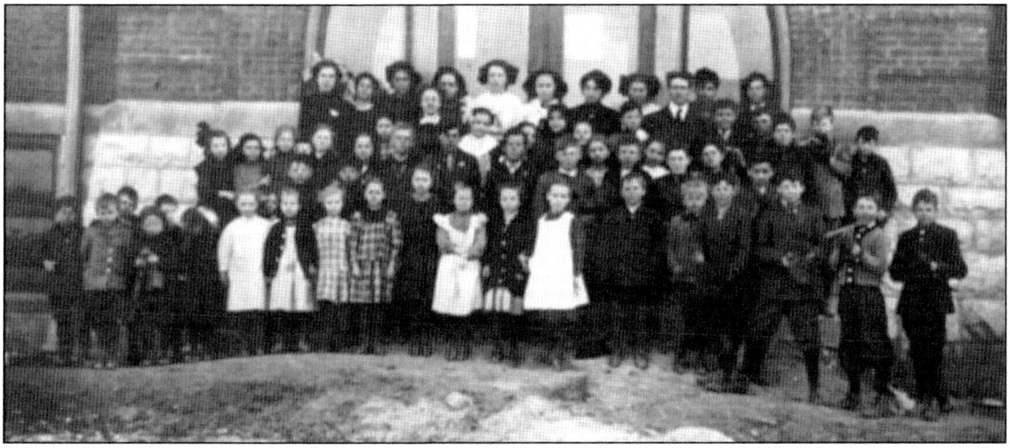

The students of the Brookwood School take time for a photograph outside of the school in 1910. (Courtesy of the Glenwood Historical Society.)

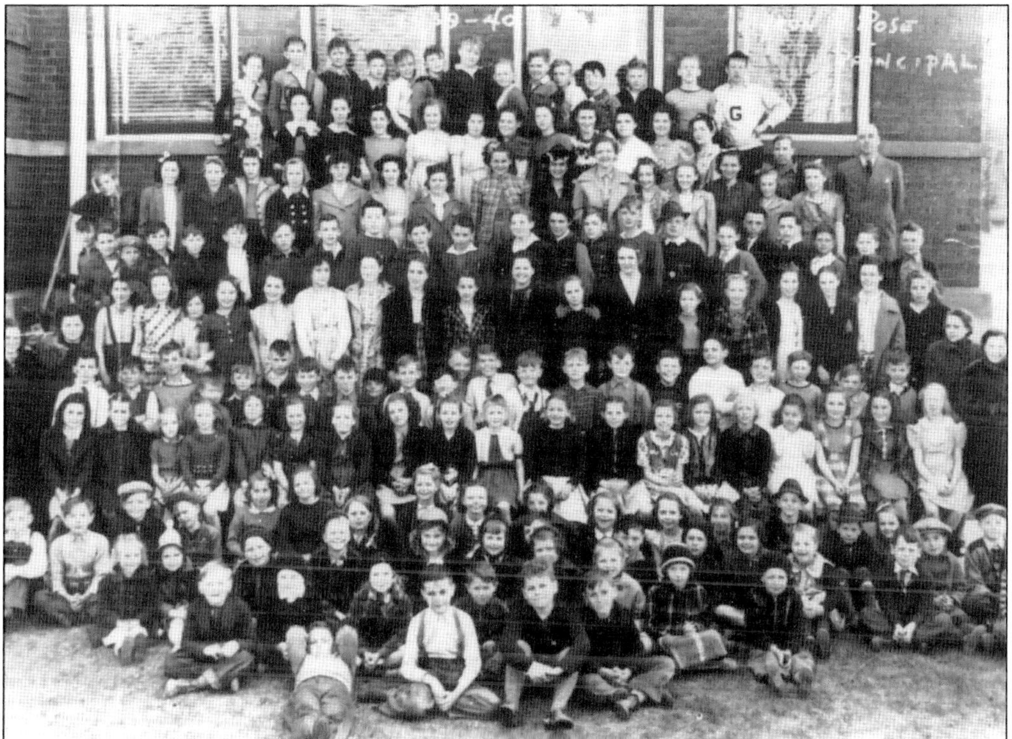

In 1940, the Brookwood student body posed for this photograph outside the school. (Courtesy of the Glenwood Historical Society.)

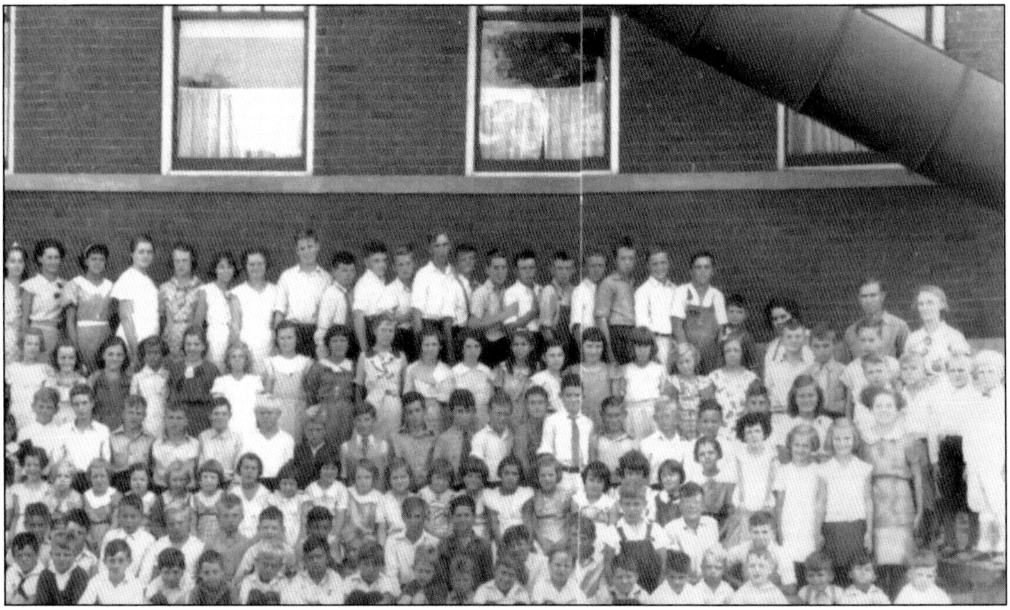

Another group of smiling Brookwood students pose for the camera. The fire escape tube is clearly visible in this image. (Courtesy of the Glenwood Historical Society.)

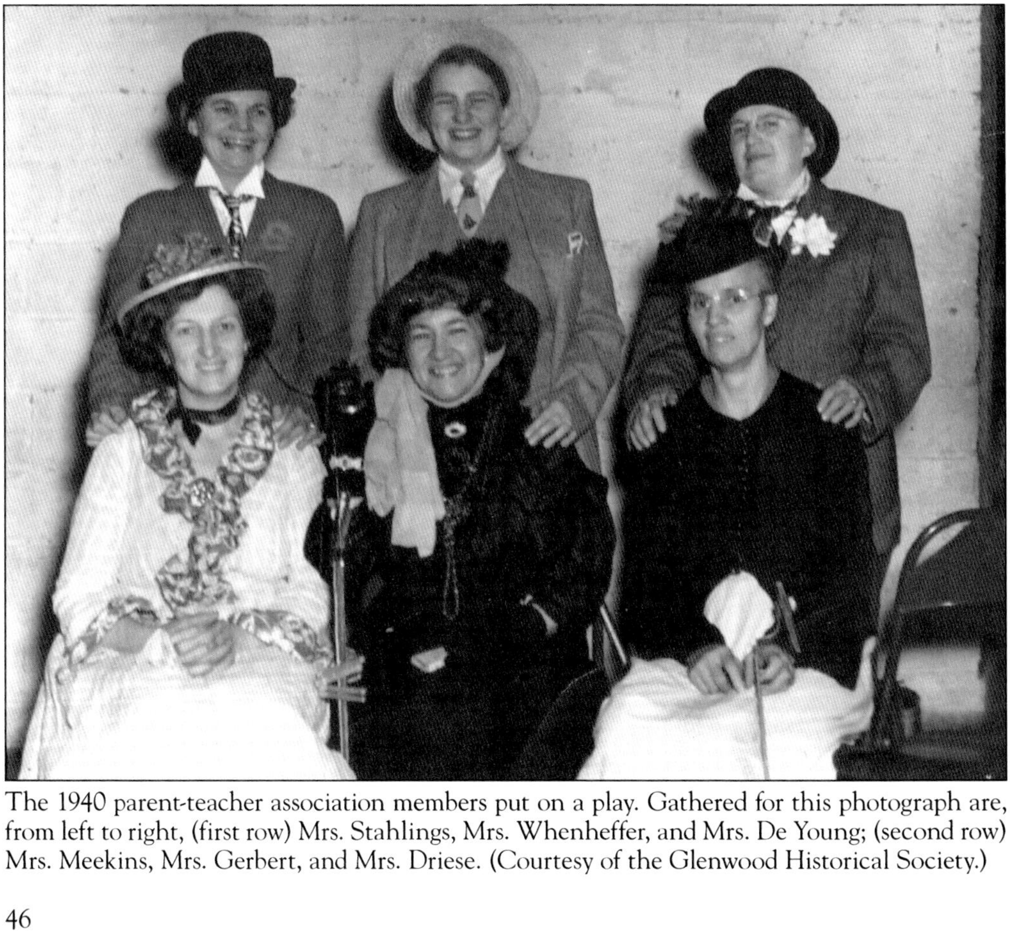

The 1940 parent-teacher association members put on a play. Gathered for this photograph are, from left to right, (first row) Mrs. Stahlings, Mrs. Whenheffer, and Mrs. De Young; (second row) Mrs. Meekins, Mrs. Gerbert, and Mrs. Driese. (Courtesy of the Glenwood Historical Society.)

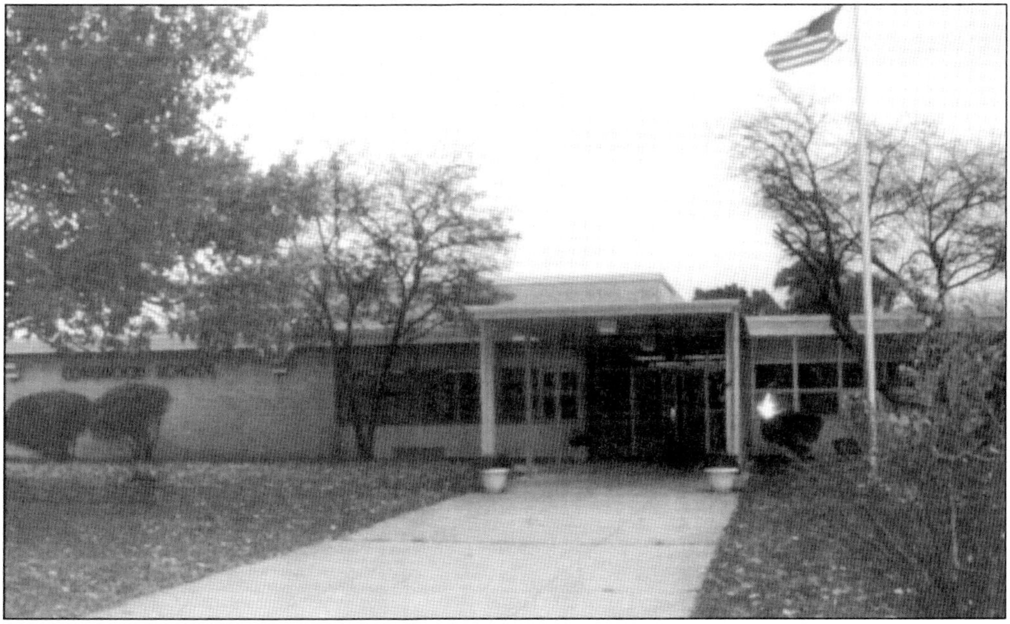

Longwood Elementary School opened in the early 1960s to serve the Glenwood Manor subdivision. (Courtesy of Brookwood School District No. 167.)

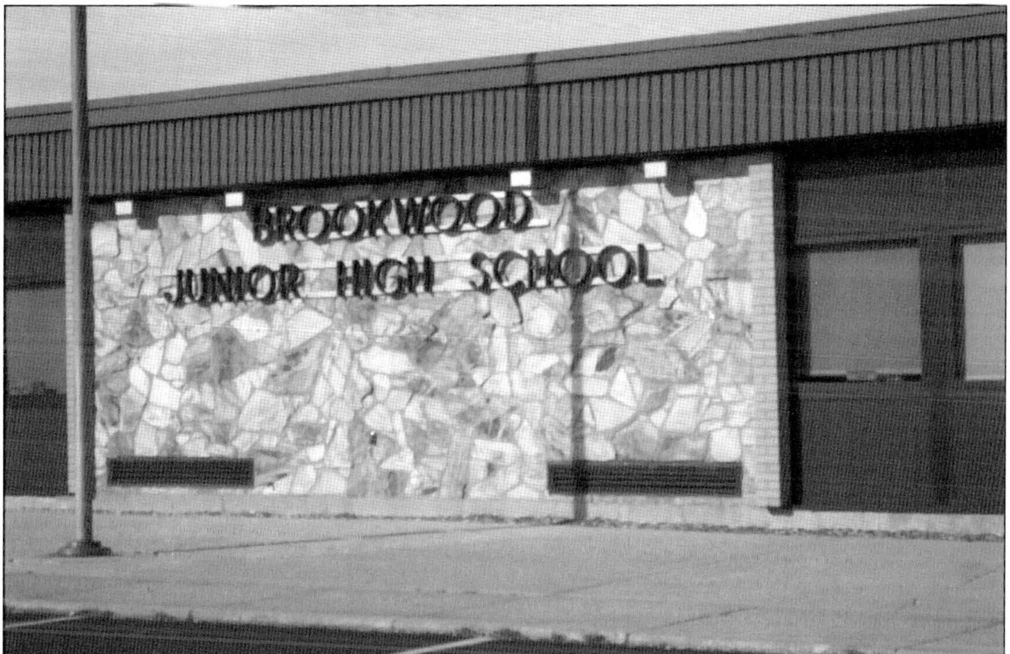

The Brookwood Junior High School opened in 1967 across the street from the original school, which then became the elementary school and is now the middle school. The creation of Glenwood Manor and Glenwood Forest subdivisions made more classrooms necessary. (Photograph by the author.)

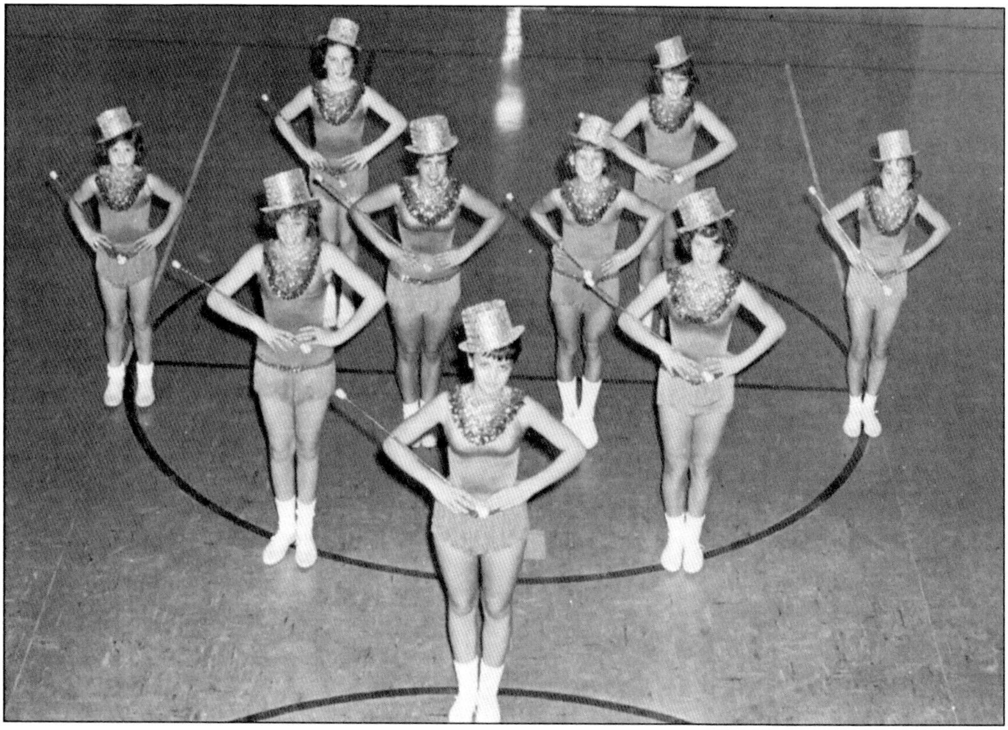

Brookwood's Senior Baton Hightoppers of 1964 are, from left to right, (first row) Beth Oliveri; (second row) Debbie Larcher and Cheryl Damon; (third row) Linda Nykaza, Cathy Nykaza, Janice Bonea, and Peggy Piazza; (fourth row) Marion Steitz and Ruth Luduigsen. (Courtesy of Brookwood School District No. 167.)

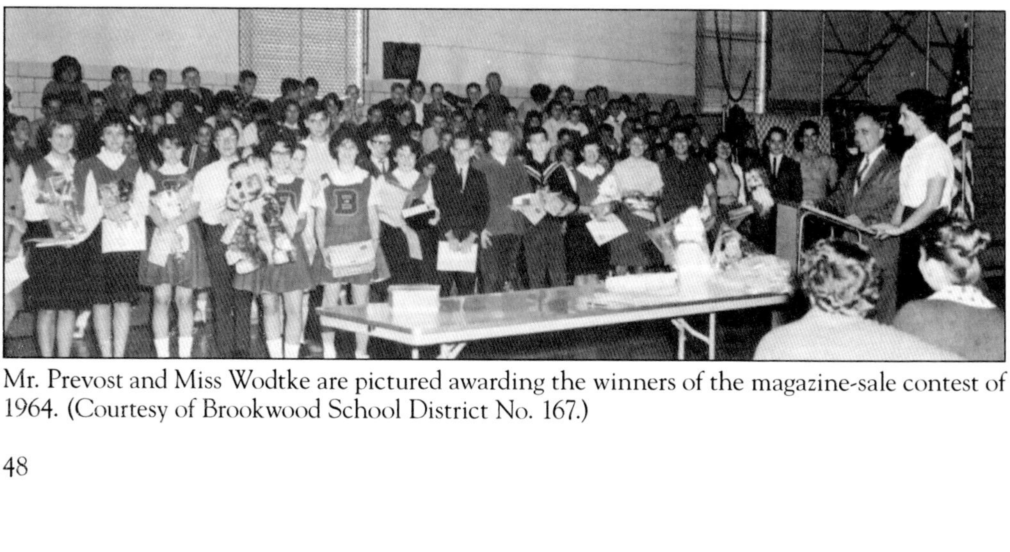

Mr. Prevost and Miss Wodtke are pictured awarding the winners of the magazine-sale contest of 1964. (Courtesy of Brookwood School District No. 167.)

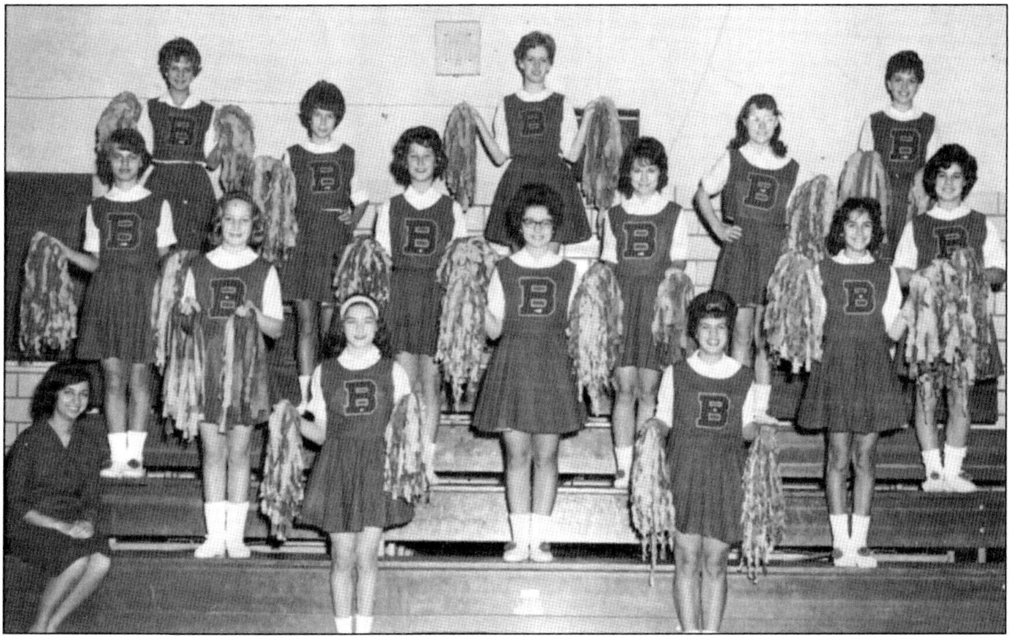

The Brookwood School cheerleading squad of 1964 are, from left to right, (first row) unidentified, Donna Bowling, and Kathy Nykaza; (second row) Mary Arnell, Vickie Bolla, and Judy Allessanrini; (third row) Janette Bertran, Cheryl Damon, Donna Fulton, and Margaret Pagoria; (fourth row) Nancy Zukauskas, Sue Dauksas, Cheryl Casey, JoAnne Miller, and Beth Oliveri. (Courtesy of Brookwood School District No. 167.)

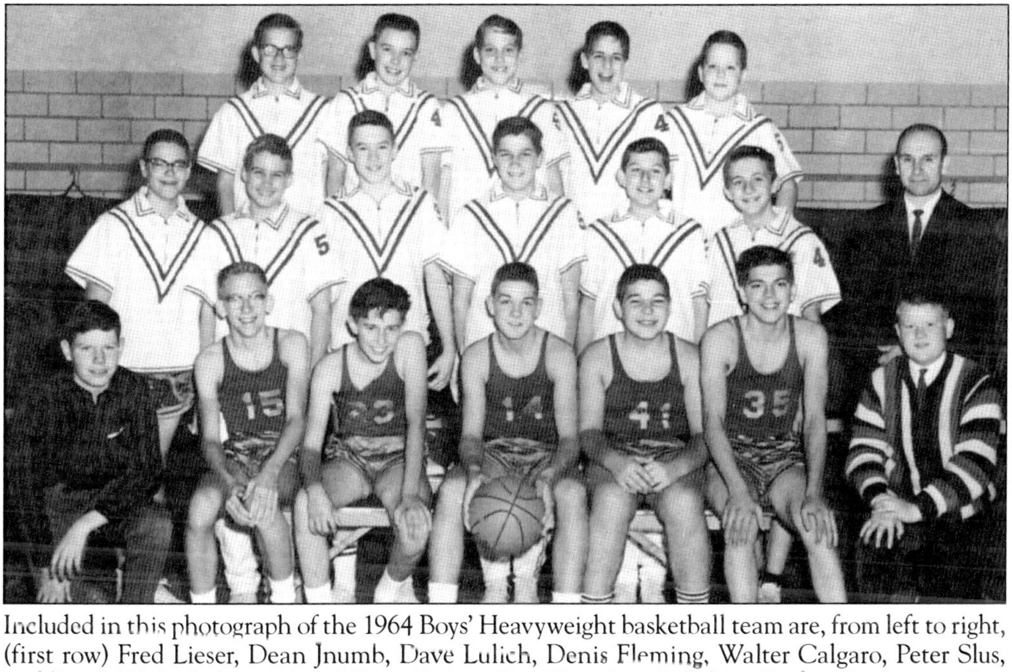

Included in this photograph of the 1964 Boys' Heavyweight basketball team are, from left to right, (first row) Fred Lieser, Dean Jnumb, Dave Lulich, Denis Fleming, Walter Calgaro, Peter Slus, and Butch Witlock; (second row) Dave Boling, Dan Fries, Jim Callahan, Rodney Ludvigsen, Ray Lemke, Jim Purlee, and coach Tony Sudar; (third row) Dennis Nicks, Jim Smith, Dan Luluga, Jim Scott, and unidentified. (Courtesy of Brookwood School District No. 167.)

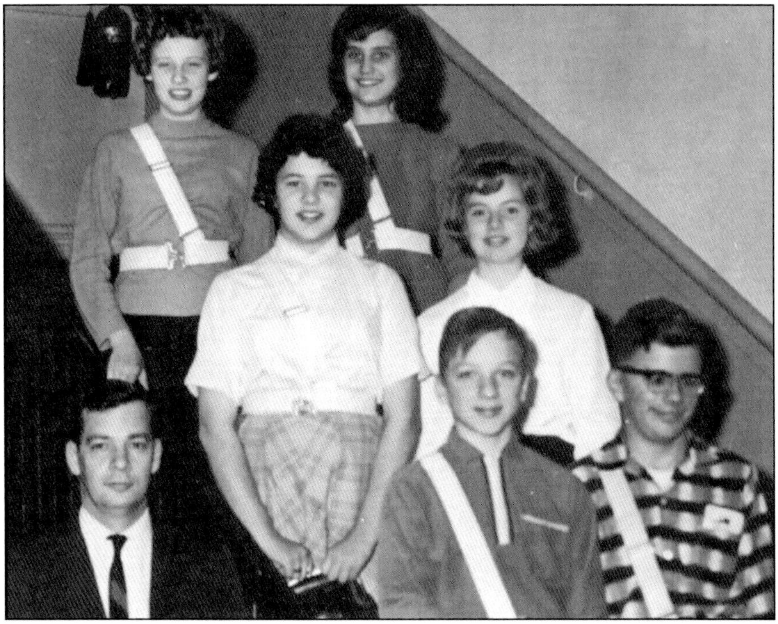

Those in this photograph of the Brookwood Safety Patrol of 1964 are, from left to right, (first row) Mr. Zachary (advisor), Ron Smith, and Terry Schickner; (second row) Geraldine Landry and Kathy Paris; (third row) Debbie Larcher and Debbie Grublesky. (Courtesy of Brookwood School District No. 167.)

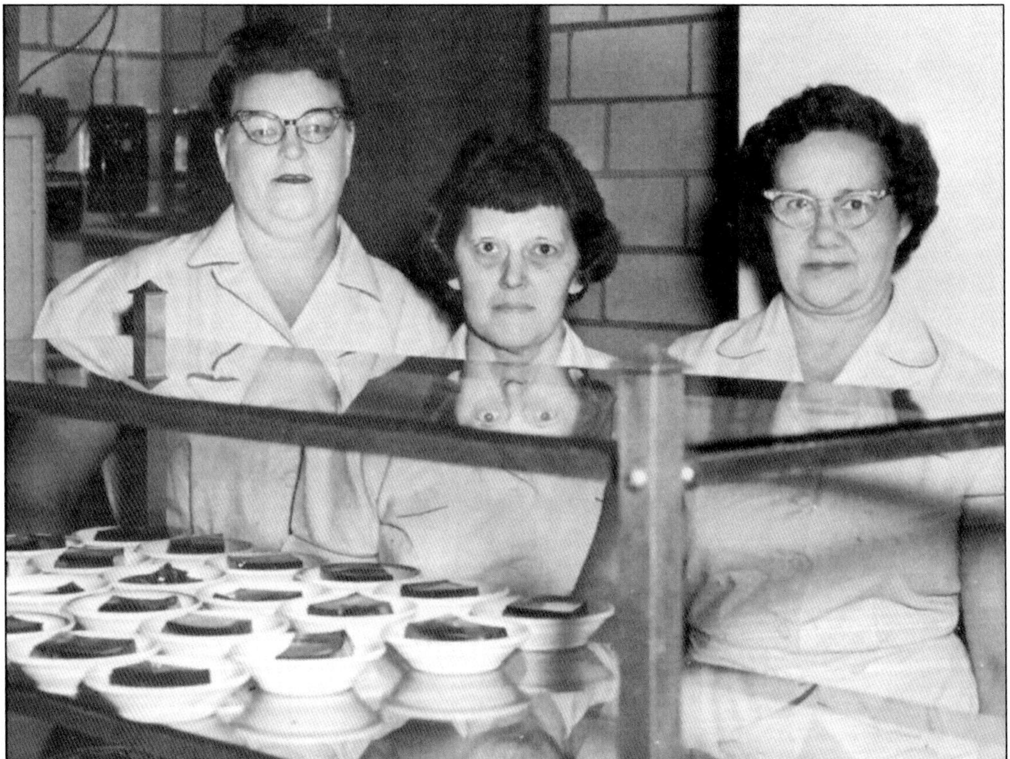

Brookwood's cafeteria staff of 1964 included, from left to right, Nellie Mergenthaler, Frances Heusmann, and Margorie Schickner. (Courtesy of Brookwood School District No. 167.)

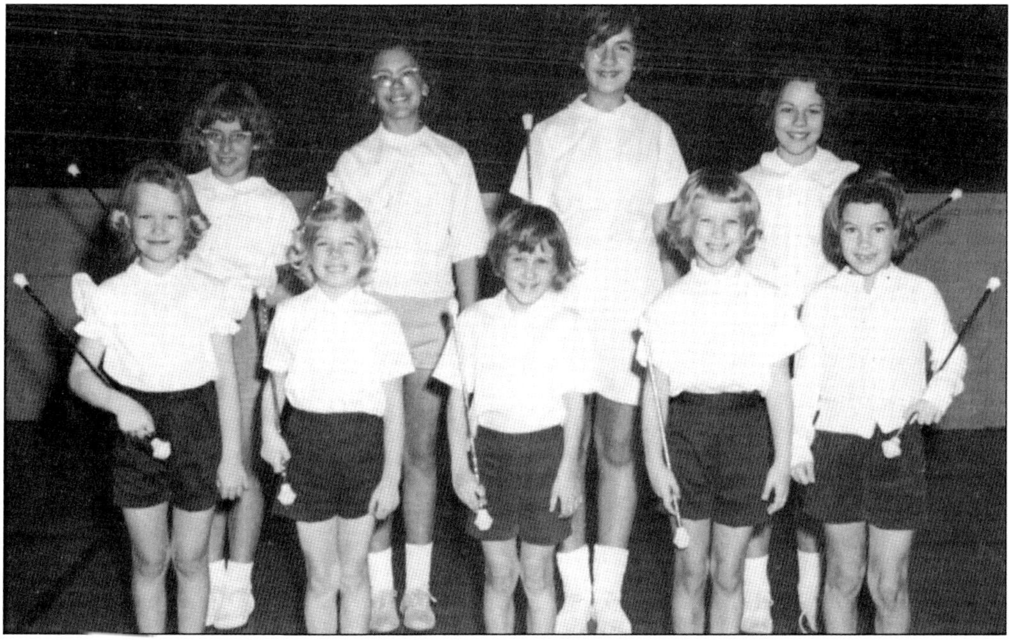

Members of Beginner Baton are, from left to right, (first row) Peggy Norman, Leanne Nelson, Cheryl Braver, Sandy Fulke, and Mary Kay Damon; (second row) Debbie Nicks, Sandra Linberg, Linda Ditola, and Susan Jackson. (Courtesy of Brookwood School District No. 167.)

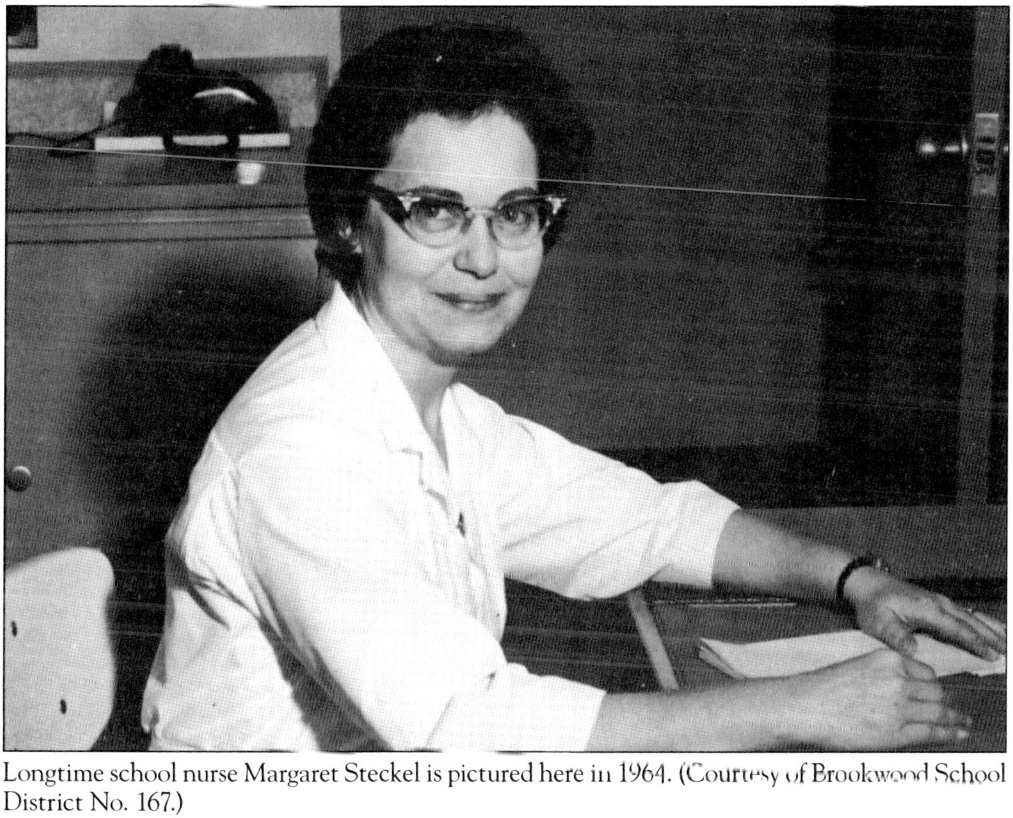

Longtime school nurse Margaret Steckel is pictured here in 1964. (Courtesy of Brookwood School District No. 167.)

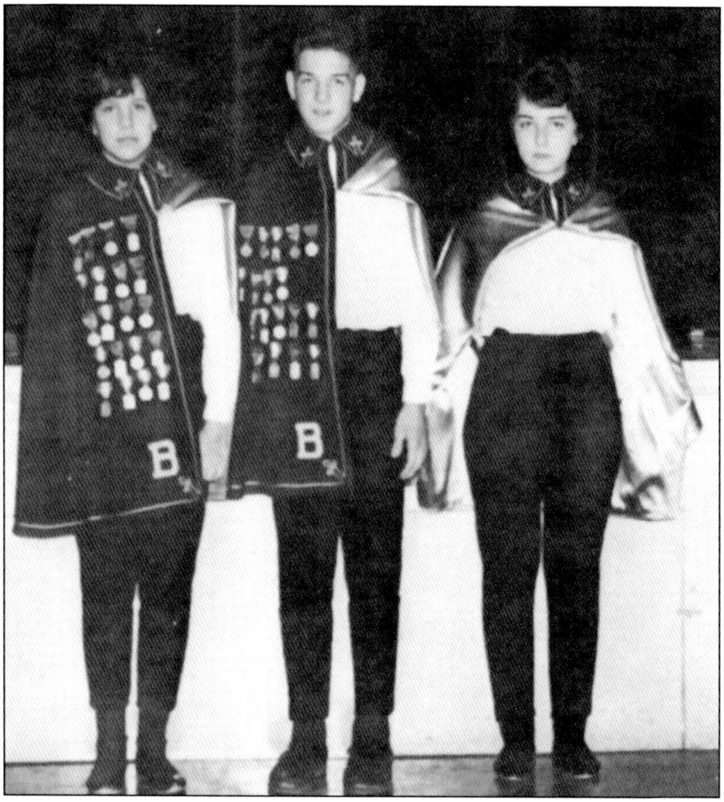

The 1964 Brookwood band officers are, from left to right, Judy Anderson, Denis Fleming, and Wendy Carney. (Courtesy of Brookwood School District No. 167.)

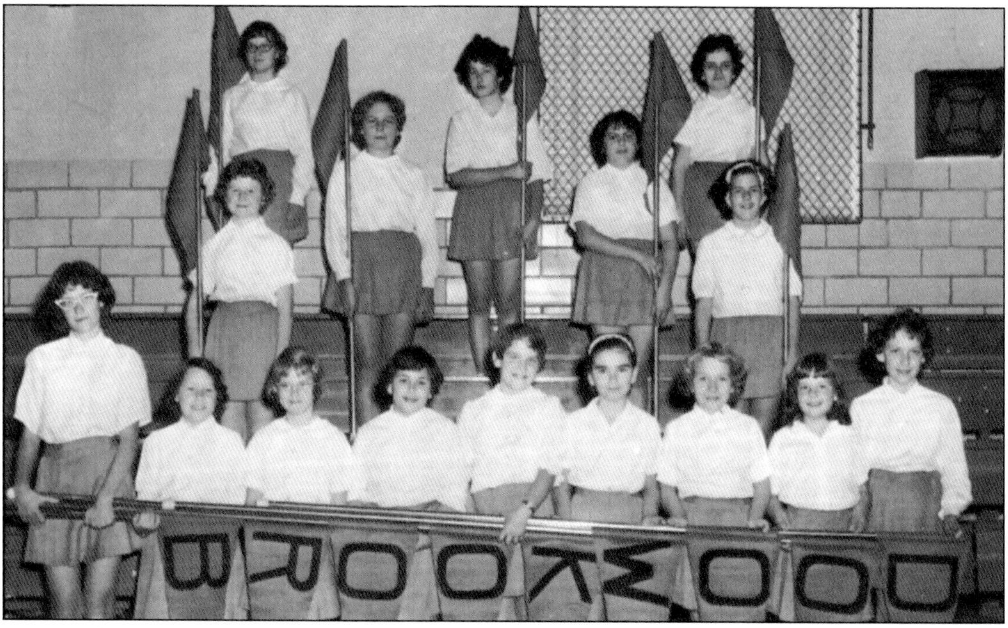

Seen in this photograph of the Brookwood Band Banner Girls of 1964 are Linda Timerlake, Diane Brown, Cathy Briggs, Paula Keeler, Karol Kersbe, Nancy Bieschne, Mary Polom, Debbie Tibbet, Carol Paris, Judy O'Brian, Debbie Wacaser, Pam Schmid, Nanette Corradetti, Vickie White, Diane Briggs, and one unidentified young lady. (Courtesy of Brookwood School District No. 167.)

The school custodians around 1965 were Fred Lockman (left) and Herb Allen. Who can remember going down to the custodian's room to clean erasers? (Courtesy of Brookwood School District No. 167.)

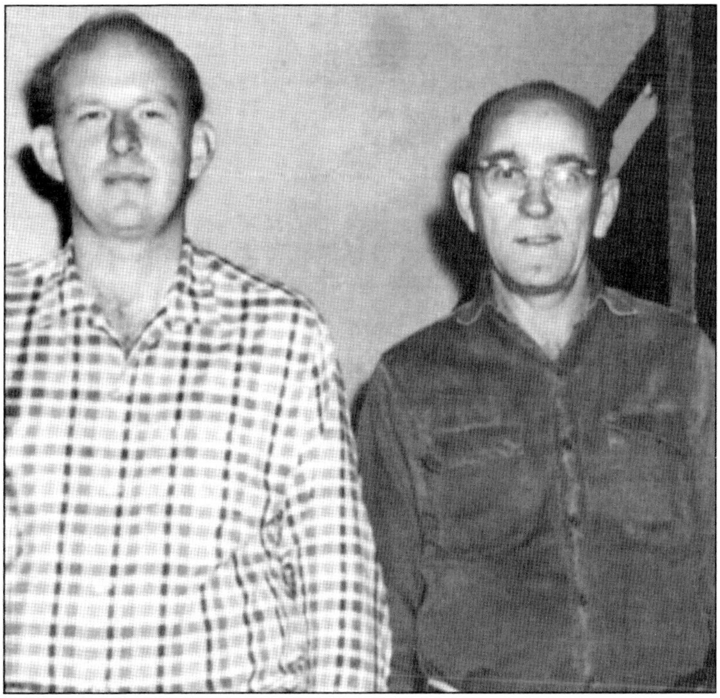

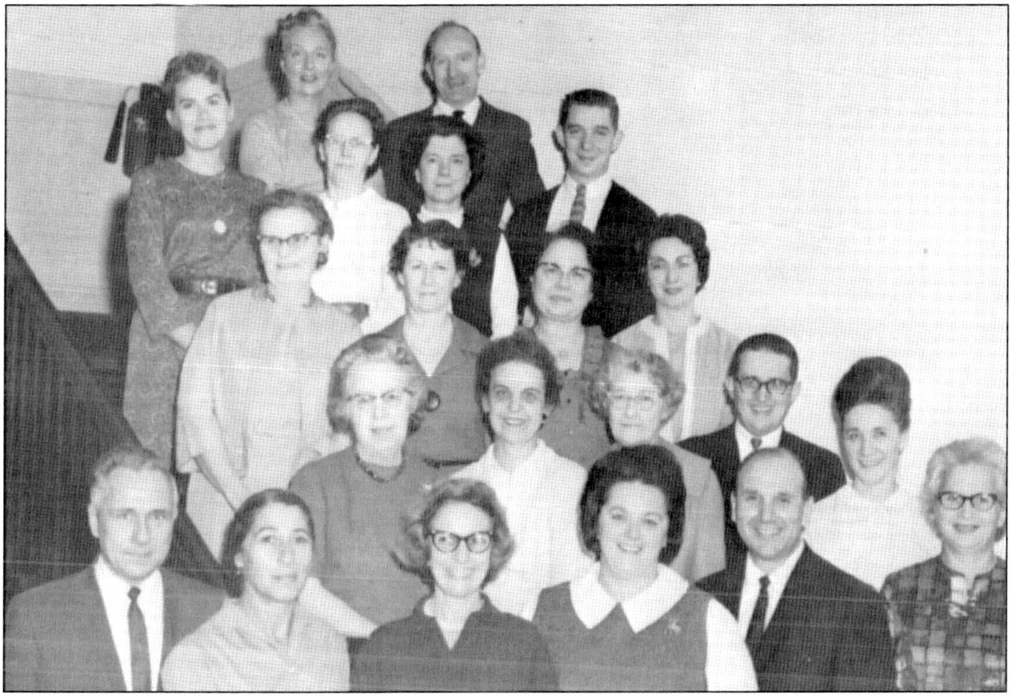

The 1966 Brookwood faculty are, from left to right, (first row) Mr. Prevost, Mrs. Marcus, Mrs. Beck, Mrs. Whittaker, Mr. Sudar, and Mrs. Hampton; (second row) Mrs. Silvery, Mrs. Clayton, Mrs. Sullivan, Mr. Havavind, and Miss Wodtke; (third row) Mrs. Paugh, Mrs. Aykens, Mrs. Bidwell, and Mrs. Lesher; (fourth row) Mrs. Drisi, Mrs. Ford, Mrs. Riddle, and Mr. Jehling; (fifth row) Mrs. Pacek and Mr. Early. (Courtesy of Brookwood School District No. 167.)

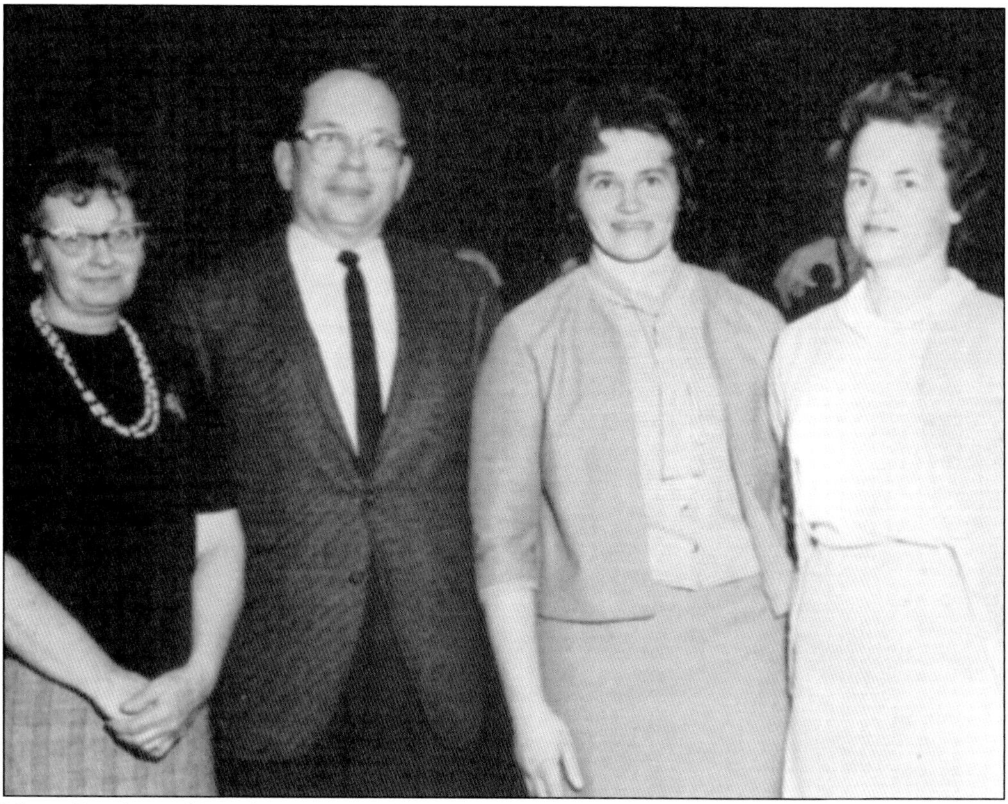

These Brookwood Band parents are, from the left to right, Mrs. Fleming, Mr. Crumbaugh, Mrs. Lowry, and Mrs. Hoffman. Crumbaugh played trombone for the Bozo's Big Top Band on WGN television for many years in the 1960s. (Courtesy of Brookwood School District No. 167.)

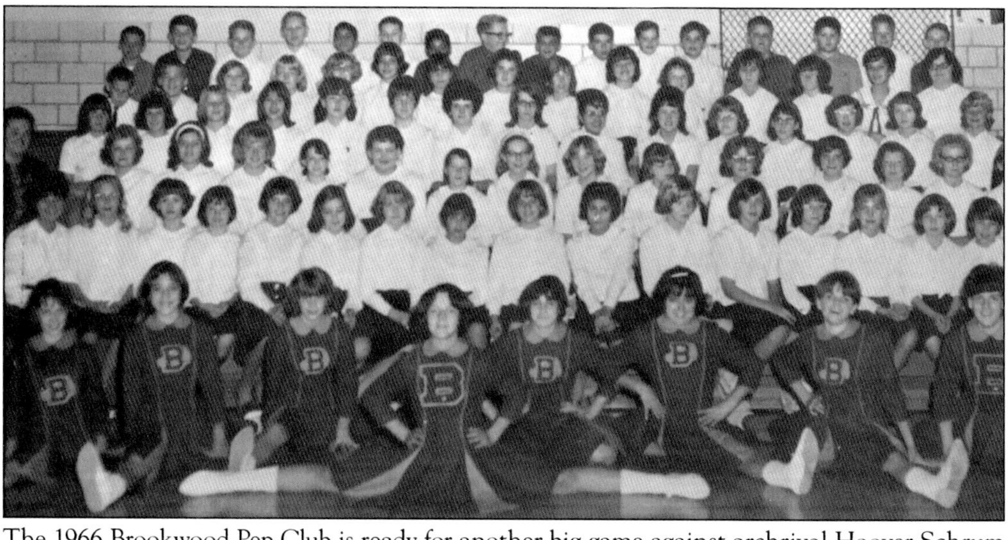

The 1966 Brookwood Pep Club is ready for another big game against archrival Hoover Schrum Memorial School of Calumet City. The advisors for Pep Club were P. Whittaker and S. Davis. (Courtesy of Brookwood School District No. 167.)

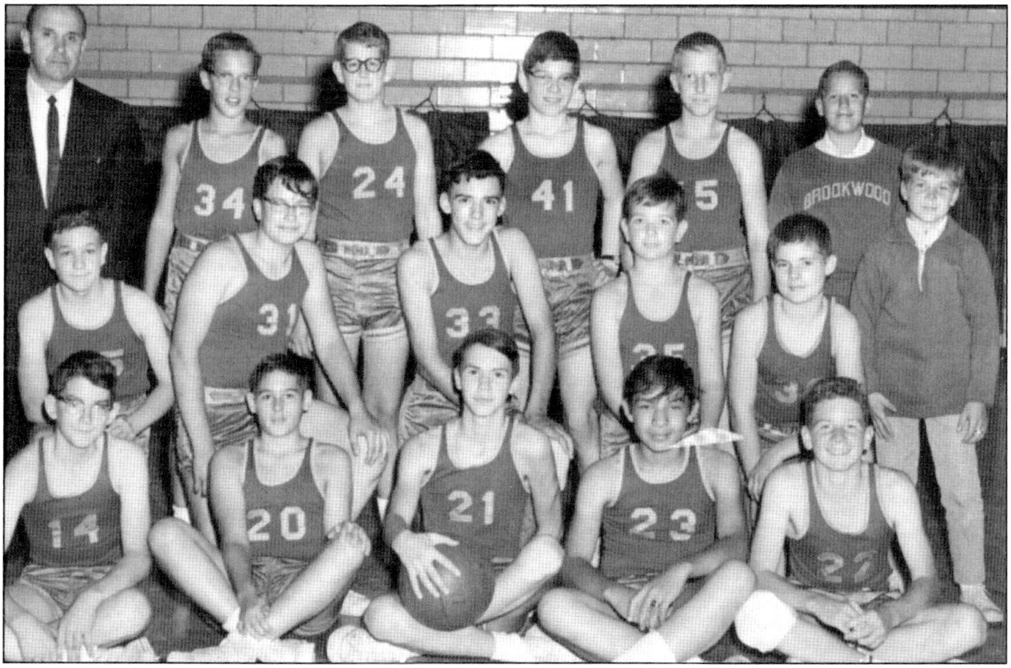

Pictured is coach Sudar's 1966 Boys' Heavyweight basketball team. Members of the team included John Johnson, David Herr, John Shockley, Charles Kats, Wayne Paris, Duane Ross, David Bohlsen, Terry Johnson, Keith Overmyer, Darren Fries, Jack Zubak, Tom Lowery, Tom Ganser, Tim Callahan, and Tony Lopez. (Courtesy of Brookwood School District No. 167.)

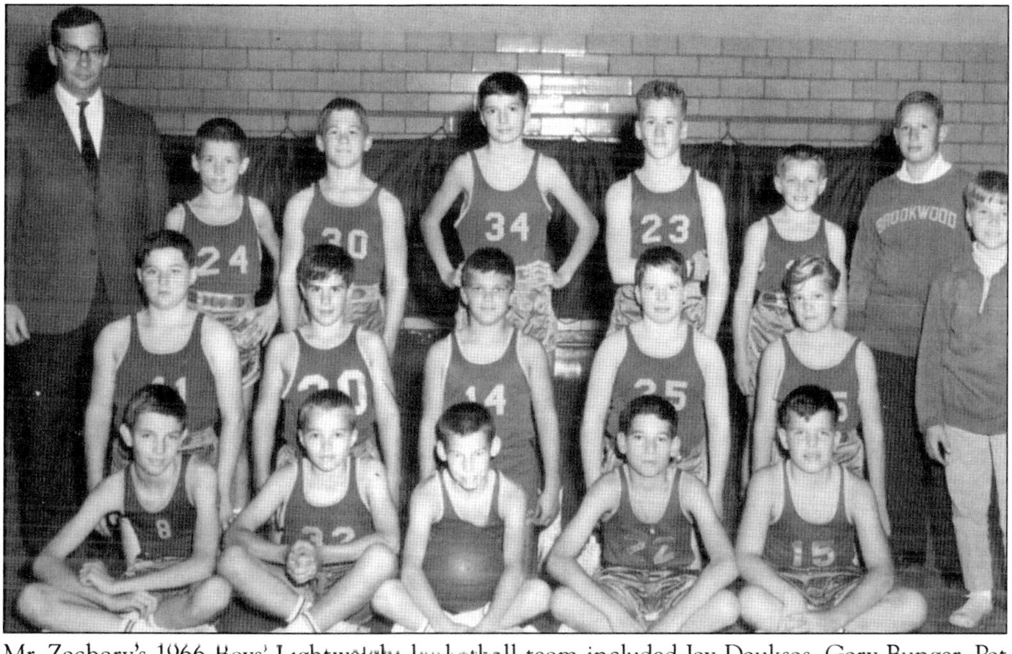

Mr. Zachary's 1966 Boys' Lightweight basketball team included Jay Dauksas, Gary Bunger, Pat Hornbeck, Bob Hoover, Ron Skubitz, Wayne Paris, Terry McLaughlin, Jan Storch, Harold Wallenber, Douglas Haney, Rick Sielof, Jack Zubak, Douglas Mushier, Steve Ashfort, Douglas Damon, Mark Bruni, and Jim Olivieri. (Courtesy of Brookwood School District No. 167.)

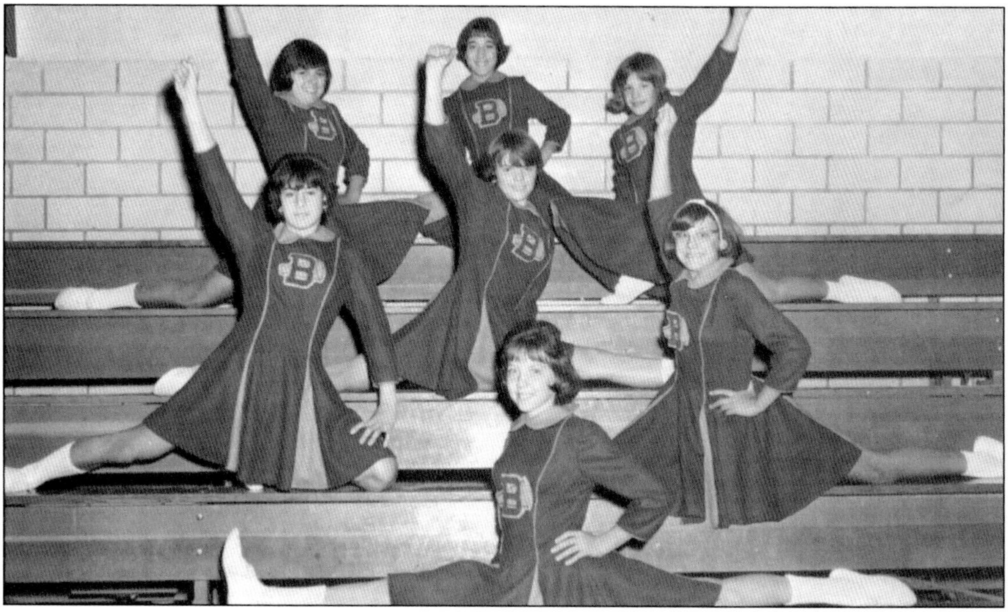

Brookwood's 1966 cheerleading squad included, from left to right, (first row) Debbie Tibbie; (second row) Mary Pagoria, Debbie Lulich, and Sandy Linborg; (third row) Joy Gregory, Peggy Piazza, and Linda Nykaza. (Courtesy of Brookwood School District No. 167.)

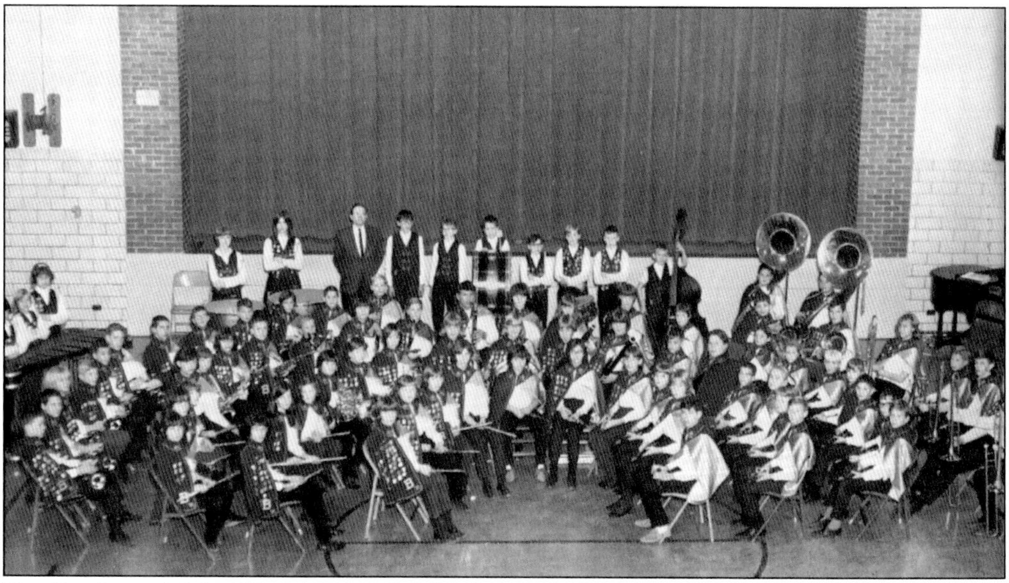

The Brookwood School Band was under the direction of Paul Crumbaugh in 1967. This would be Crumbaugh's last year as director of the band due to a disabling automobile accident. (Courtesy of Brookwood School District No. 167.)

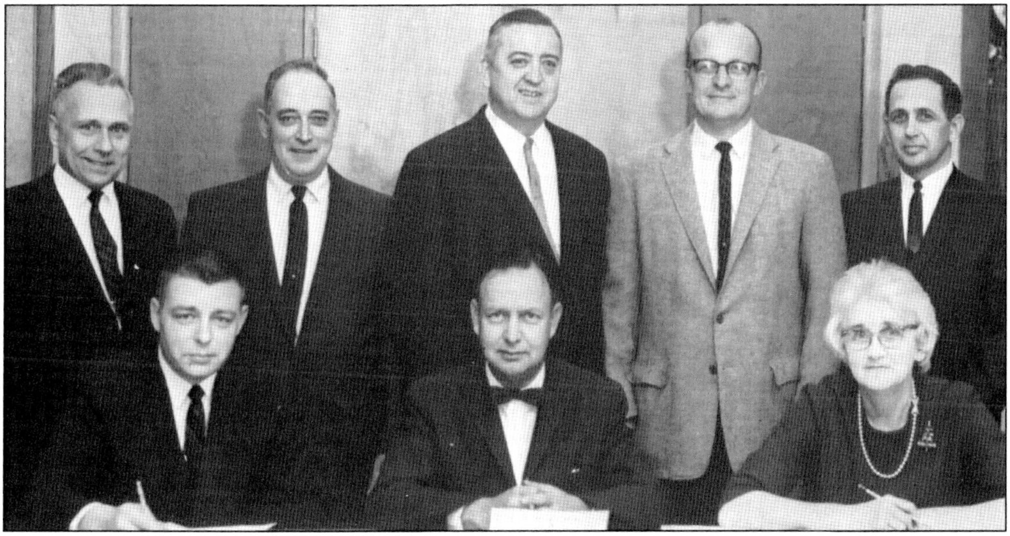

The 1967 Brookwood School Board of Education included, from left to right, (first row) R. Hoffman, W. Nygren, and Mrs. Croston; (second row) L. Prevost, Mr. Gregory, B. Herr, Mr. Zuidema, and R. Hibbs. (Courtesy of Brookwood School District No. 167.)

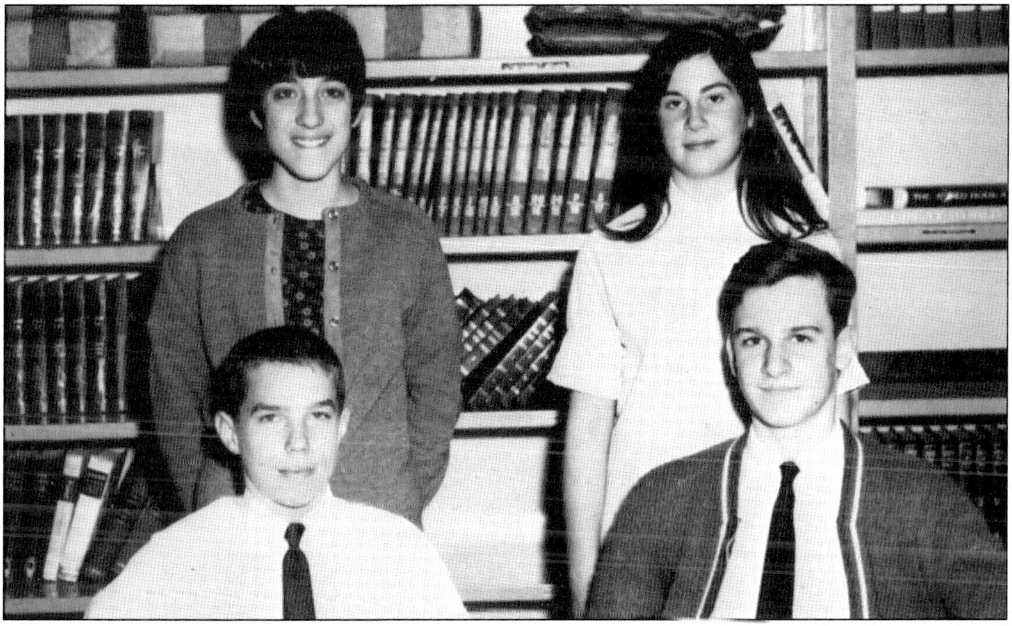

The Brookwood School eighth-grade officers for 1967 were, from left to right, (first row) Jeff Mykleby (vice president) and Roger Smiley (president), (second row) Peggy Piazza (treasurer) and Karen Greco (secretary). (Courtesy of Brookwood School District No. 167.)

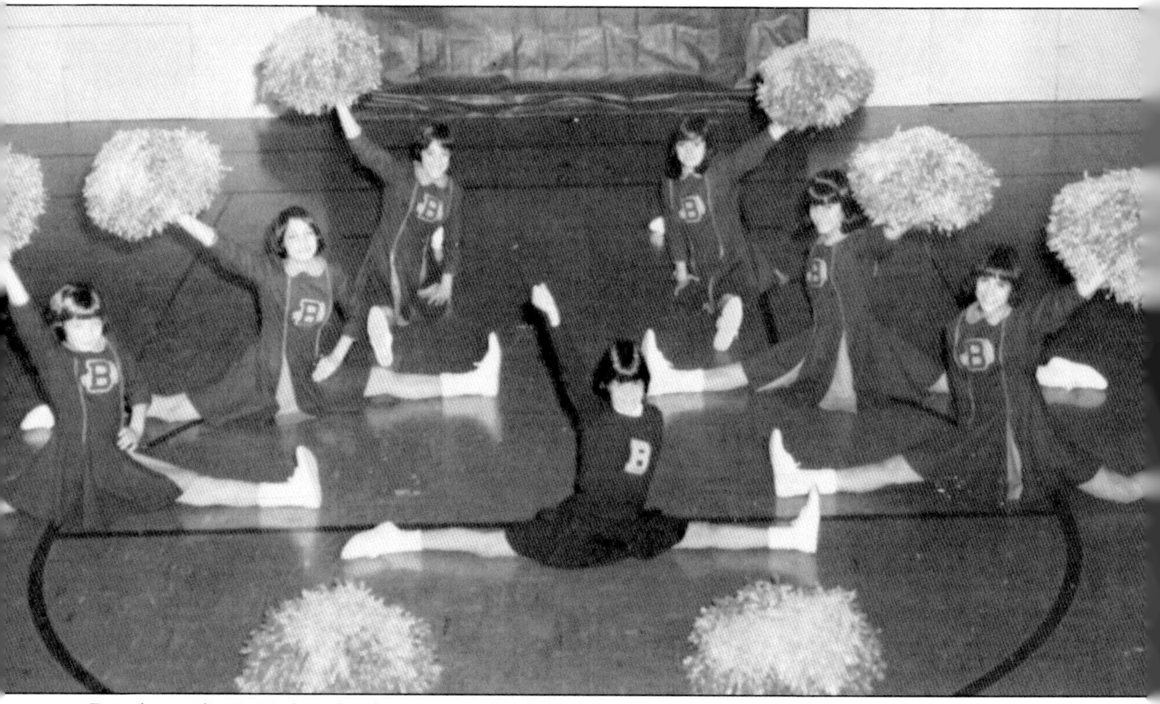

Brookwood's 1967 cheerleaders posing for this photograph are, from left to right, Ann Blackmore, Debbie Grau, Peggy Piazza, Joy Gregory, Vivian Portelli, Joni Allessanrini, and Pattie Oliveri. (Courtesy of Brookwood School District No. 167.)

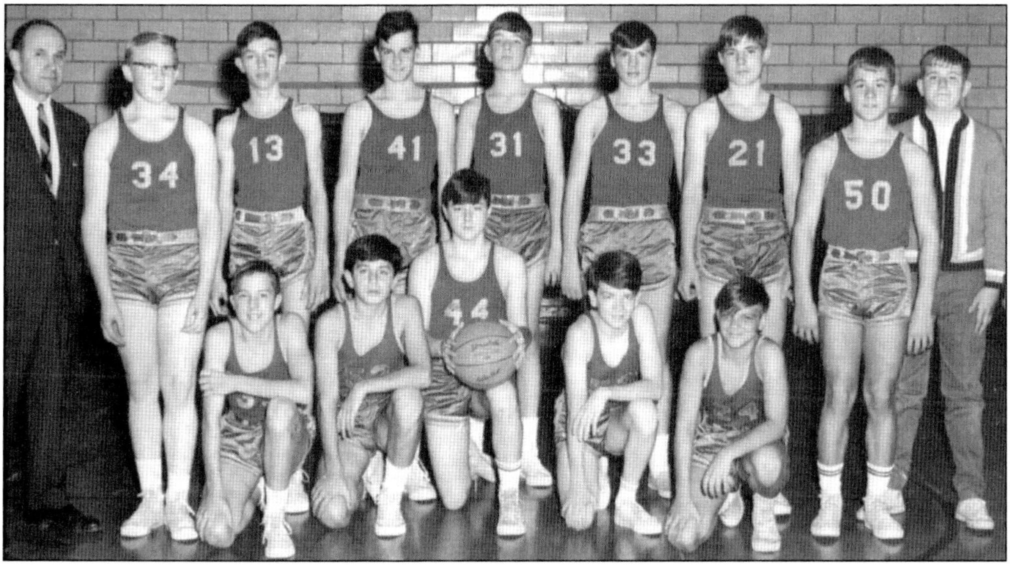

The Brookwood Boys' Heavyweight basketball team of 1967 included, from left to right, (first row) Tom Meyrick, Phillip Genarelli, Terry McLaughlin, Garret Angelich, and Harold Wallenberg; (second row) coach Sudar, Jim Martinmaki, Doug Mushier, Roger Smiley, Keith Overmyer, Scott Johnson, Darrin Fries, Gary Bunger, and Tom Godfrey. (Courtesy of Brookwood School District No. 167.)

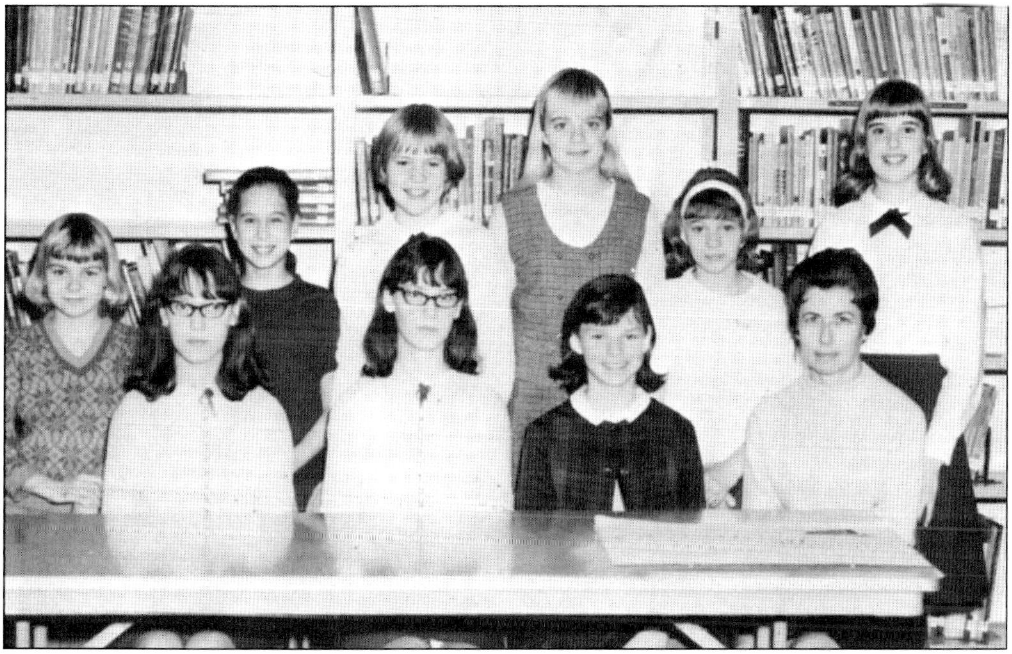

The library assistants in 1967 are, from left to right, (first row) Doris Miller, Betty Miller, Reva Bertrand, and faculty advisor Mrs. Nygren; (second row) Terri Zubak, Lucky Jones, Ruth Pohlmann, Marilyn Douglas, Judy Gabor, and Janet Staton. (Courtesy of Brookwood School District No. 167.)

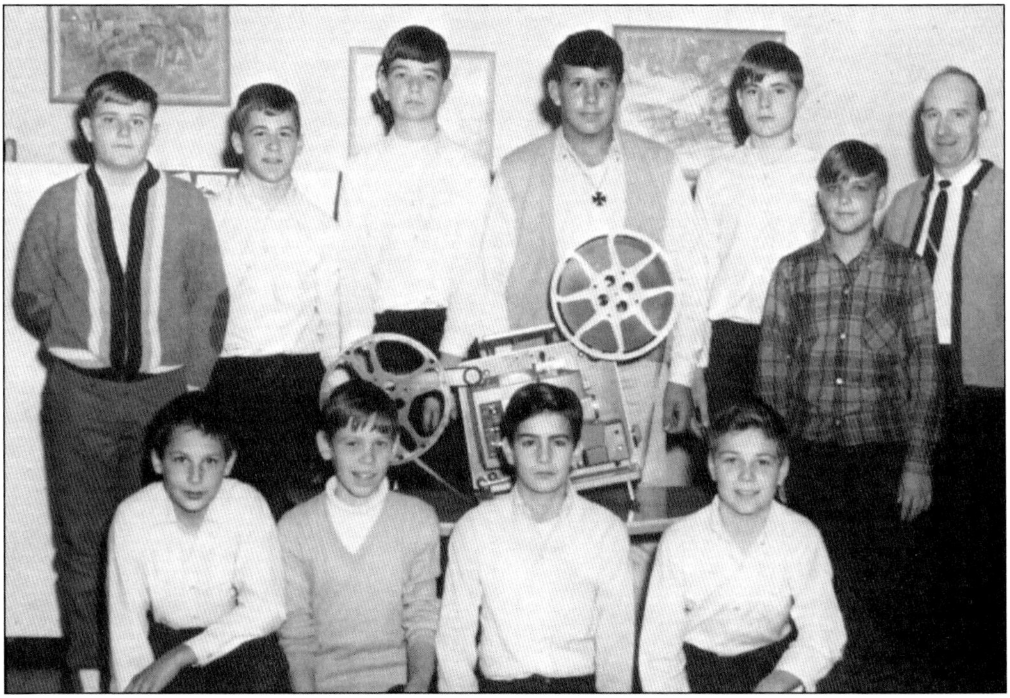

The school projectionists who kept the films rolling in 1967 were, from left to right, (first row) Bob Schmelzer, John Baczynski, John Pagoria, and Lak Zubak; (second row) Tom Godfrey, Gary Bunger, Keith Overmyer, Charlie Anderson, Darrin Fries, Harold Wallenberg, and Mr. Early. (Courtesy of Brookwood School District No. 167.)

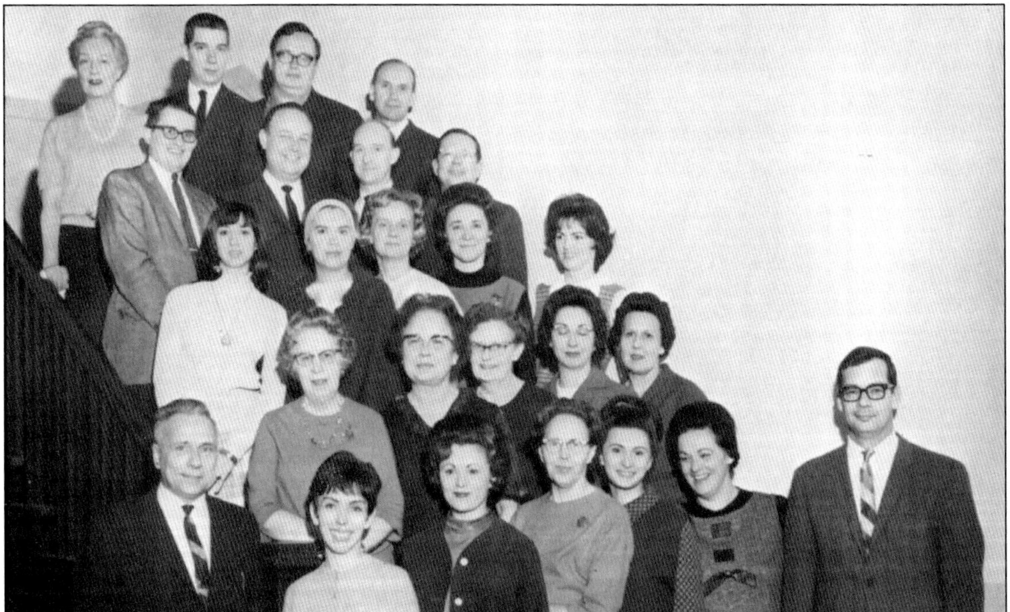

The 1967 faculty had increased in size from 1966 with staff additions that included Mr. Wentzel teaching music, Mr. Angel teaching language arts, and Mrs. Harrington teaching science. (Courtesy of Brookwood School District No. 167.)

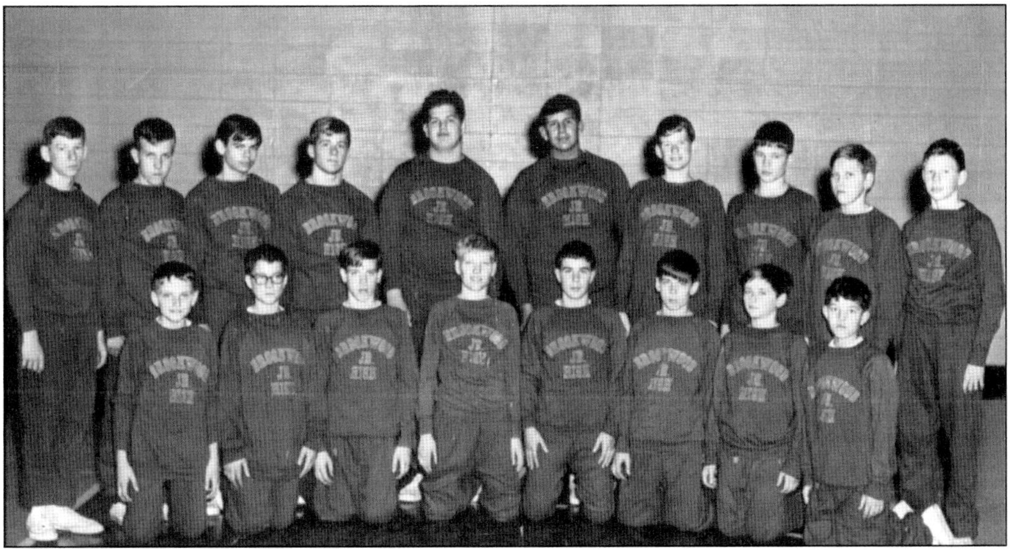

The Brookwood Junior High track team for 1968 were, from left to right, (first row) Ron Skubisz, Bob Wilcox, Chuck Dill, Kirk Rimsnider, Jan Storch, Jay Dauksas, Tony Satalic, and Steve Hatfield; (second row) Ted Chuchla, Jeff Whalen, Randy Sailsberry, Gary Bunger, John Honza, Charley Anderson, Darrel Heasley, Peter Callahan, Wayne Slusinski, and Bob Harvey. (Courtesy of Brookwood School District No. 167.)

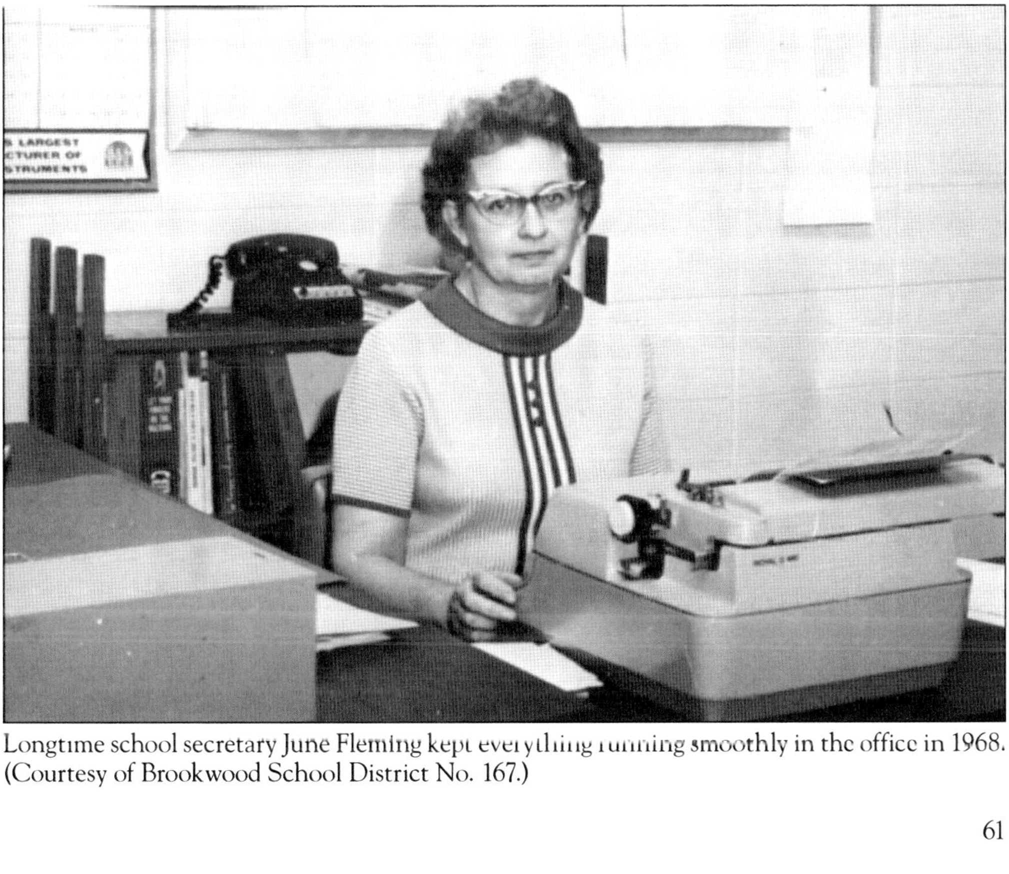

Longtime school secretary June Fleming kept everything running smoothly in the office in 1968. (Courtesy of Brookwood School District No. 167.)

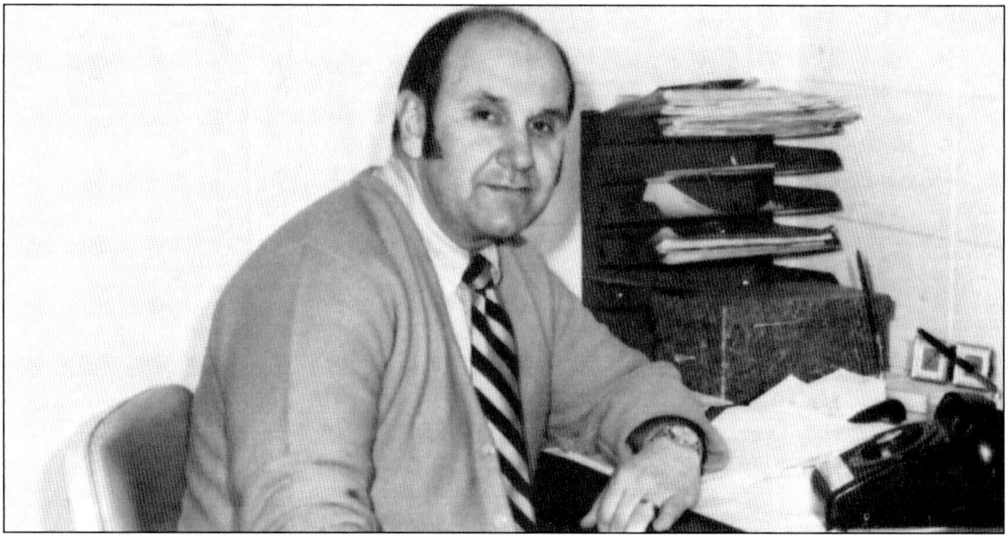

Coach Sudar became an advisor after giving up coaching because his son began participating in the sports program at Brookwood's archrival, Hoover Schrum Memorial School of Calumet City, Illinois. He did not want to coach against him. (Courtesy of Brookwood School District No. 167.)

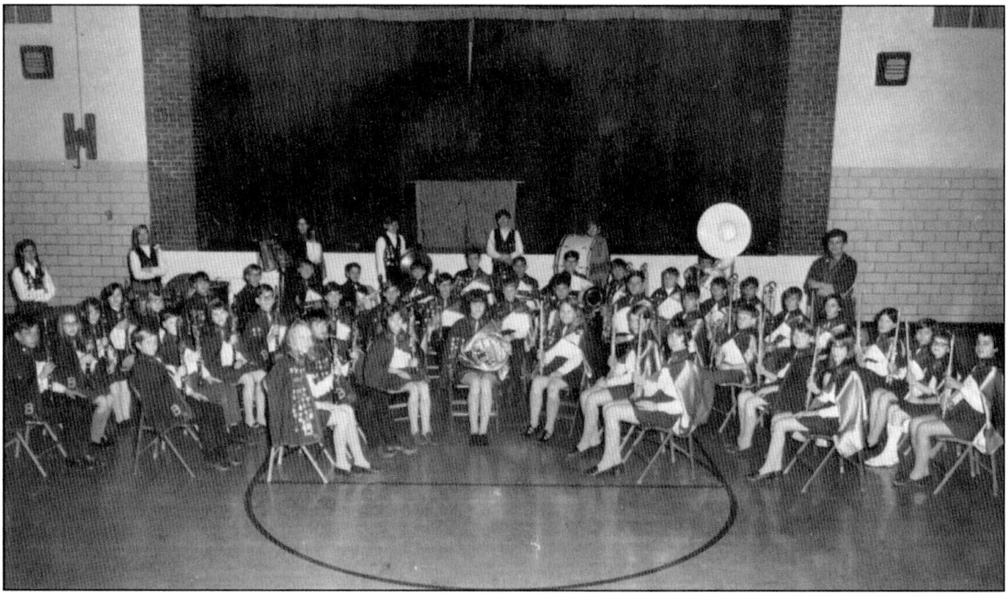

Francis Smet was director of the Brookwood Concert Band of 1969. Anyone who went to Brookwood will recognize the location of the photograph. (Courtesy of Brookwood School District No. 167.)

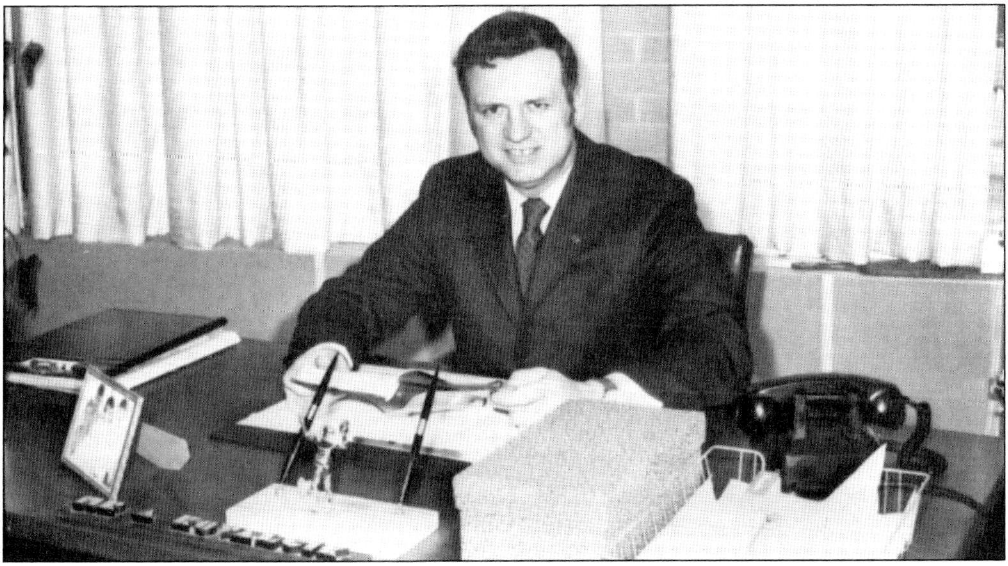

Alfred Kovalcik was the Brookwood Junior High principal in 1970. (Courtesy of Brookwood School District No. 167.)

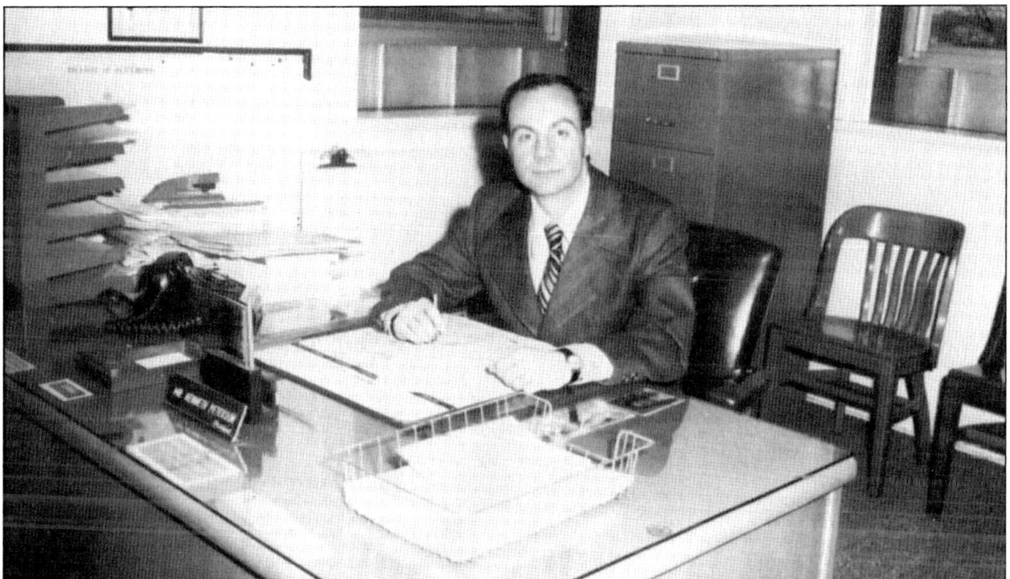

Kenneth A. Peterson was teaching social studies at the junior high in 1967, but by 1971, at the time of this photograph, he was principal. He would later become superintendent of Brookwood School District No. 167. (Courtesy of Brookwood School District No. 167.)

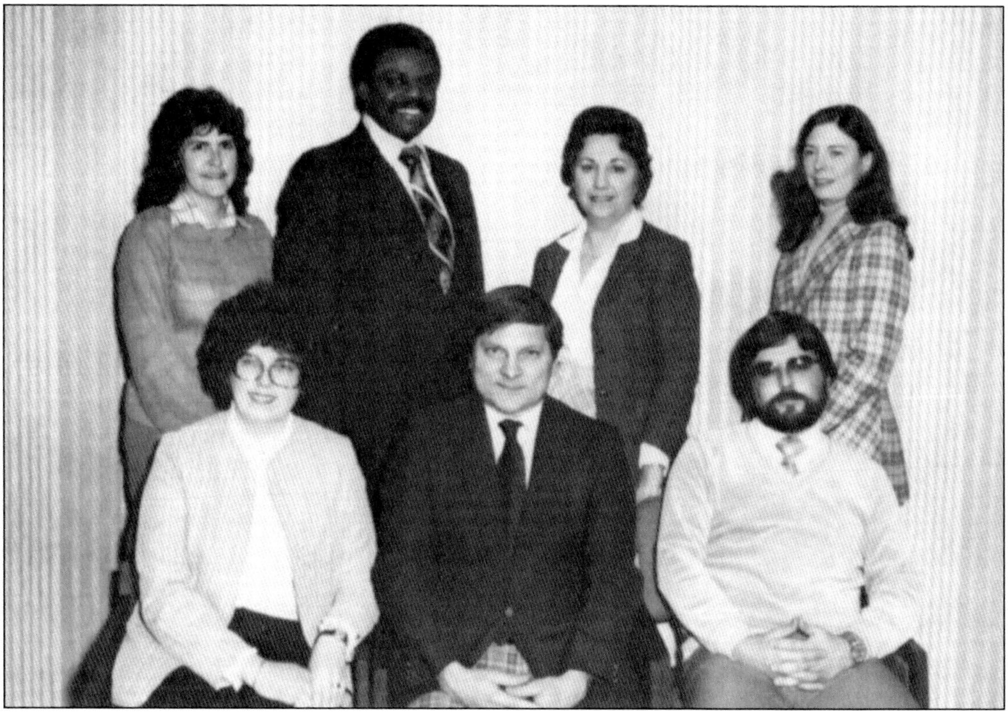

Members of the Brookwood School Board of Education in 1981 were, from left to right, (first row) Betty Wentzel, Walter Nykaza, and Richard Nylander; (second row) Kay Bult, Charles Pulliam, Lucy Claus, and Jane Winningham. (Courtesy of Brookwood School District No. 167.)

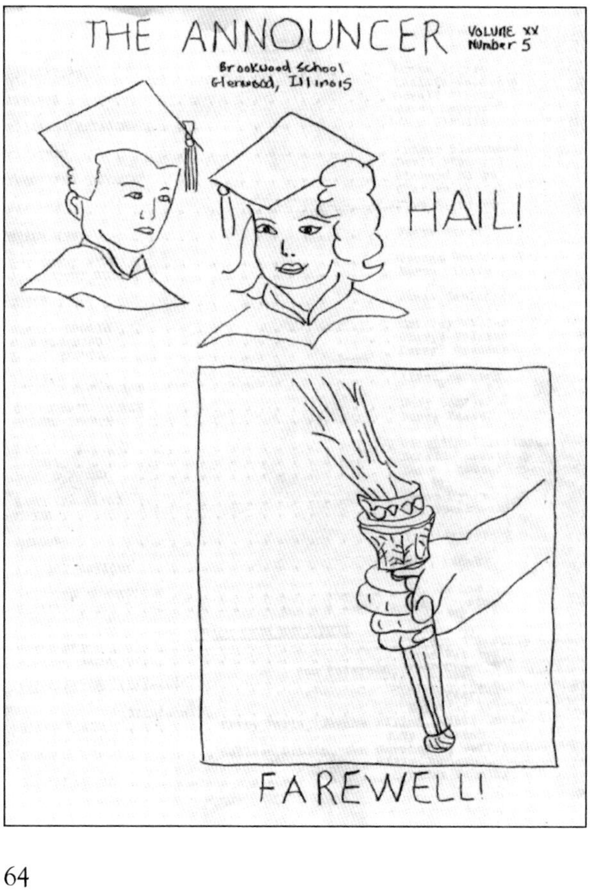

The *Announcer* was Brookwood's school newspaper. This cover is from the June 1962 issue. (Courtesy of Brookwood School District No. 167.)

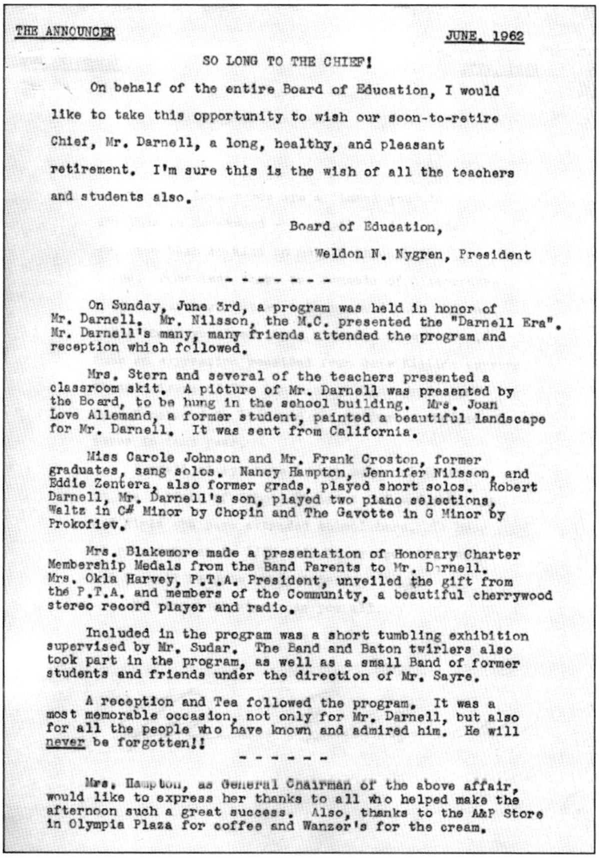

THE ANNOUNCER JUNE, 1962

SO LONG TO THE CHIEF!

On behalf of the entire Board of Education, I would like to take this opportunity to wish our soon-to-retire Chief, Mr. Darnell, a long, healthy, and pleasant retirement. I'm sure this is the wish of all the teachers and students also.

Board of Education,

Weldon N. Nygren, President

- - - - - - -

On Sunday, June 3rd, a program was held in honor of Mr. Darnell. Mr. Nilsson, the M.C. presented the "Darnell Era". Mr. Darnell's many, many friends attended the program and reception which followed.

Mrs. Stern and several of the teachers presented a classroom skit. A picture of Mr. Darnell was presented by the Board, to be hung in the school building. Mrs. Joan Love Allemand, a former student, painted a beautiful landscape for Mr. Darnell. It was sent from California.

Miss Carole Johnson and Mr. Frank Croston, former graduates, sang solos. Nancy Hampton, Jennifer Nilsson, and Eddie Zentera, also former grads, played short solos. Robert Darnell, Mr. Darnell's son, played two piano selections, Waltz in C# Minor by Chopin and The Gavotte in G Minor by Prokofiev.

Mrs. Blakemore made a presentation of Honorary Charter Membership Medals from the Band Parents to Mr. Darnell. Mrs. Okla Harvey, P.T.A. President, unveiled the gift from the P.T.A. and members of the Community, a beautiful cherrywood stereo record player and radio.

Included in the program was a short tumbling exhibition supervised by Mr. Sudar. The Band and Baton twirlers also took part in the program, as well as a small Band of former students and friends under the direction of Mr. Sayre.

A reception and Tea followed the program. It was a most memorable occasion, not only for Mr. Darnell, but also for all the people who have known and admired him. He will never be forgotten!!

- - - - - -

Mrs. Hampton, as General Chairman of the above affair, would like to express her thanks to all who helped make the afternoon such a great success. Also, thanks to the A&P Store in Olympia Plaza for coffee and Wanzer's for the cream.

A write-up from the June 1962 edition of the *Announcer* concerned the retirement of longtime superintendent Mr. Darnell. He would be replaced by Mr. Prevost. (Courtesy of Brookwood School District No. 167.)

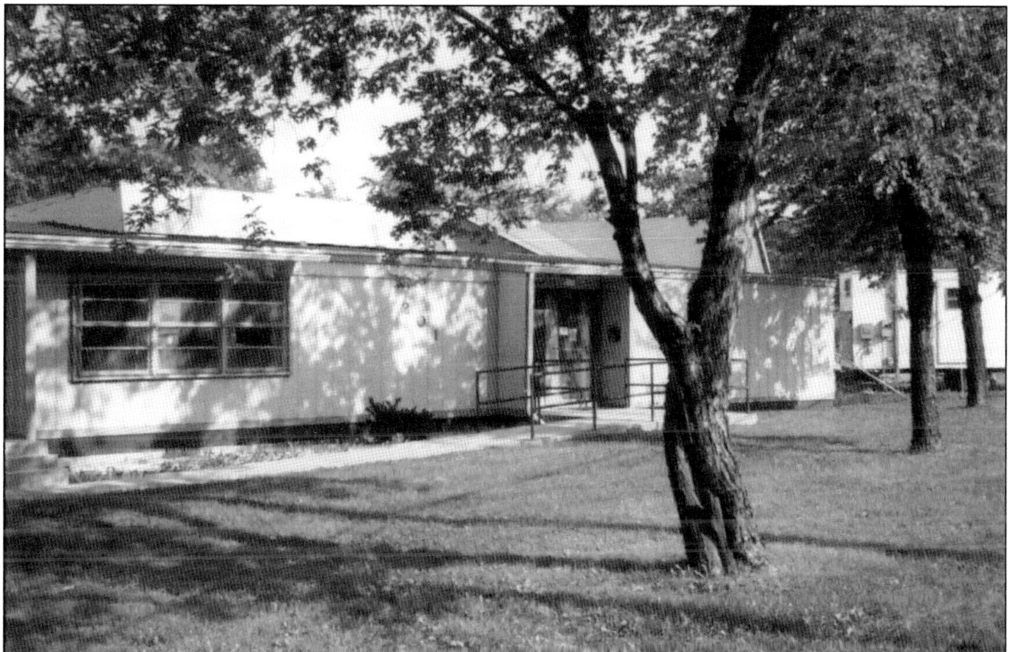

The Brookwood School District No. 167 administration building is pictured as it looked in 1989. A new building would be constructed soon. (Courtesy of Brookwood School District No. 167.)

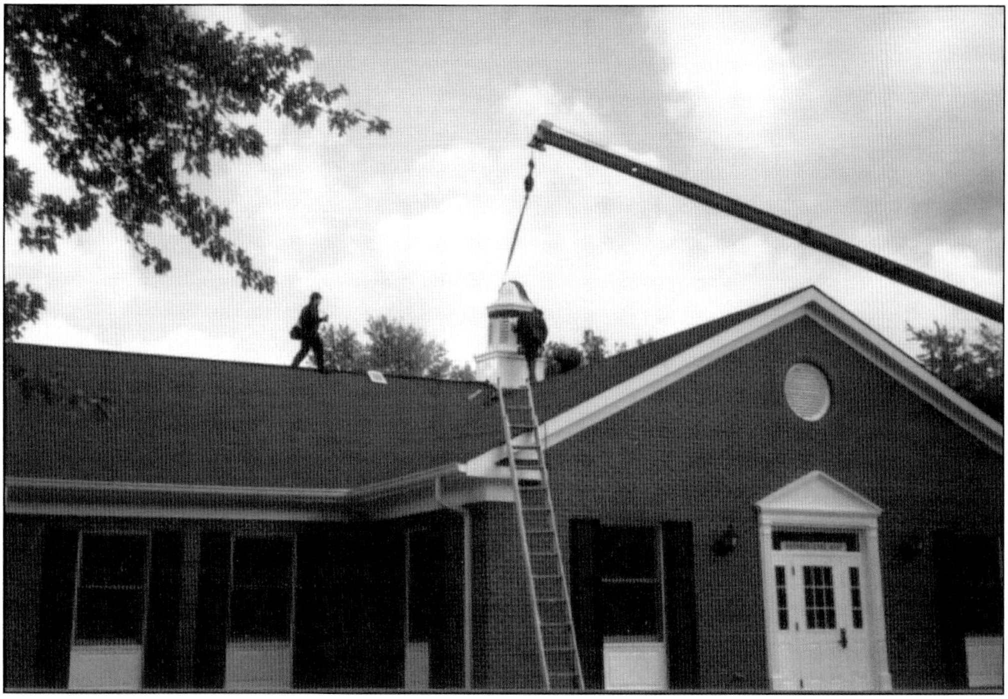

In this image, the district's new administration building is being topped off on October 10, 1990. (Courtesy of Brookwood School District No. 167.)

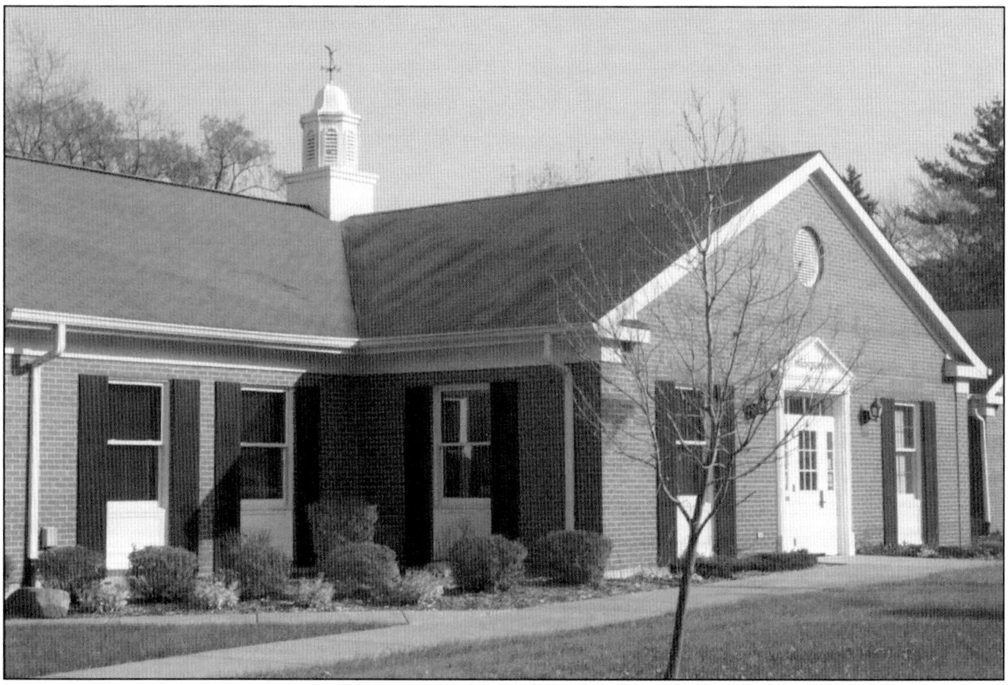

The Brookwood School District Administration and Diagnostic Building is pictured as it appears today. (Photograph by the author.)

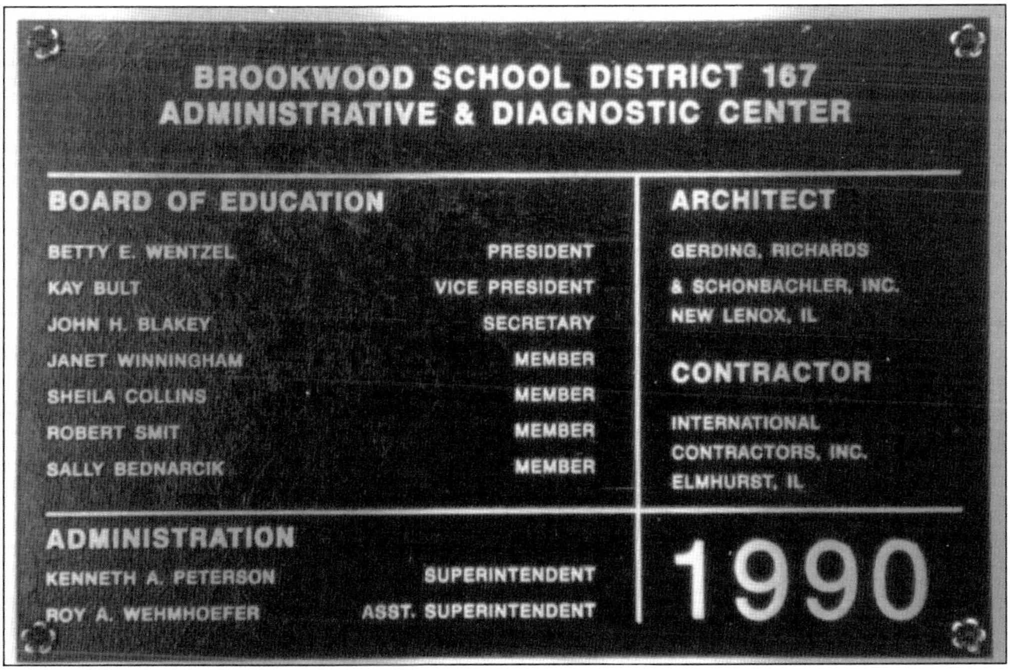

This plaque on the wall inside the District Administration and Diagnostic Building commemorates its construction and the people involved. (Photograph by the author.)

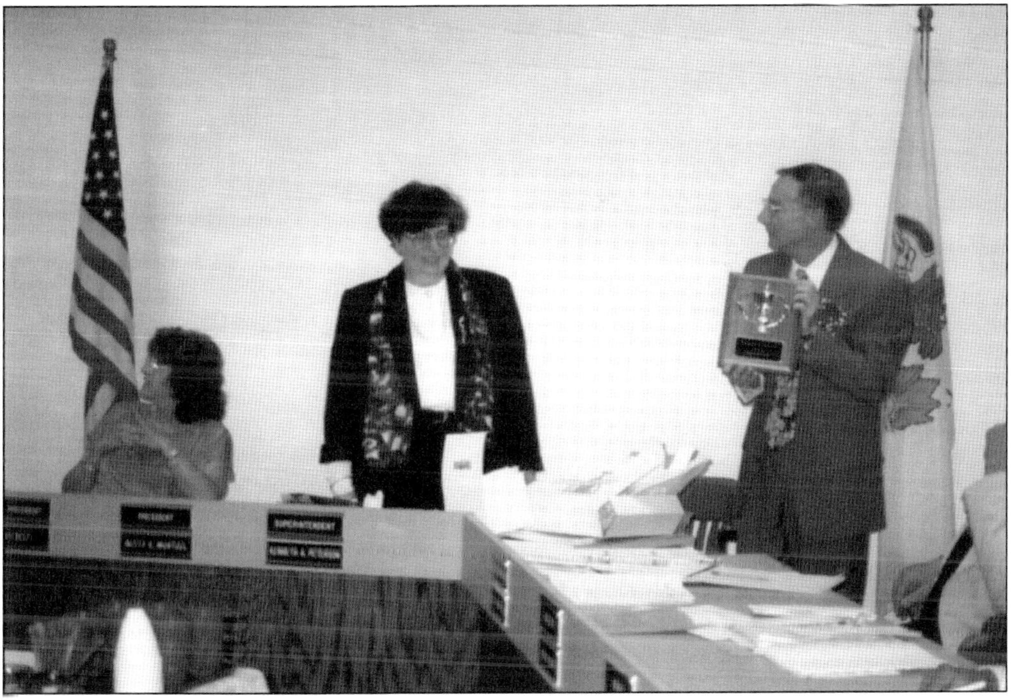

On May 9, 1994, the Brookwood School Board of Education honored Supt. Kenneth A. Peterson on his retirement. Pictured from left to right are school board vice president Kay Bult, school board president Betty Wentzel, and Kenneth A. Peterson. (Courtesy of Brookwood School District No. 167.)

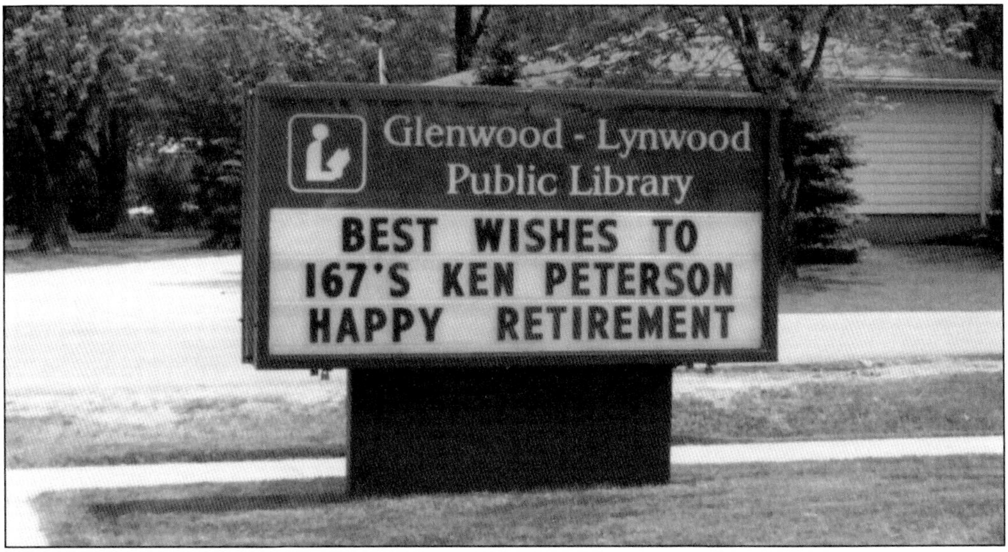

The Glenwood-Lynwood Public Library's sign presents a warm sentiment for Ken Peterson on his retirement. For some time before they moved to their new building on Stony Island Avenue in Lynwood, the library was on Brookwood School property at the corner of Glenwood-Lansing Road and Eberhart Avenue. (Courtesy of Brookwood School District No. 167.)

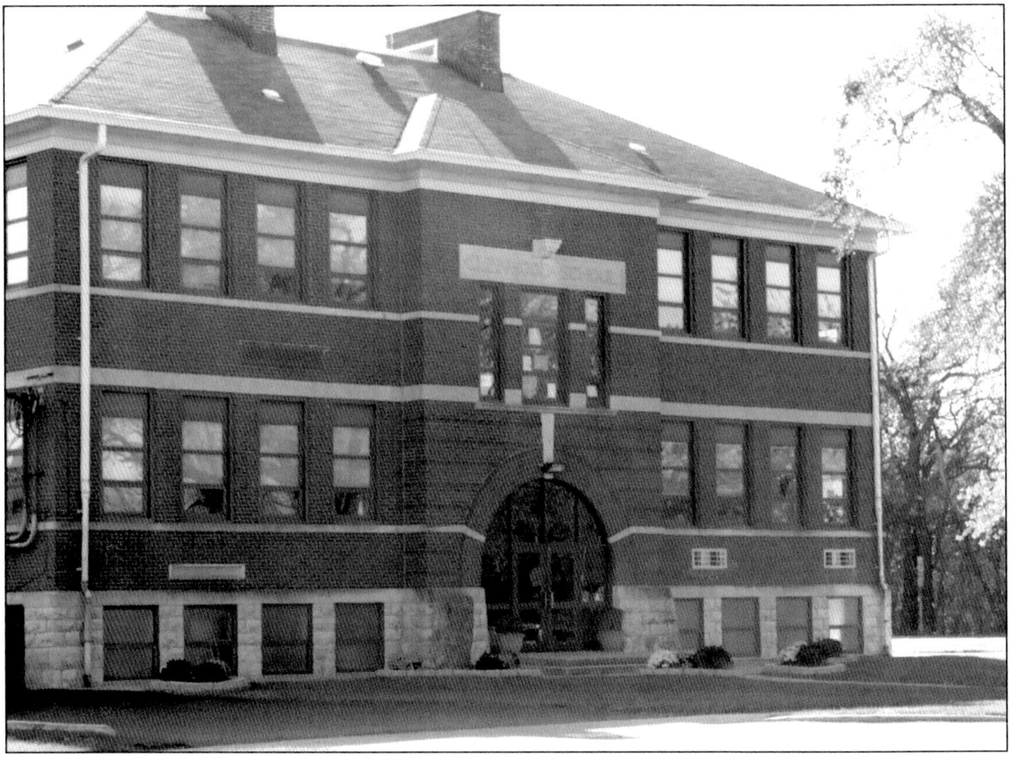

The original brick Brookwood School now serves as the district's middle school. Brookwood School District No. 167 is now composed of two elementary schools, one middle school, and one junior high school. The third-floor fire escape tubes were removed some time ago. (Photograph by the author.)

Three

The Glenwood School for Boys and Girls

Intertwined with the history of the village of Glenwood is that of the Glenwood School. Through the work and vision of some very determined minds, what is now known as the Glenwood School for Boys and Girls came to fruition in the last part of the 19th century. Founded on February 8, 1887, by Oscar Dudley, who—with the help of other men, including Robert Todd Lincoln (son of Abraham Lincoln)—received a state charter to operate the first school. The school started with 10 boys housed in the Norwood Hotel in Norwood Park, Illinois. The school was officially known as Illinois Manual Training School Farm for a while. In 1911, the name would be changed to the Glenwood Manual Training School.

The Glenwood School was built in 1890 on a 300-acre site known as Rural Glen, which was donated by Milton George in 1889. It began as a home for boys 8 to 16 years in age whose original homes had become unsuitable due to death, desertion, divorce, unsuitable guardianship, or any number of other unfortunate situations. Early on, the school placed emphasis on teaching the manual arts, including printing, cabinetmaking, plumbing, horticulture, plumbing, electrical work, engineering, farm dairy and creamery training, forestry, kitchen training, and baking. The boys attended academic classes during part of the day, and the other part of the day was dedicated to vocational training. At one time, the school maintained a large dairy herd and a full, working farm that provided much of the food consumed at the school. Fully accredited by the state, the school provides classes through the 10th grade. High school students in their junior and senior years attend Bloom High School in nearby Chicago Heights. In 1948, the school changed its name to Glenwood School for Boys. Beginning in 2001, Glenwood enrolled girls in its day program. On June 10, 2003, Glenwood opened its first residential cottage for girls.

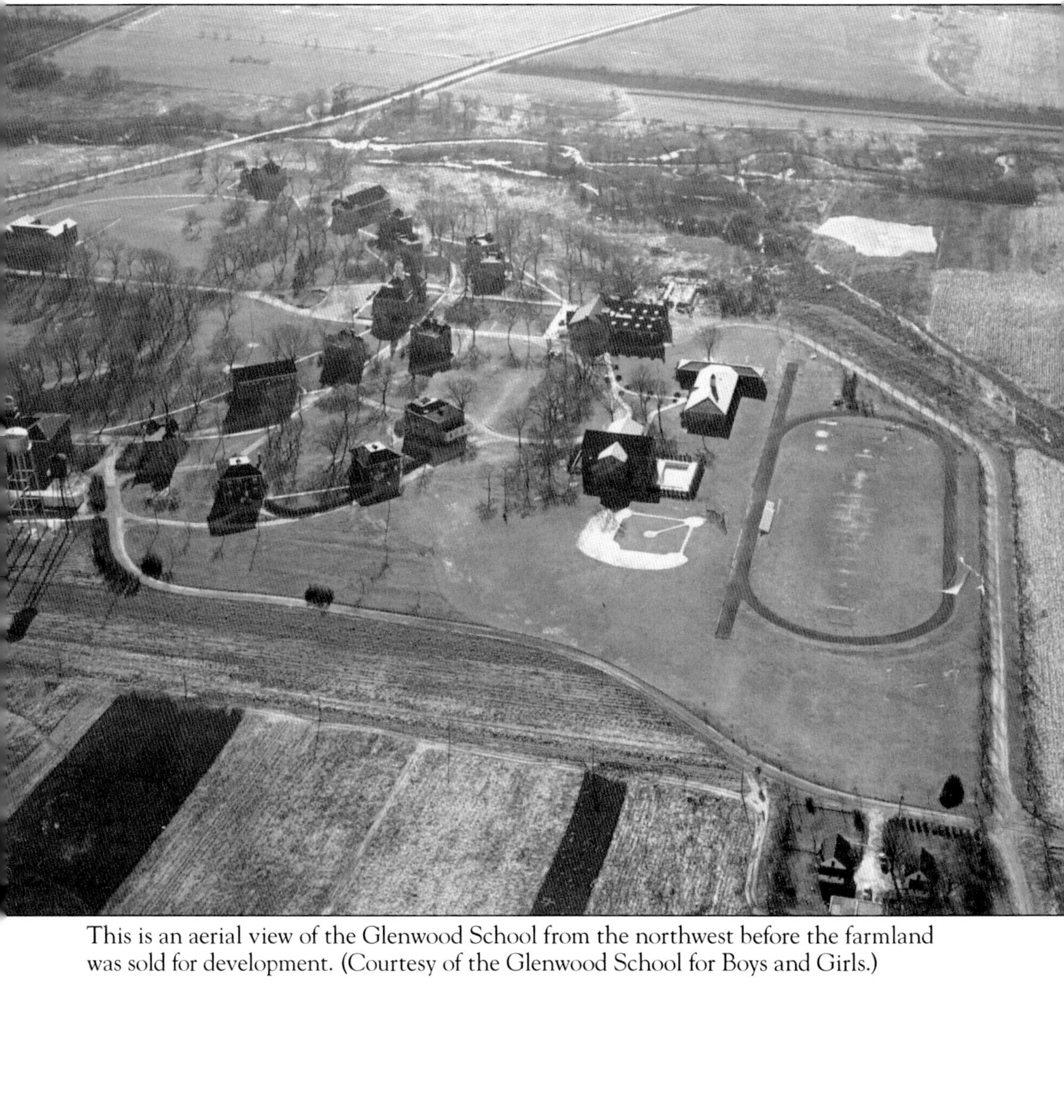

This is an aerial view of the Glenwood School from the northwest before the farmland was sold for development. (Courtesy of the Glenwood School for Boys and Girls.)

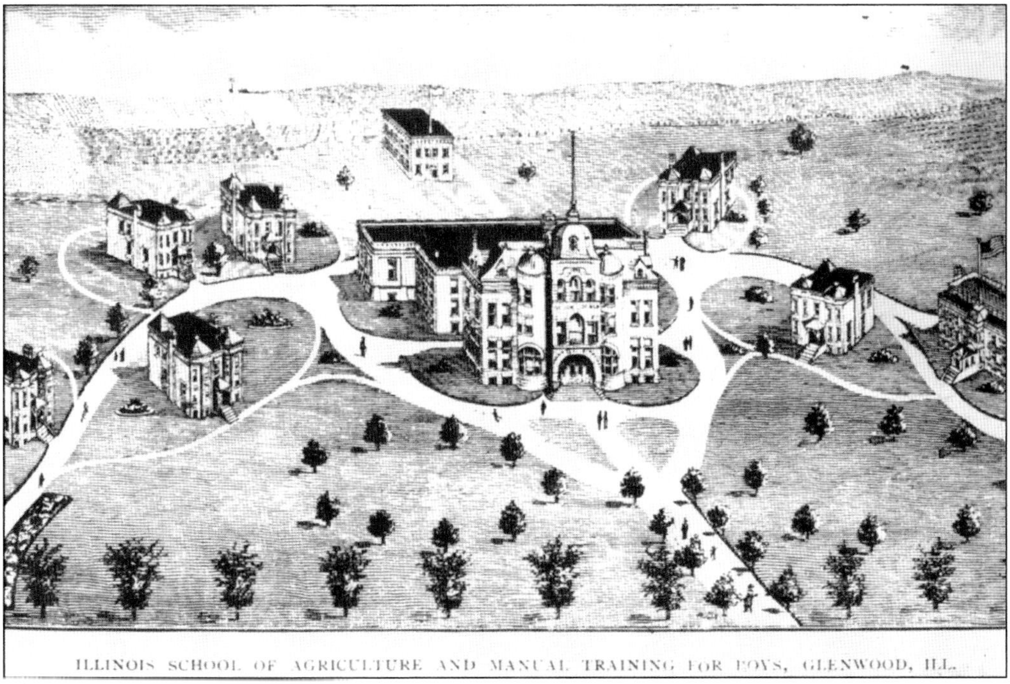

This is an artist's rendering of the Glenwood School, referred to here as the Illinois School of Agriculture and Manual Training for Boys. (Courtesy of the Glenwood School for Boys and Girls.)

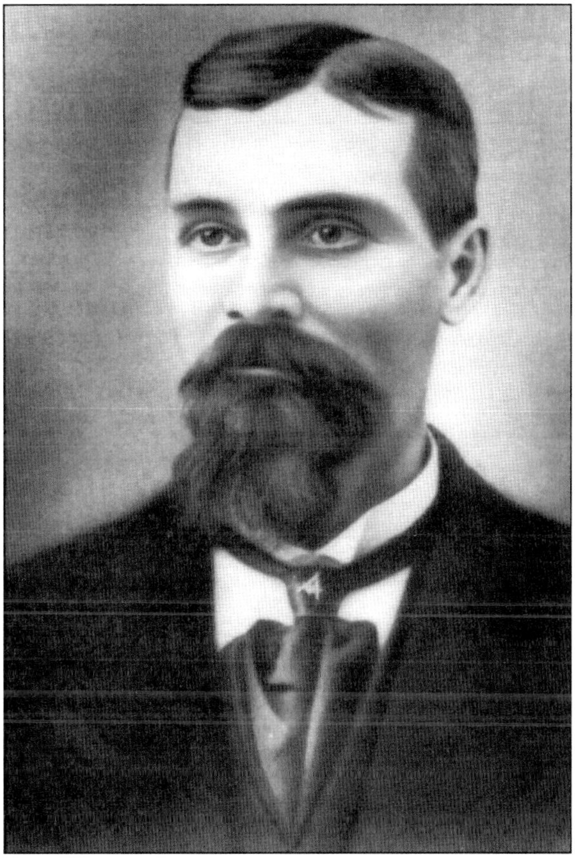

Glenwood Manual Training School founder, Oscar Dudley, served in the Union army during the Civil War. (Courtesy of the Glenwood School for Boys and Girls.)

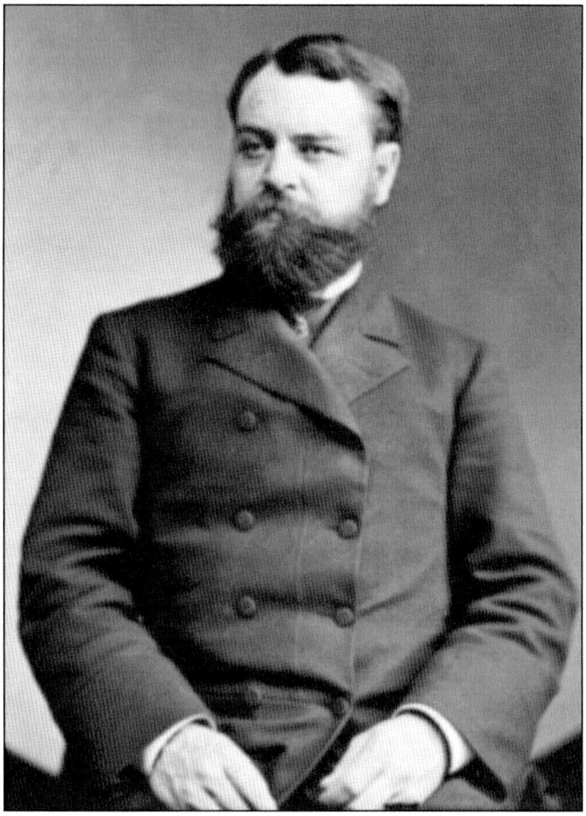

Robert Todd Lincoln, son of Abraham Lincoln, was one of the men who helped Oscar Dudley get the school up and running. (Private collection.)

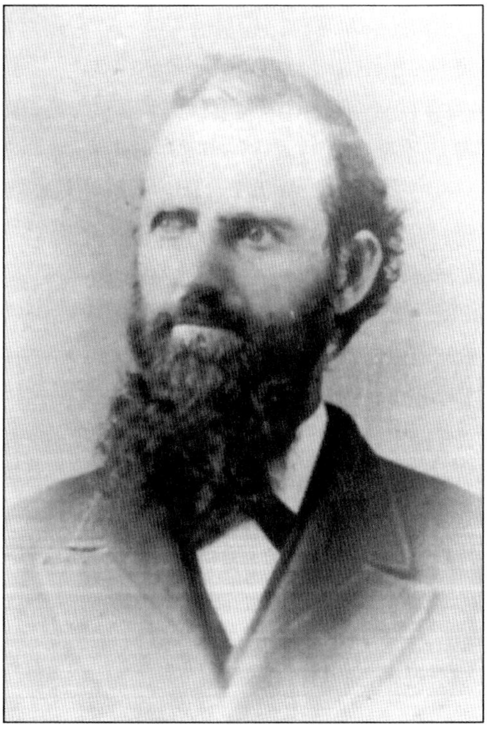

In 1889, Milton George donated 300 acres of farmland to the school with the stipulation that additional funds were to be raised to provide the necessary buildings. (Courtesy of the Glenwood School for Boys and Girls.)

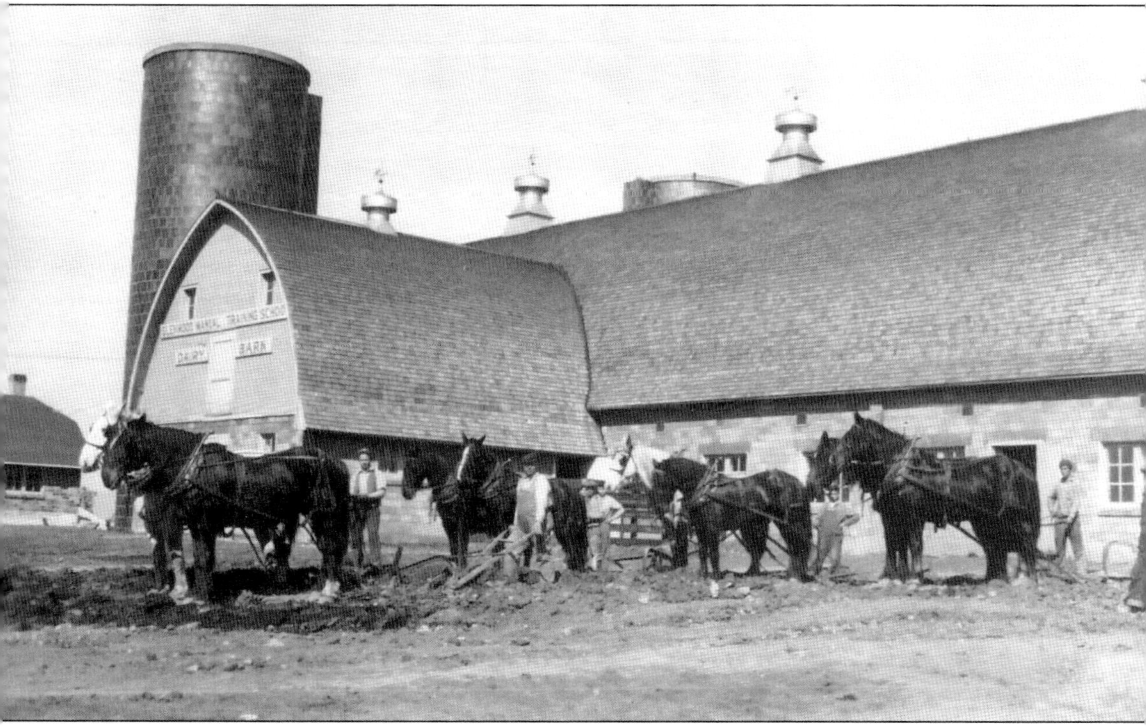

At the Glenwood Manual Training School, the emphasis in the early days, as the name implied, was on teaching the manual arts. (Courtesy of the Glenwood School for Boys and Girls.)

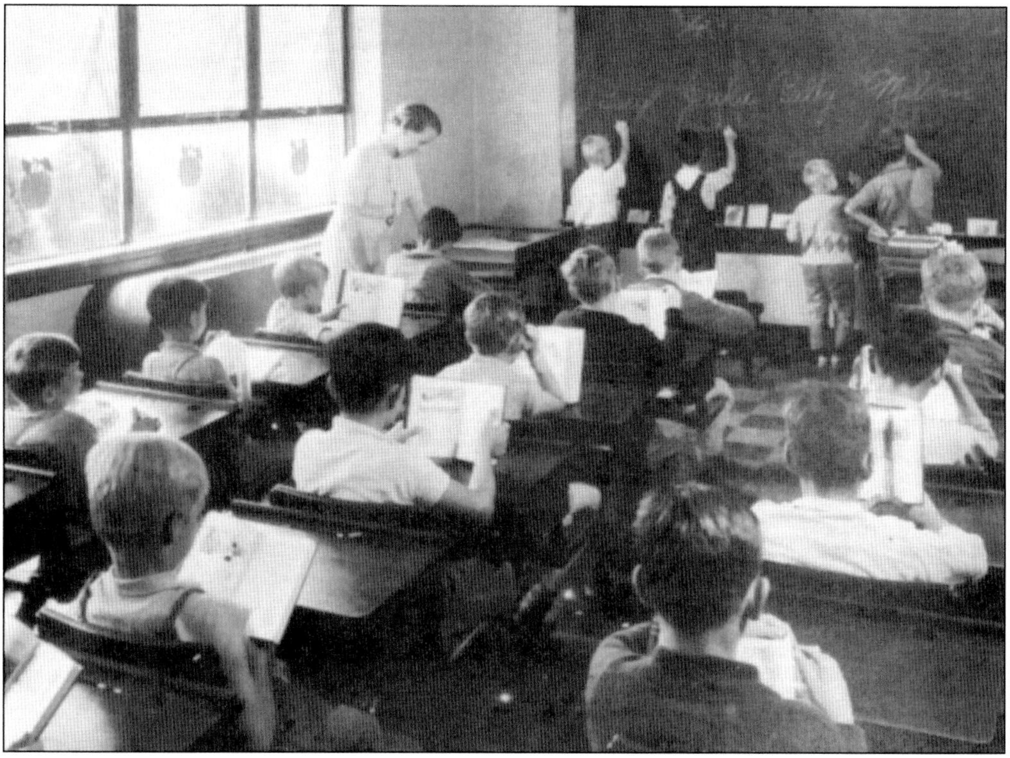

Milton George wrote the following in the document deeding the land to the school: "Through such an enterprise (as Glenwood) . . . hundreds of boys may be trained in a way to become good and useful citizens, and at the same time, a rectory tide of humanity turned back toward the rural districts to offset the one now streaming into the great cities." (Courtesy of the Glenwood School for Boys and Girls.)

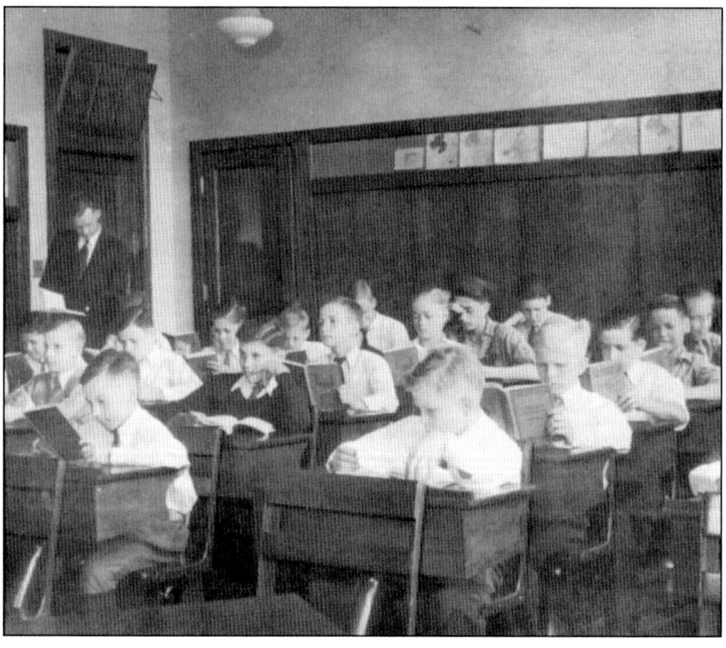

At about the time this photograph was taken, the village of Glenwood was promoting itself as the home of the Glenwood School. (Courtesy of the Glenwood School for Boys and Girls.)

In 1903, when this photograph was taken, the Glenwood School was officially known as Illinois Manual Training School Farm. The name would be changed to the Glenwood Manual Training School in 1911. (Courtesy of the Glenwood School for Boys and Girls.)

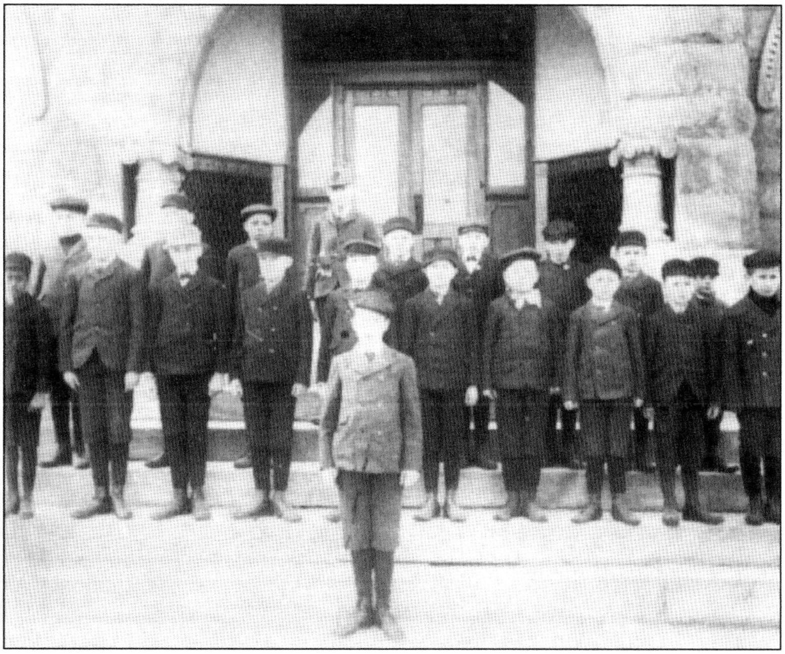

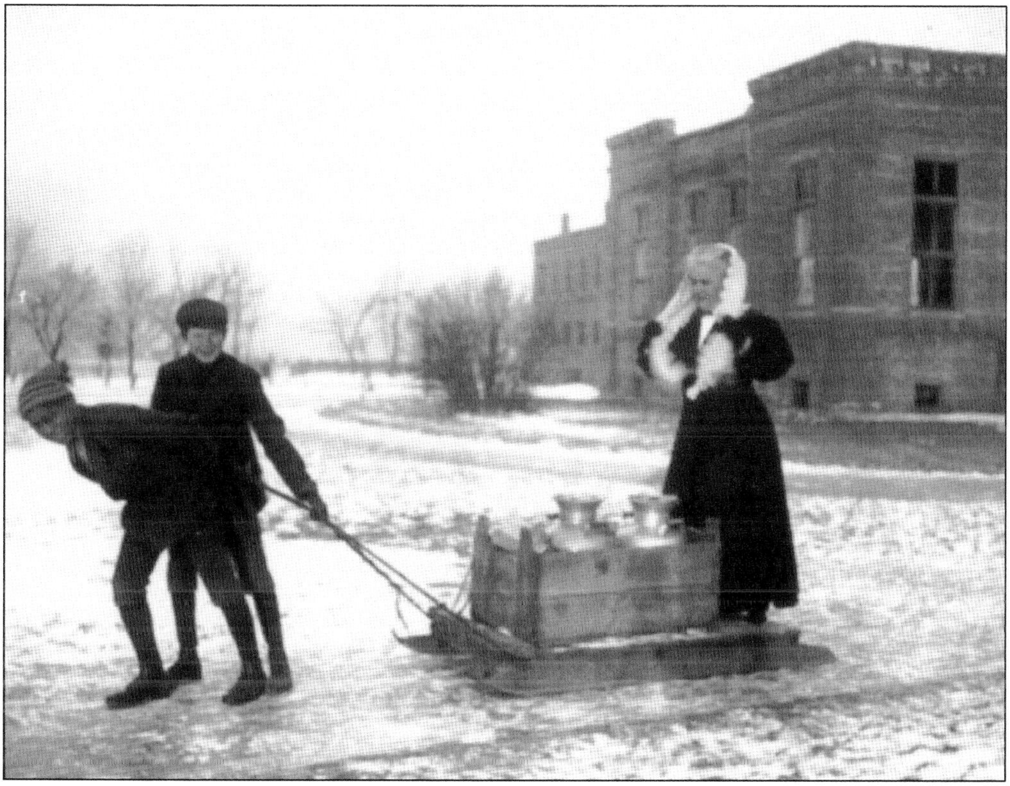

The boys could always count on fresh milk from the school's very own dairy farm. (Courtesy of the Glenwood School for Boys and Girls.)

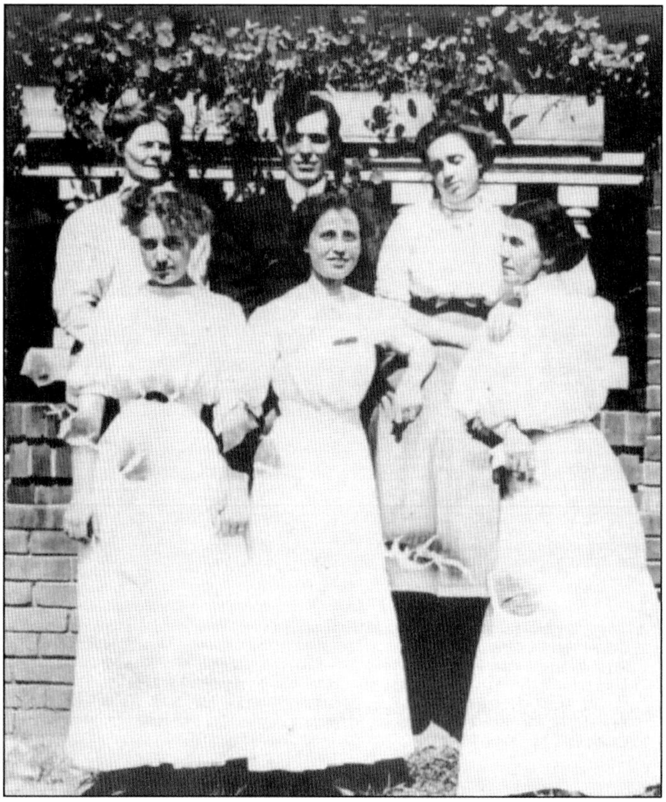

The dedicated faculty of the Glenwood Manual Training School pose for a photograph in 1912. (Courtesy of the Glenwood School for Boys and Girls.)

The school building is now used as the maintenance building (physical plant) and for storage. (Courtesy of the Glenwood School for Boys and Girls.)

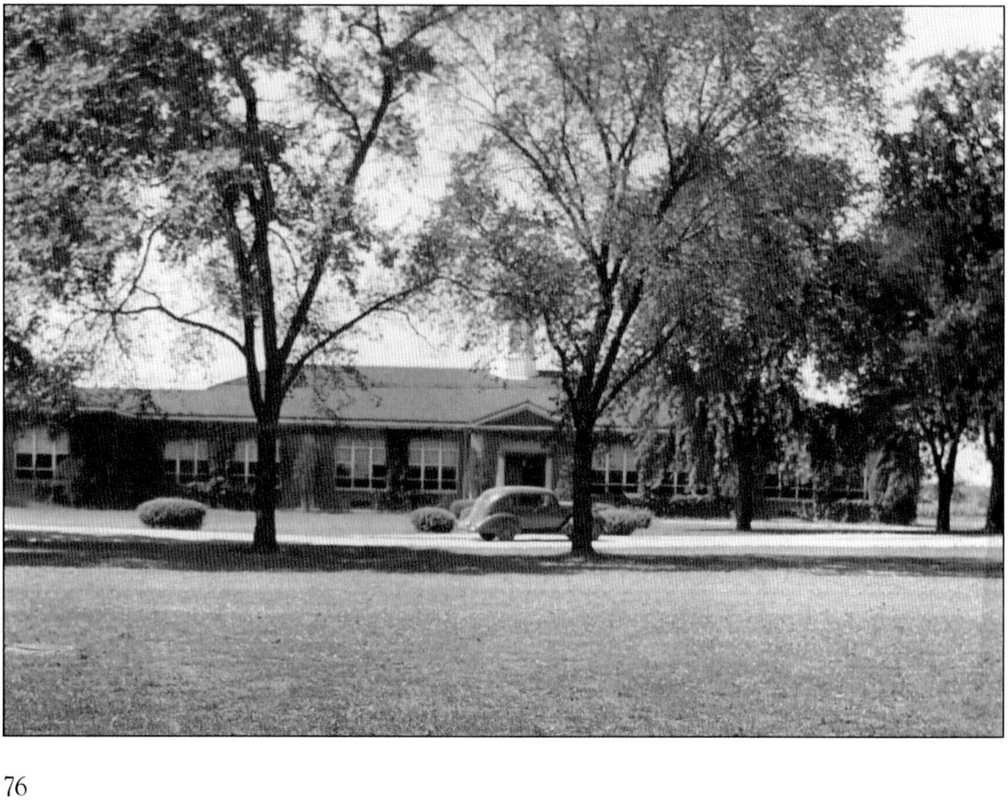

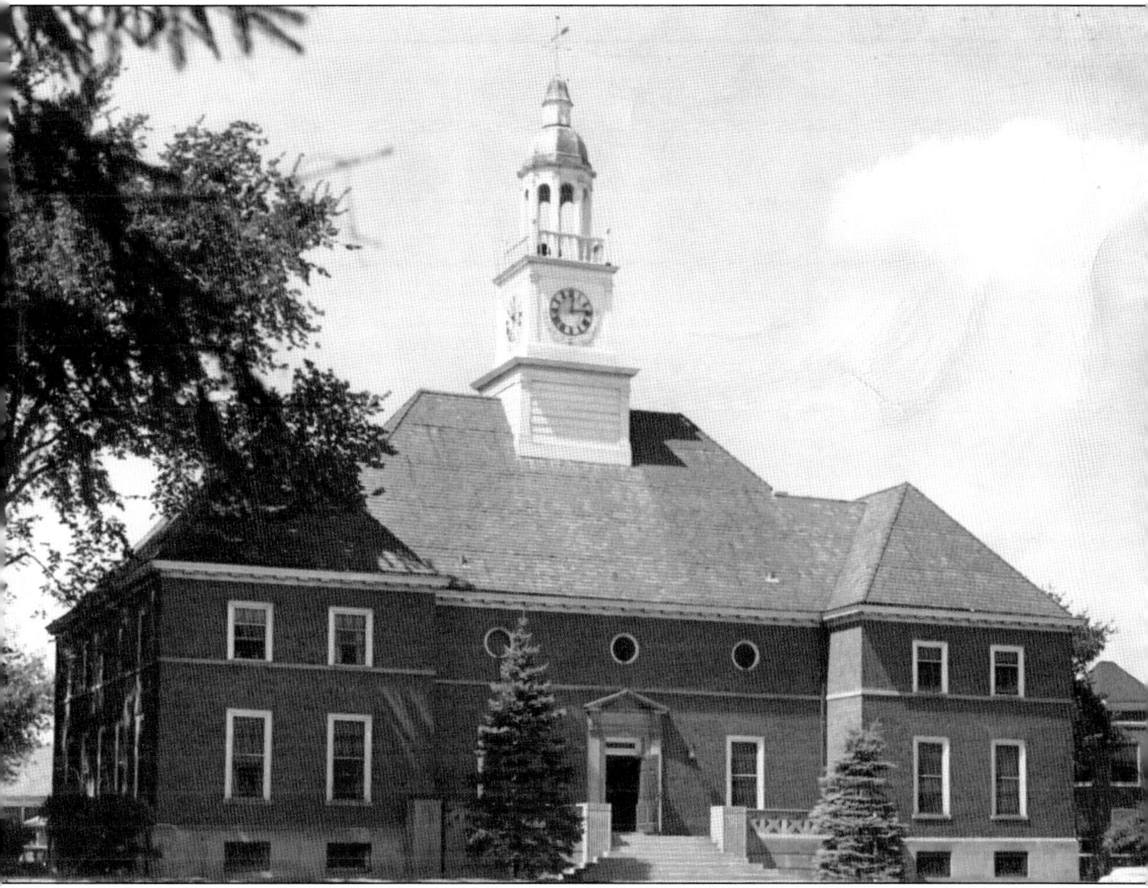

The E.B. Butler Administration Building was named in honor of the former president of the school, Edward Burgess Butler. Samuel Insull, who—among other things—was responsible for the construction of the Chicago Civic Opera House in 1929, gave the dedication address. (Courtesy of the Glenwood School for Boys and Girls.)

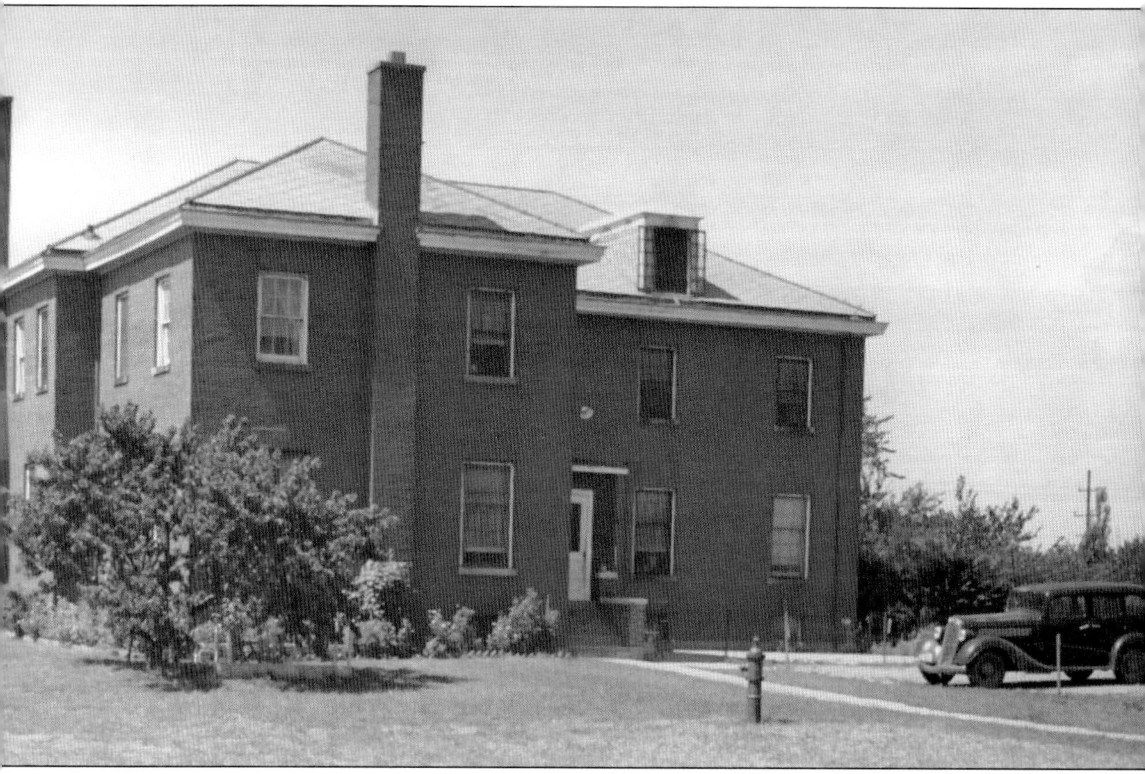

Built in the 1920s, Countryman Cottage was a residence hall used by older boys who were training in agriculture. It was a gift from Issac B. Countryman of Dixon, Illinois, in memory of his wife, Elizabeth. (Courtesy of the Glenwood School for Boys and Girls.)

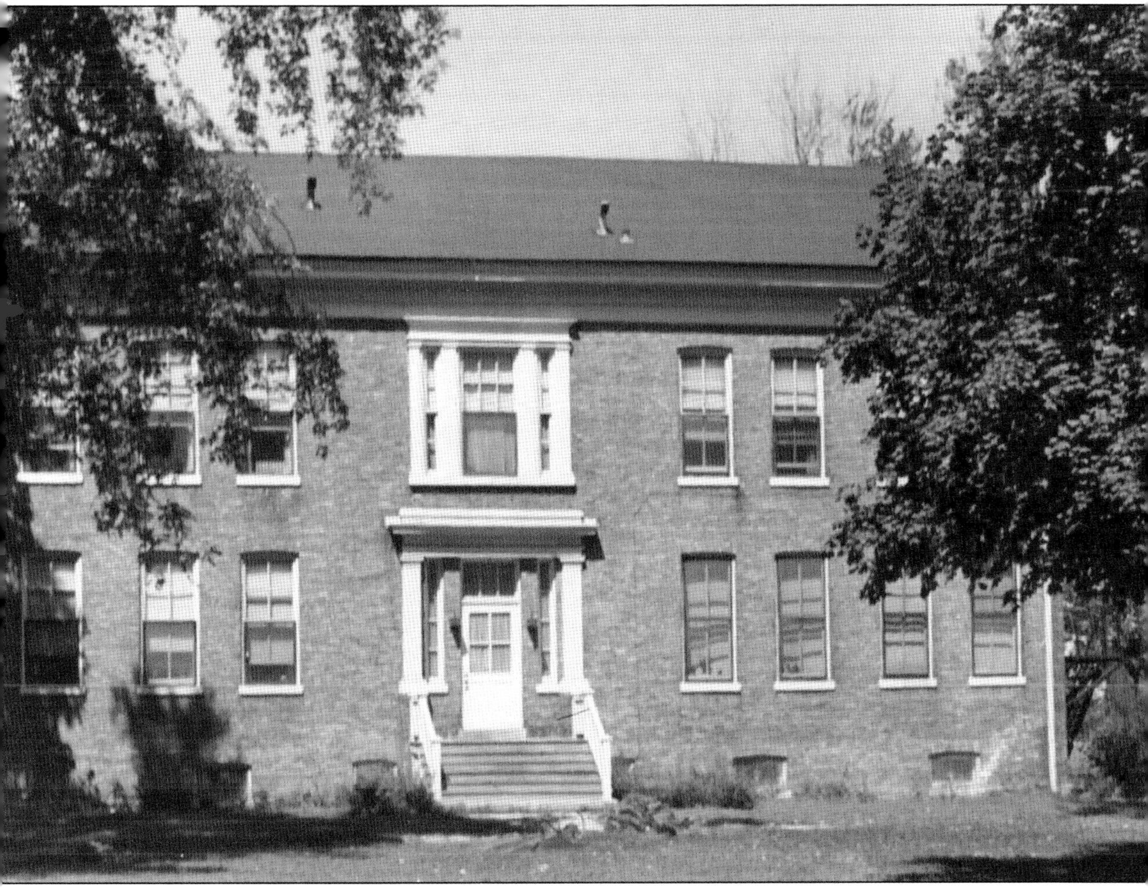

The Milton George Building was erected in 1889 and was the first structure on the school property. Originally built as a classroom through a gift from the Women's Club of Chicago, it was remodeled into a residence hall in 1907. At that time, it was given the name Milton George. (Courtesy of the Glenwood School for Boys and Girls.)

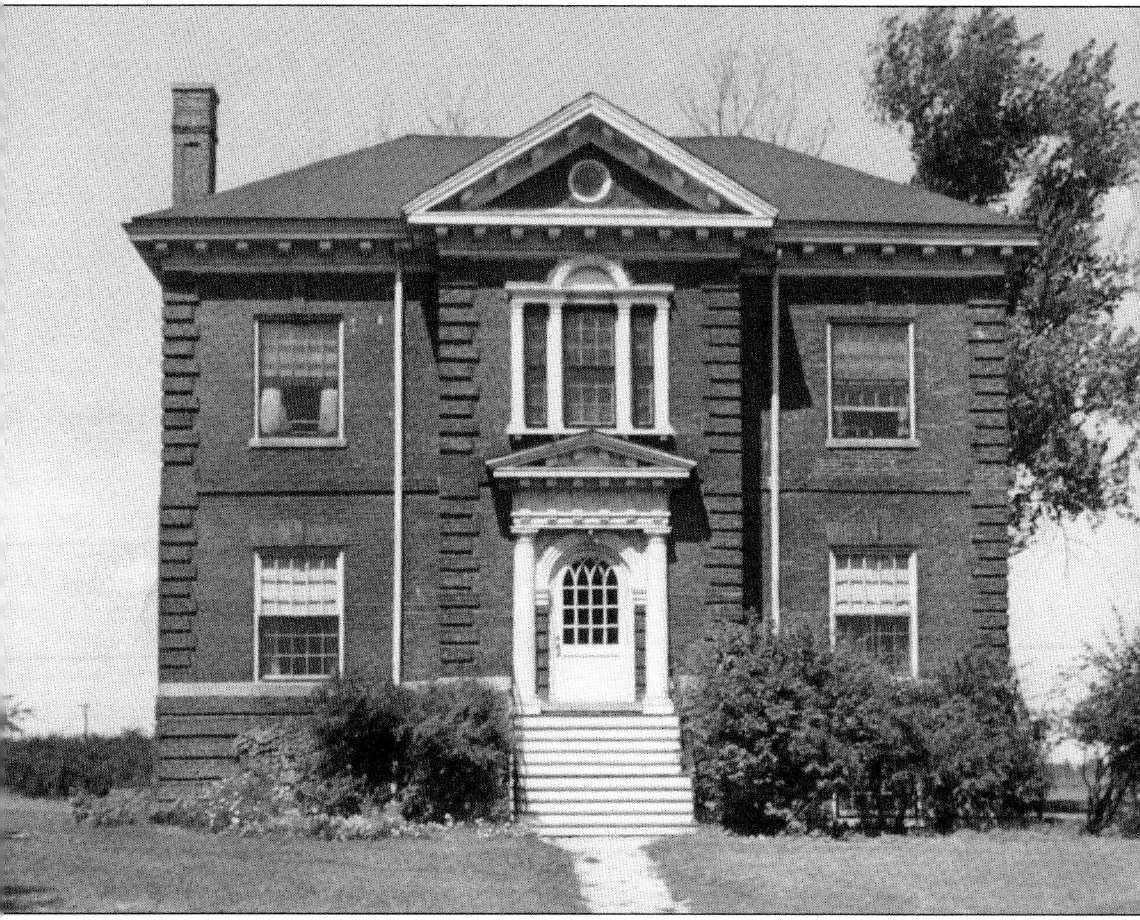

Washington Cottage was built in 1903 as one of the gifts of the Commercial Club of Chicago. (Courtesy of the Glenwood School for Boys and Girls.)

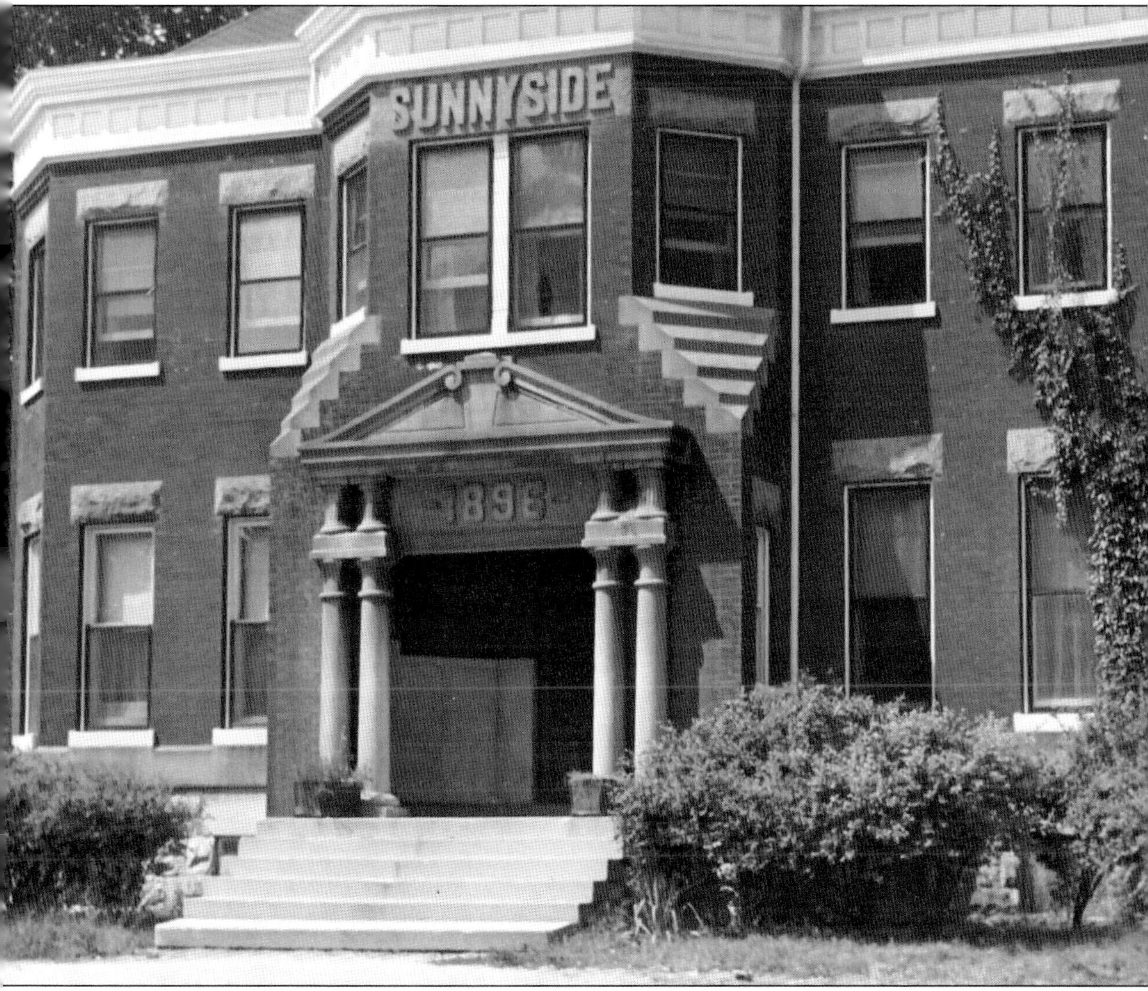

Sunnyside Cottage, built in 1896, was given this name because donor Charles A. Spring Jr. wanted to remain anonymous. (Courtesy of the Glenwood School for Boys and Girls.)

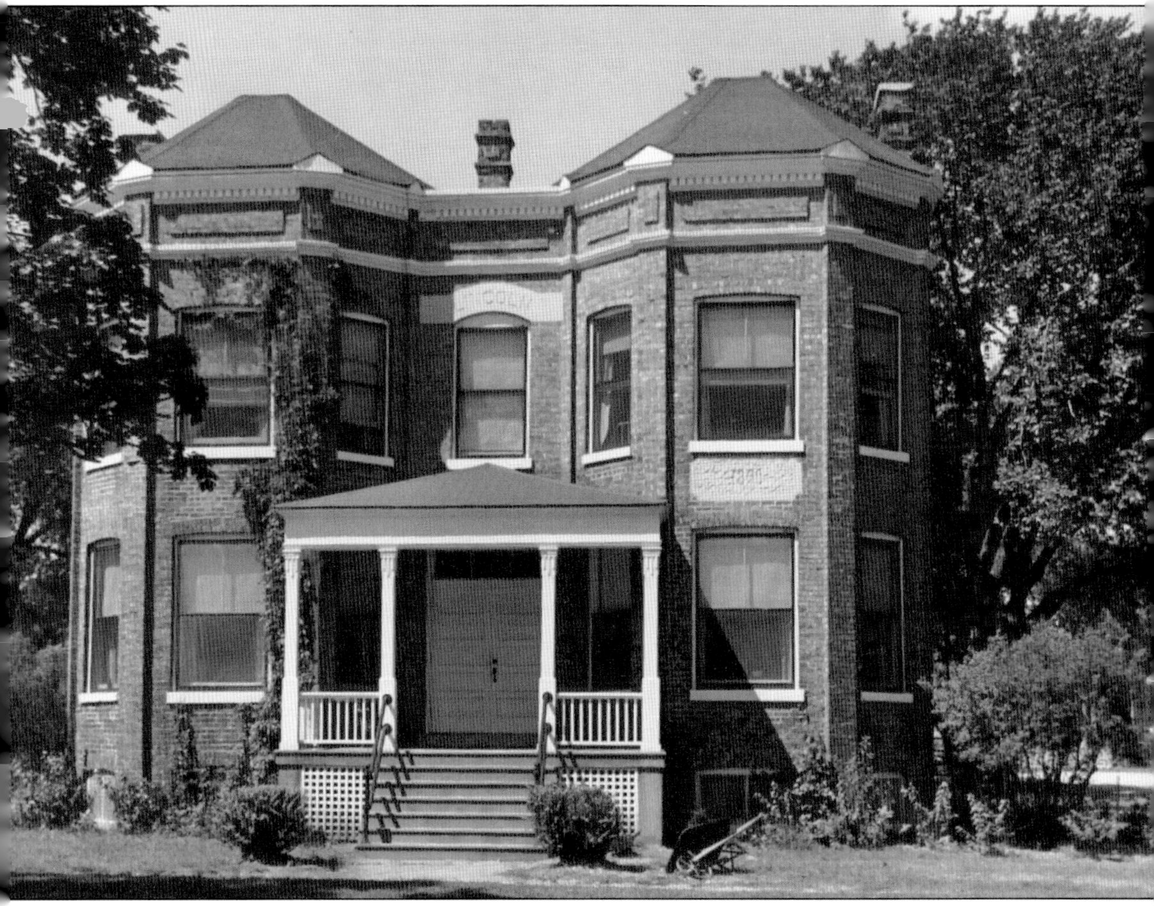

Lincoln Cottage was built in 1890 and named for the 16th president of the United States, Abraham Lincoln. (Courtesy of the Glenwood School for Boys and Girls.)

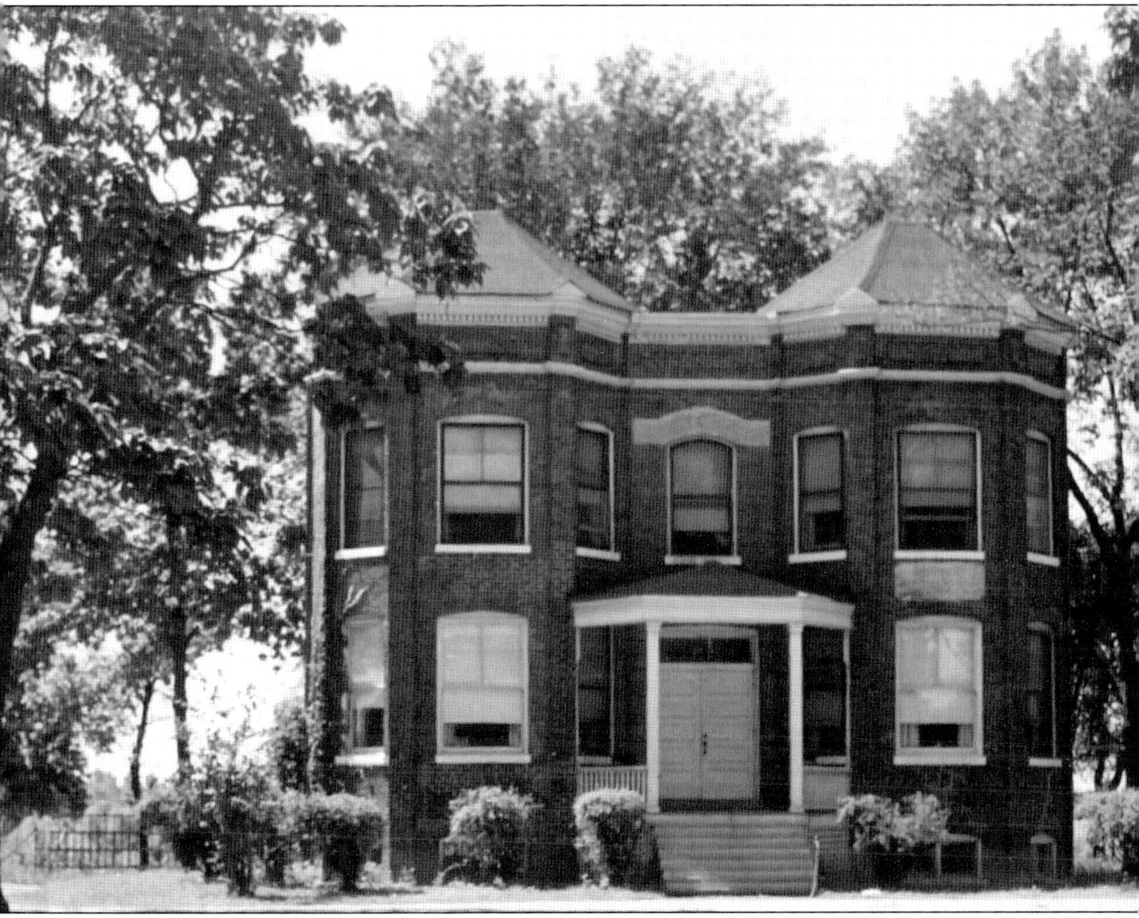
The Beecher Cottage, built in 1890, was a gift of Mrs. Jerome Beecher. (Courtesy of the Glenwood School for Boys and Girls.)

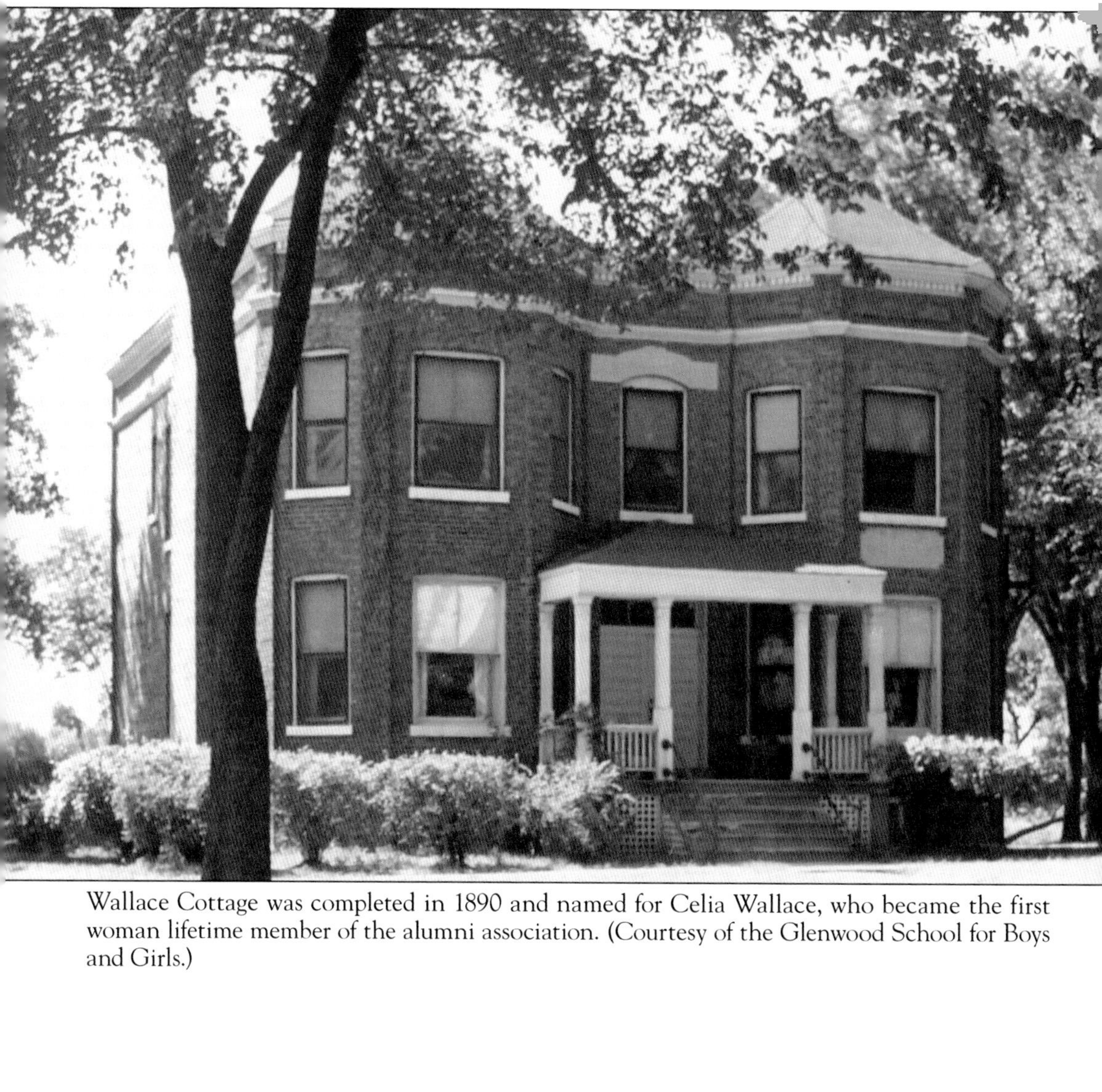

Wallace Cottage was completed in 1890 and named for Celia Wallace, who became the first woman lifetime member of the alumni association. (Courtesy of the Glenwood School for Boys and Girls.)

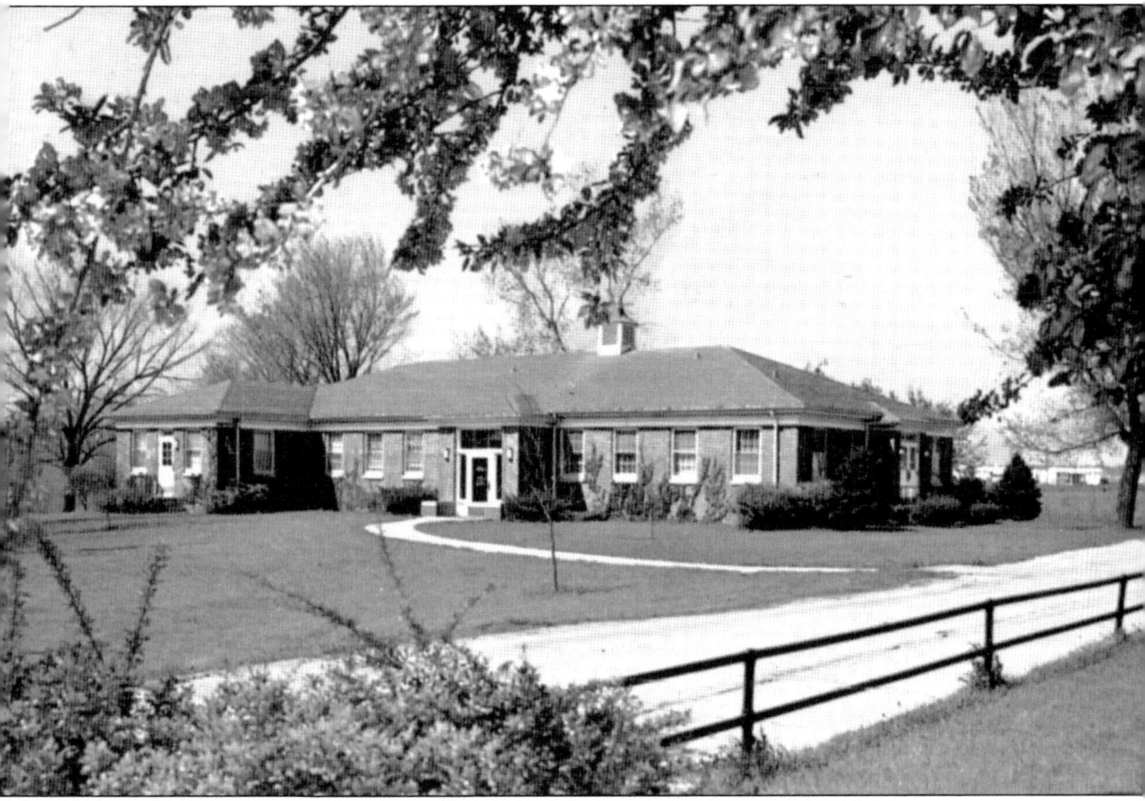

The Borland Infirmary once provided medical and dental care to the residents of the Glenwood School. (Courtesy of the Glenwood School for Boys and Girls.)

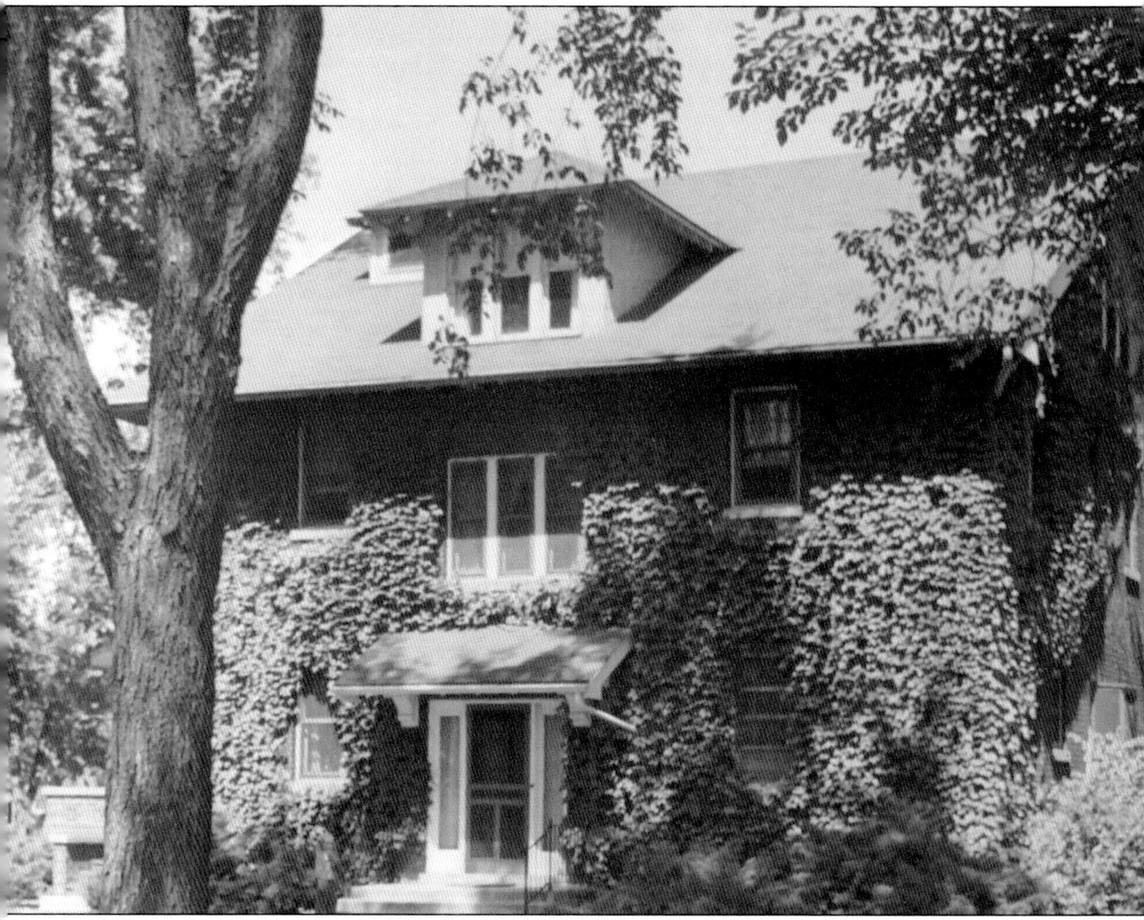

Ryerson Cottage was built in 1911 as the gift of Martin A. Ryerson. In 1957, it was remodeled with funds provided by the Service Club of Chicago to serve as an honor cottage for older students. (Courtesy of the Glenwood School for Boys and Girls.)

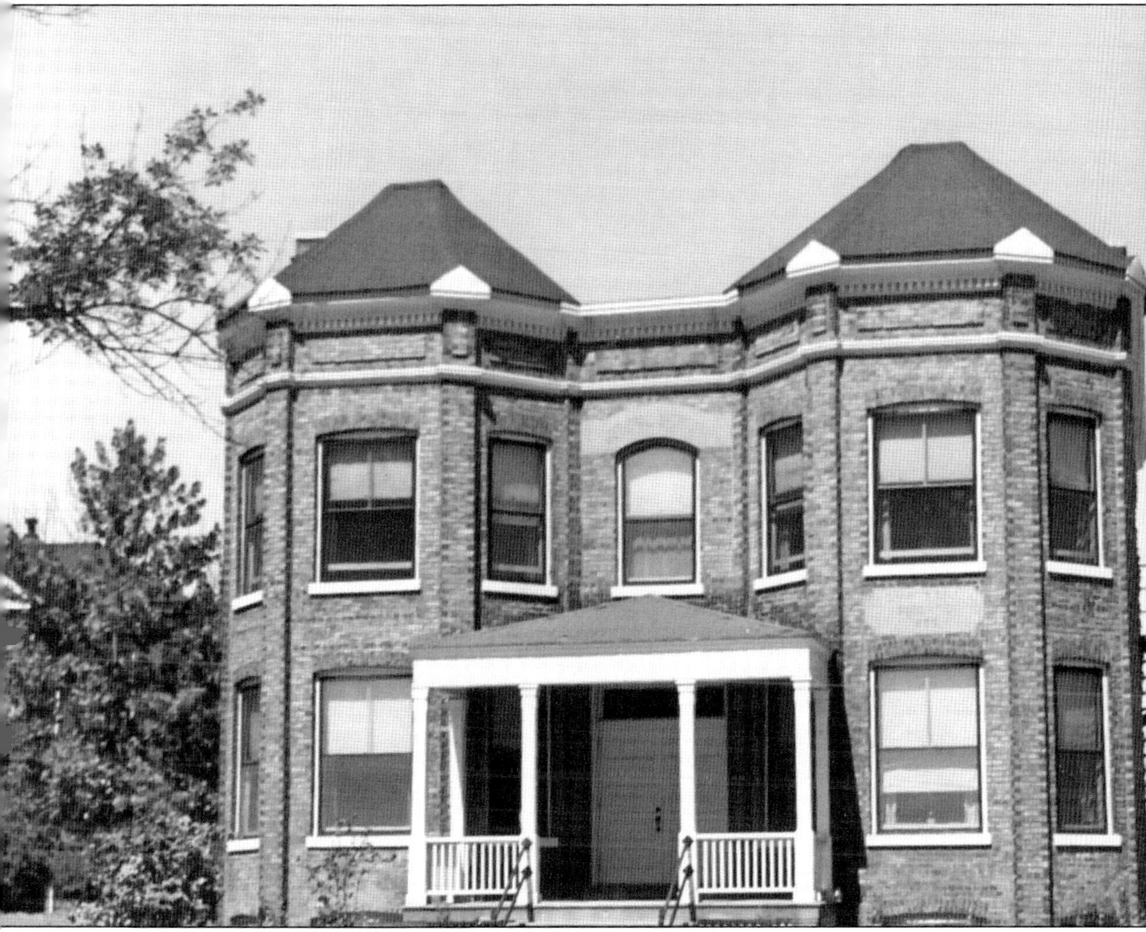

Sheridan Cottage, named for Civil War general Phillip Sheridan, was built in 1896 with a $5,000 gift from the Charity Ball Association. (Courtesy of the Glenwood School for Boys and Girls.)

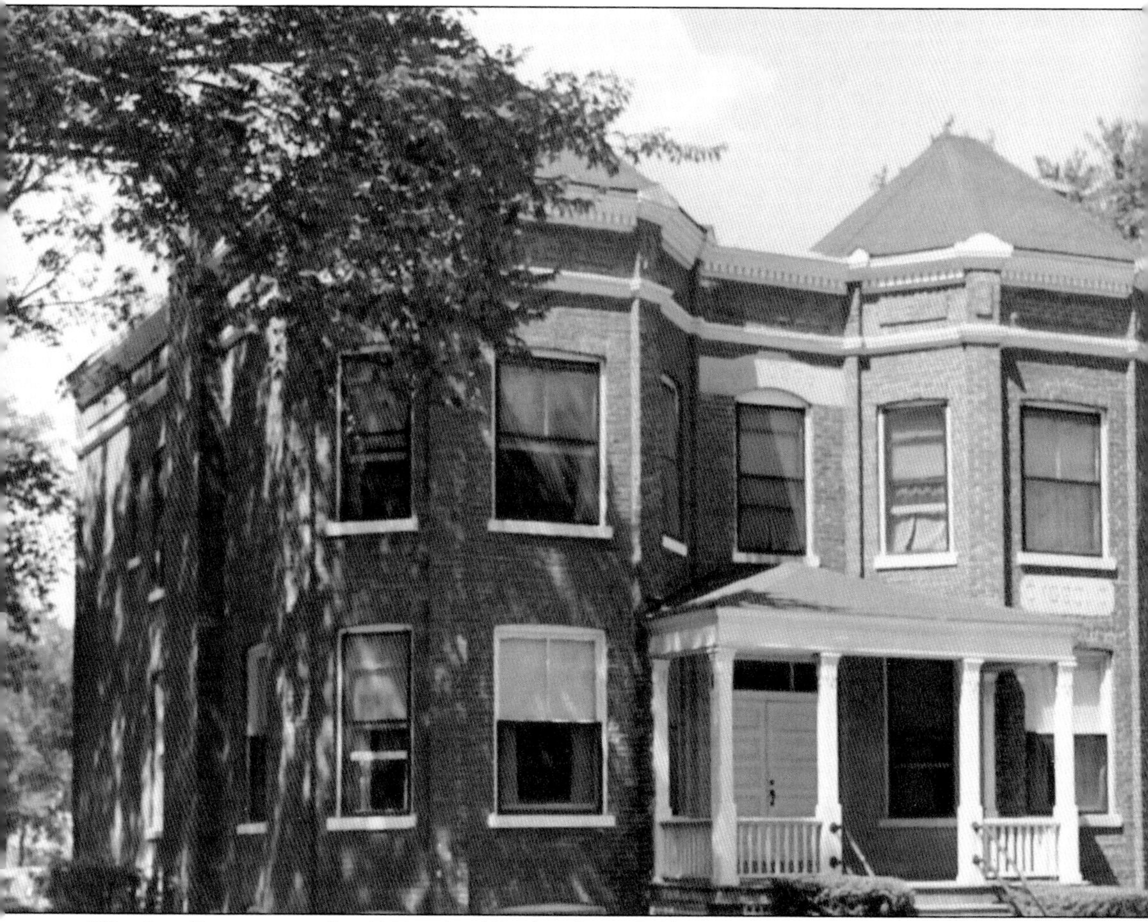

Windsor Cottage was the 1890 gift of Frederick Haskell. (Courtesy of the Glenwood School for Boys and Girls.)

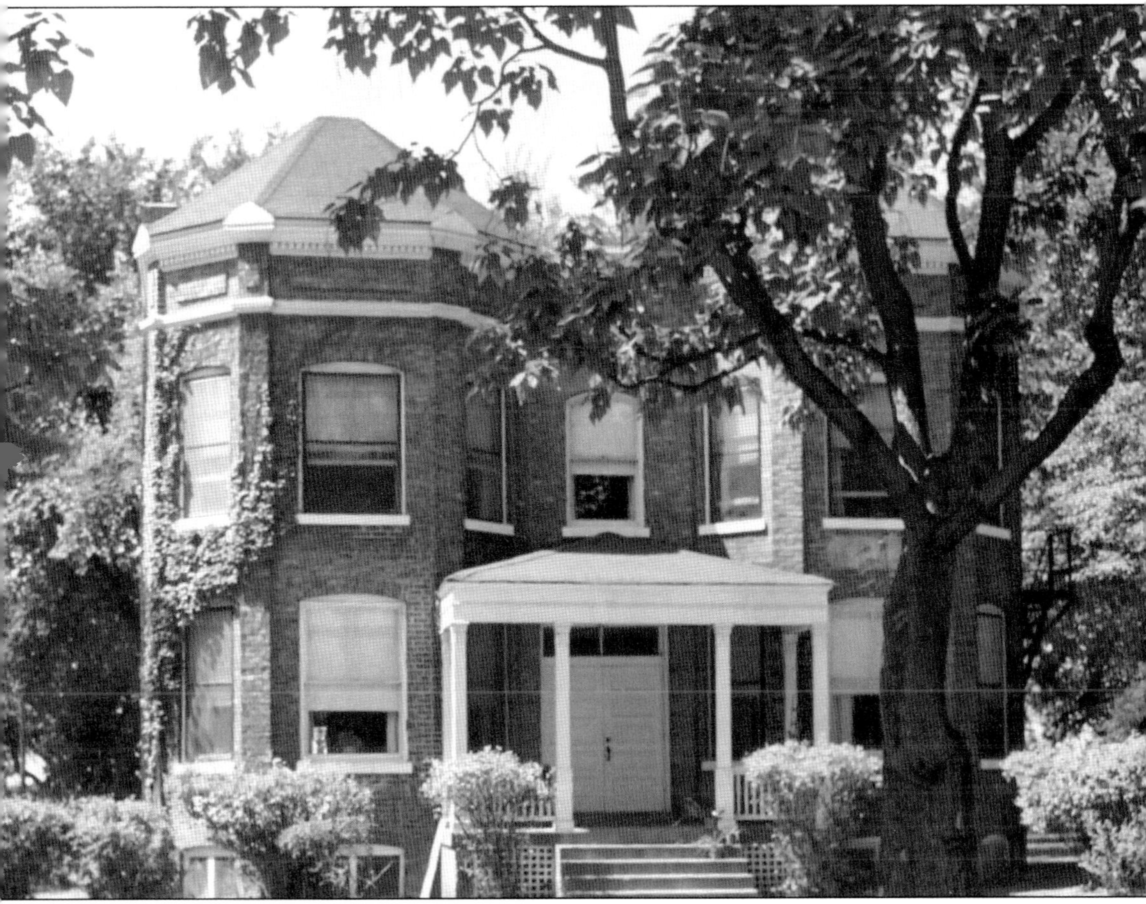

Pope Cottage was built in 1892 through a gift from Mrs. Charles B. Pope in memory of her husband. (Courtesy of the Glenwood School for Boys and Girls.)

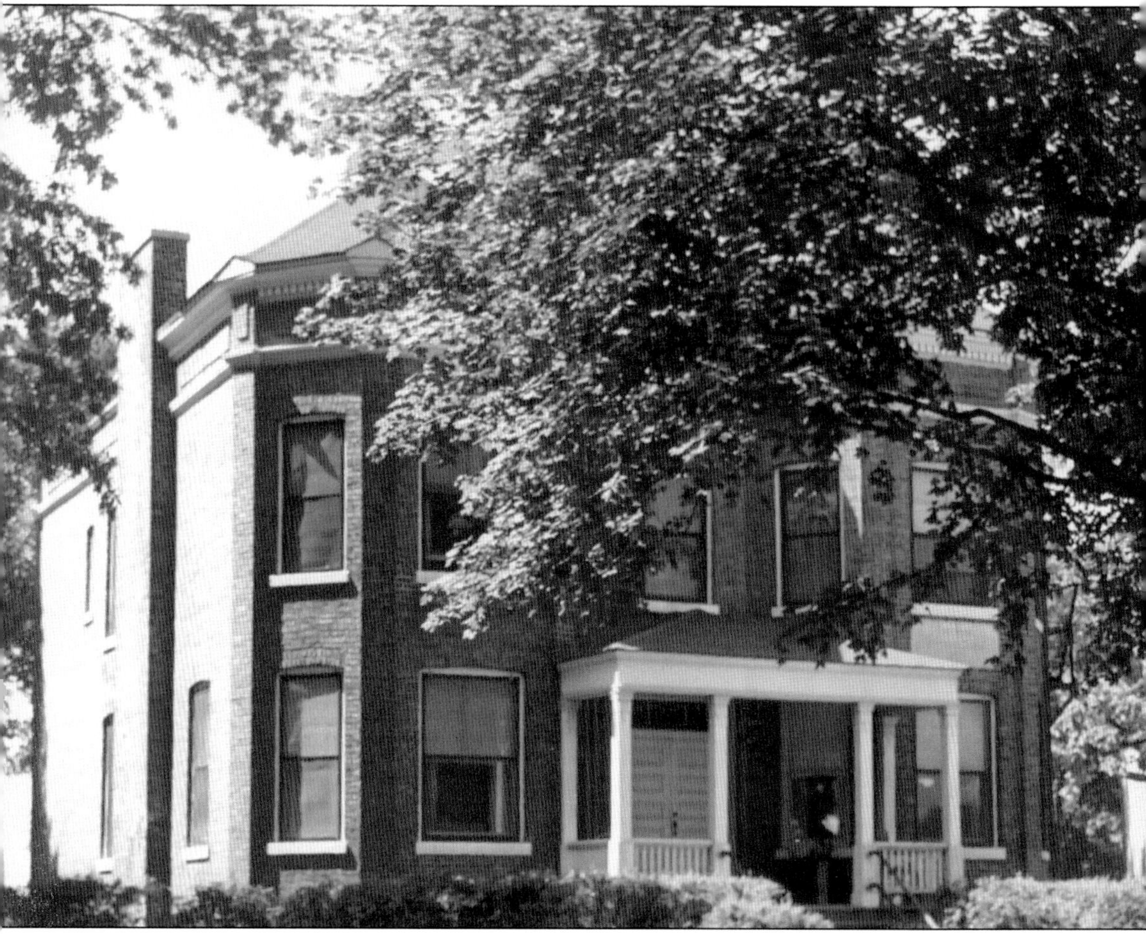

In 1890, Plymouth Cottage was one of the first five built. None of them are still standing. (Courtesy of the Glenwood School for Boys and Girls.)

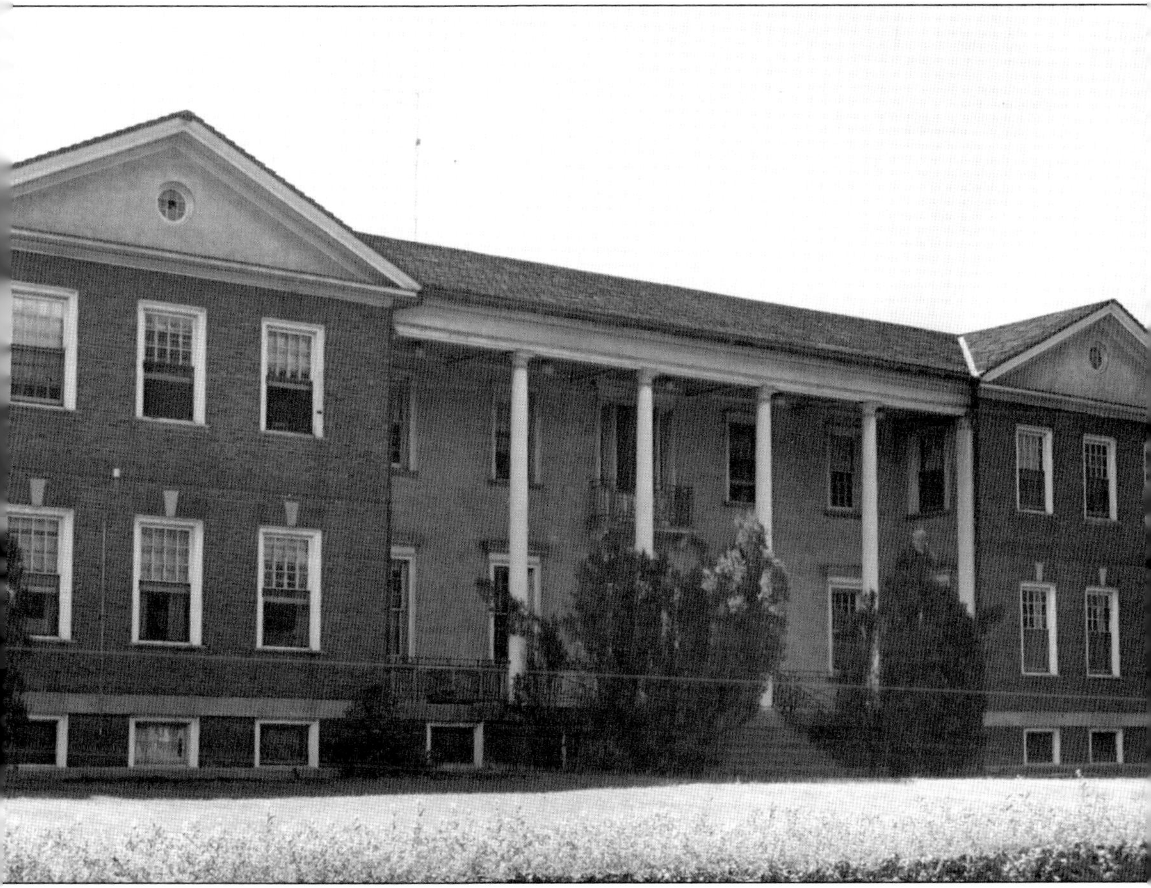

Spalding Hall was built through a gift from Mrs. Robert McElwee in memory of her father, Jesse Spalding. The building of Spalding Hall made it possible to expand the school's program for older boys. (Courtesy of the Glenwood School for Boys and Girls.)

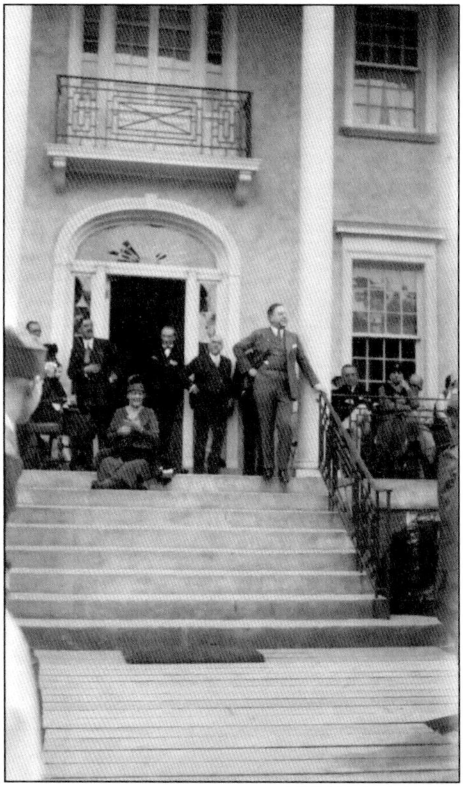

Pres. Norman C. Mather speaks from the steps of Spalding Hall at its opening ceremony in 1928. It was the only residence building on campus then referred to as "hall." (Courtesy of the Glenwood School for Boys and Girls.)

Gen. Frederick Dent Grant, son of Ulysses S. Grant, watches (with arms folded) the boys' drill on Flag Day in 1906. (Courtesy of the Glenwood School for Boys and Girls.)

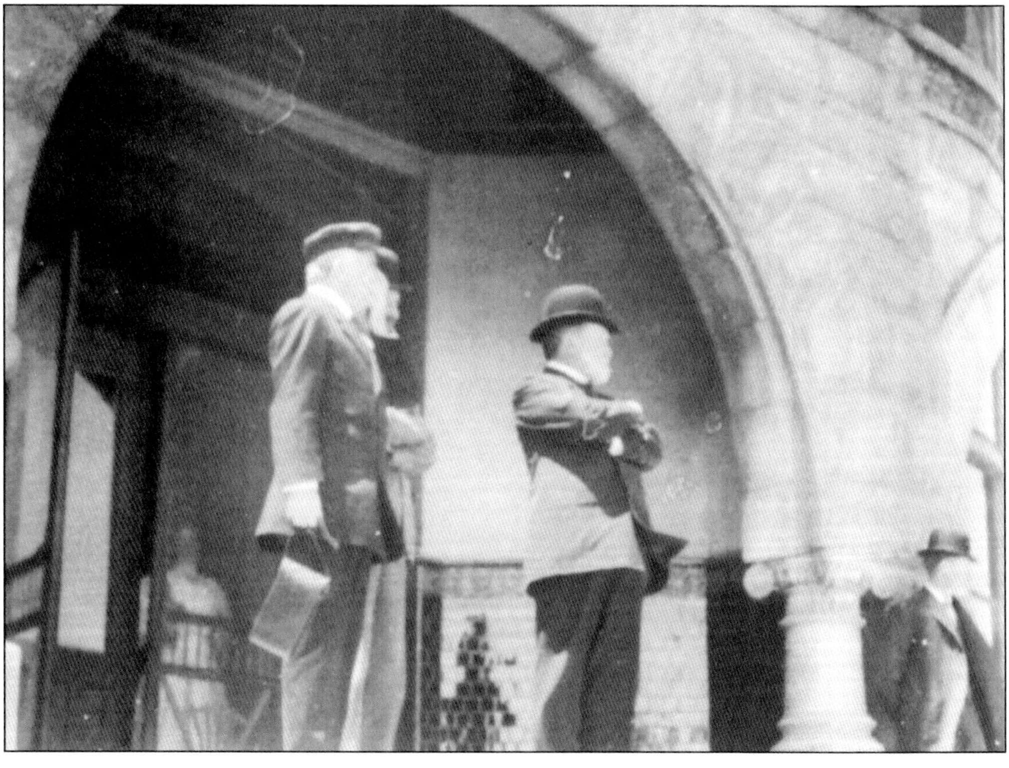

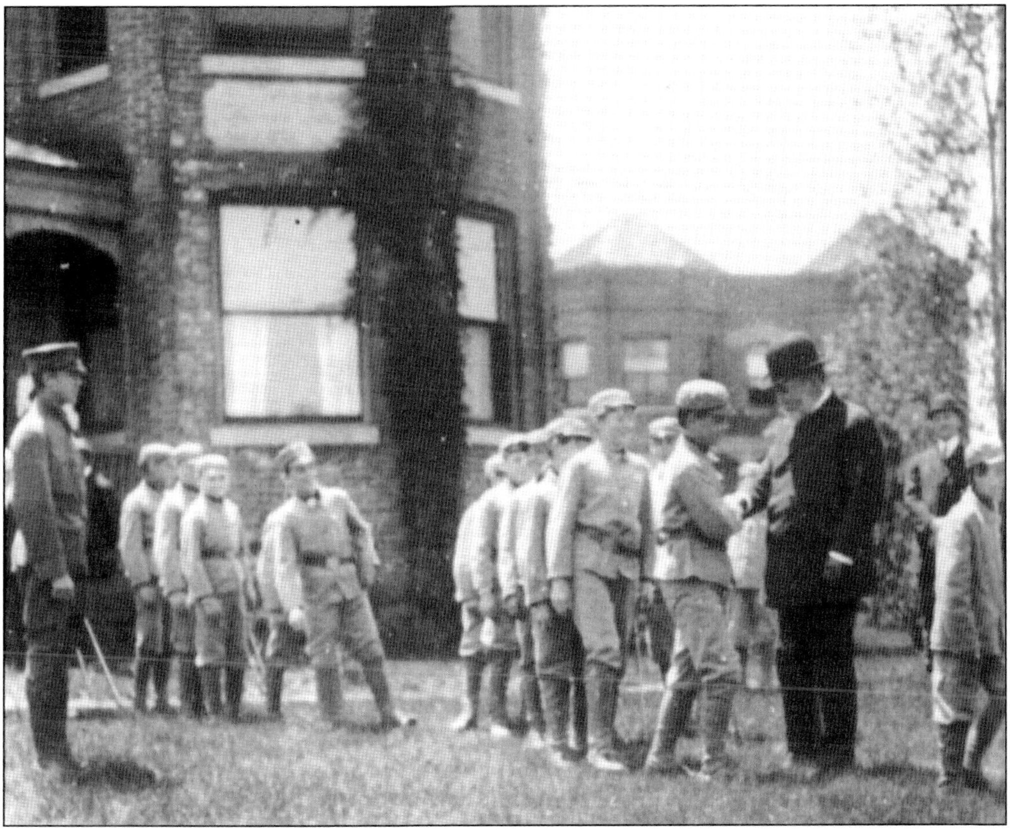

Gen. Frederick Dent Grant is pictured shaking hands with some of the Glenwood boys on Flag Day in 1906. (Courtesy of the Glenwood School for Boys and Girls.)

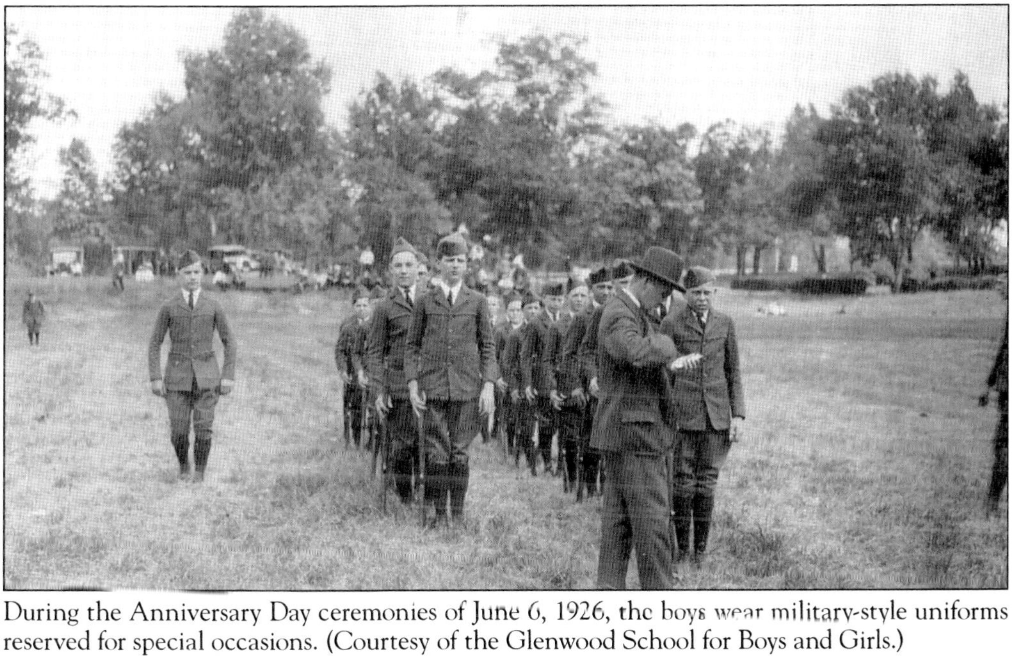

During the Anniversary Day ceremonies of June 6, 1926, the boys wear military-style uniforms reserved for special occasions. (Courtesy of the Glenwood School for Boys and Girls.)

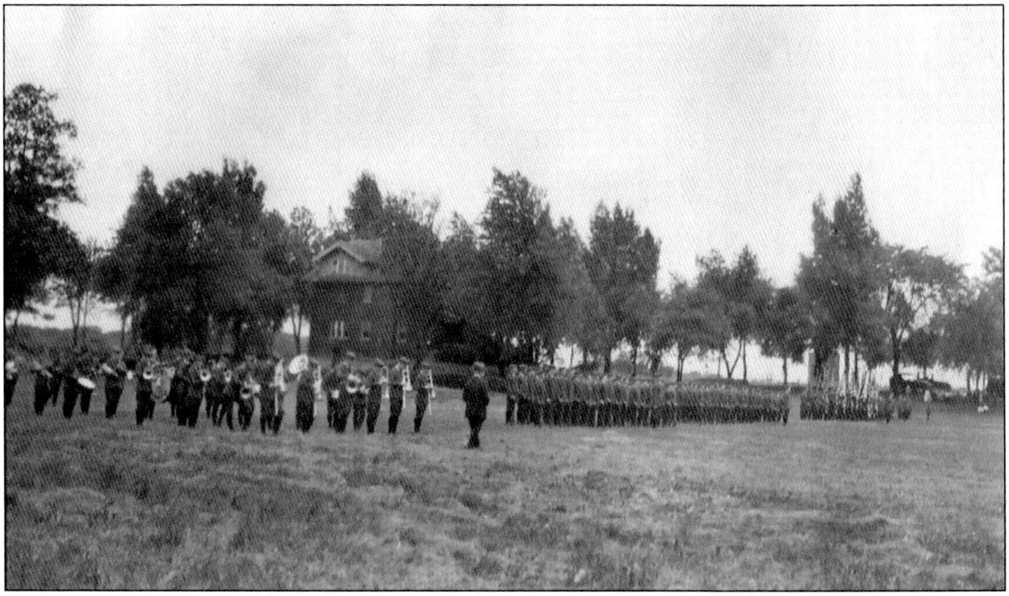

The boys line up for the day's festivities on Anniversary Day, June 6, 1926. (Courtesy of the Glenwood School for Boys and Girls.)

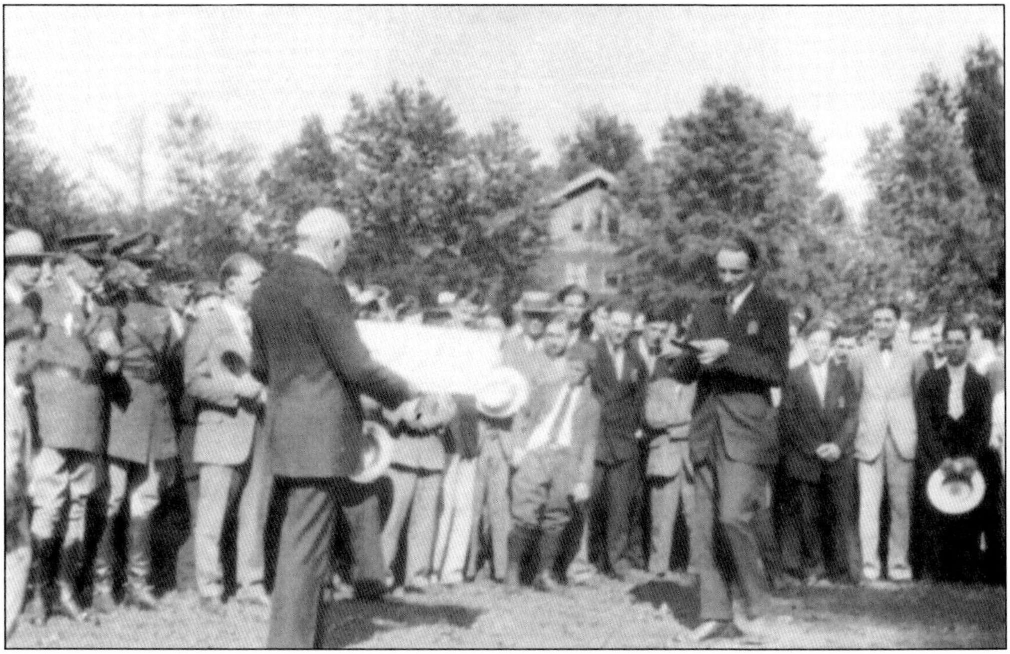

In June 1927 Glenwood alumnus and now architect Bernard Klekamp presented to school president Edward Butler (seen here with his back to the camera) the plans for an entrance gate to be dedicated in Butler's honor. At the time, Butler said "Boys, nothing could please me better than this gateway-this open gate, with arms stretching out to welcome you and your children and your children's children and thousands of boys throughout this state who need Glenwood's care." Four months later the gate was completed. Edward Butler died in February 1928 after 32 years of leadership at the Glenwood School. (Courtesy of the Glenwood School for Boys and Girls.)

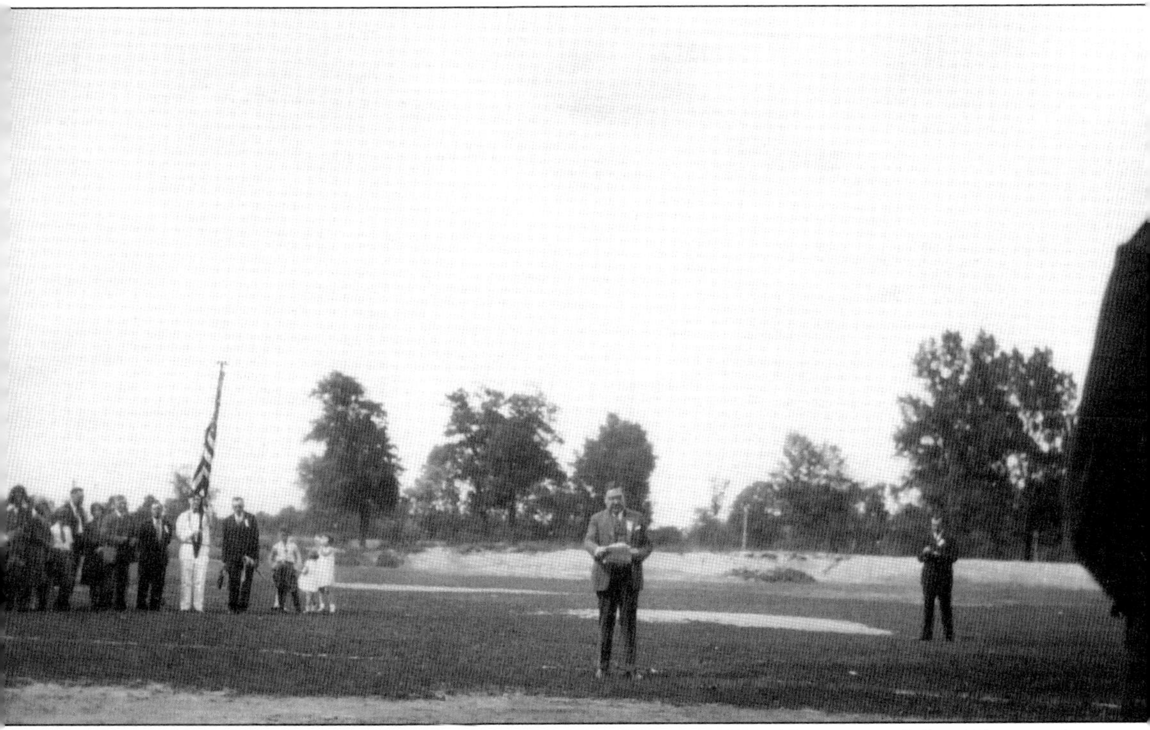

Norman C. Mather gives a speech on Anniversary Day in 1929. (Courtesy of the Glenwood School for Boys and Girls.)

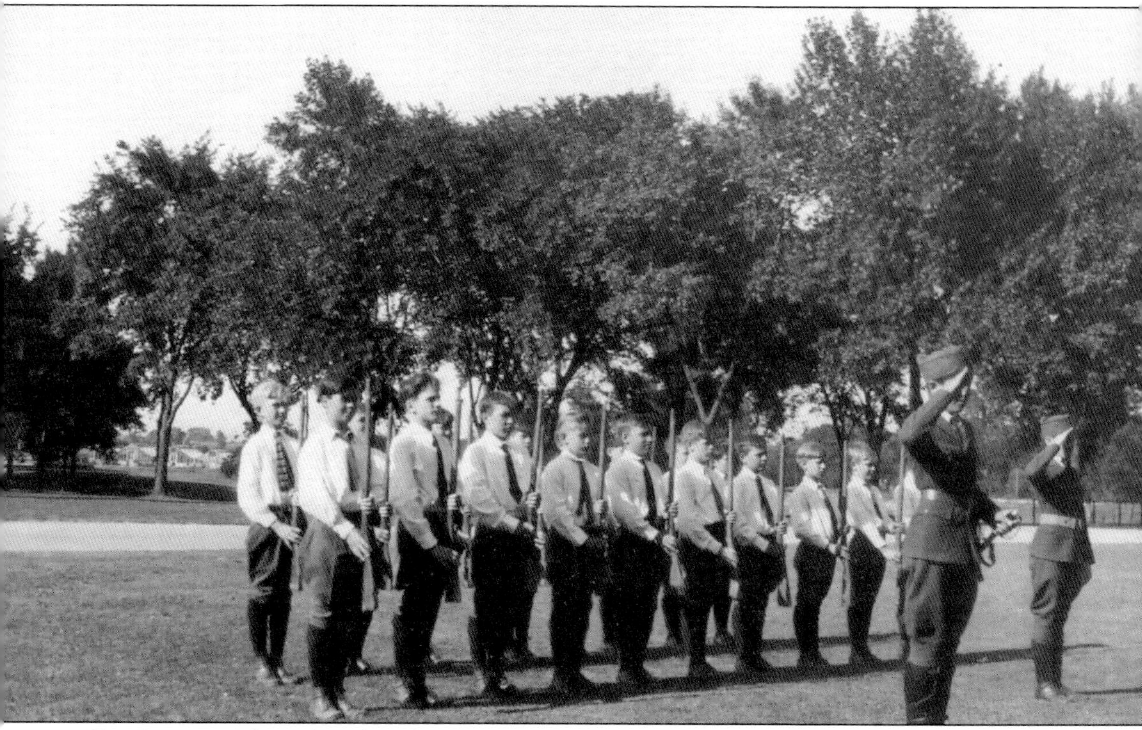

Flag Day is celebrated at the Glenwood School in 1929. (Courtesy of the Glenwood School for Boys and Girls.)

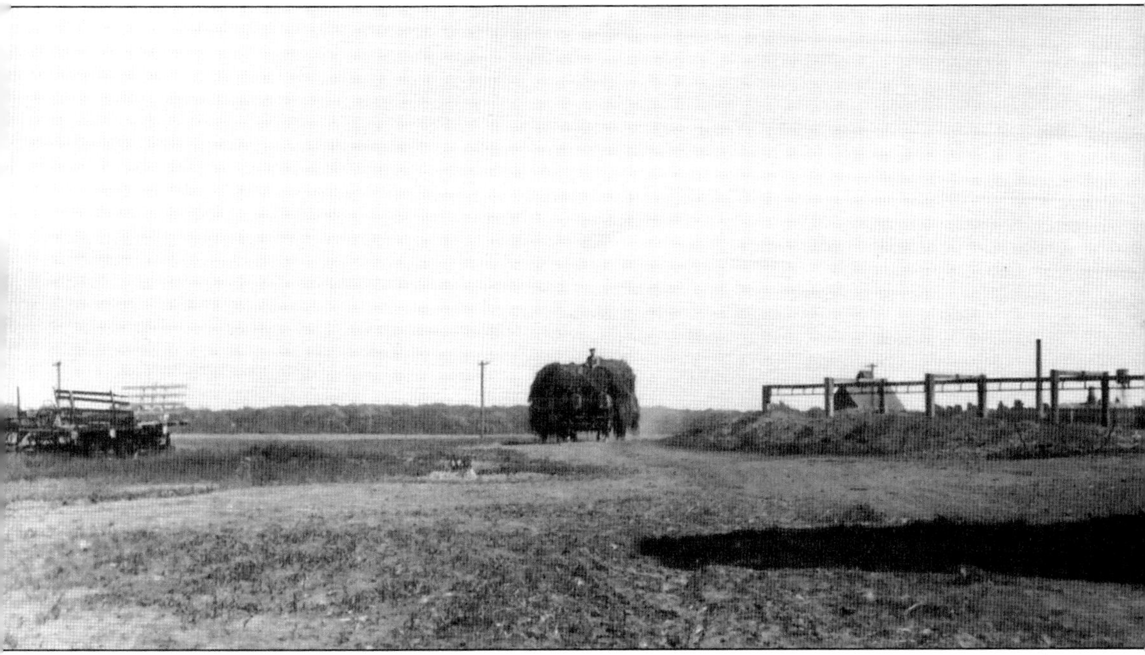

On his 50th birthday, which happened to be in the same year as the 50th anniversary of the school, Julius Rosenwald gave the school funds to buy the 50-acre Meister farm located immediately south of the school property. By 1940, the school property included 551 acres. (Courtesy of the Glenwood School for Boys and Girls.)

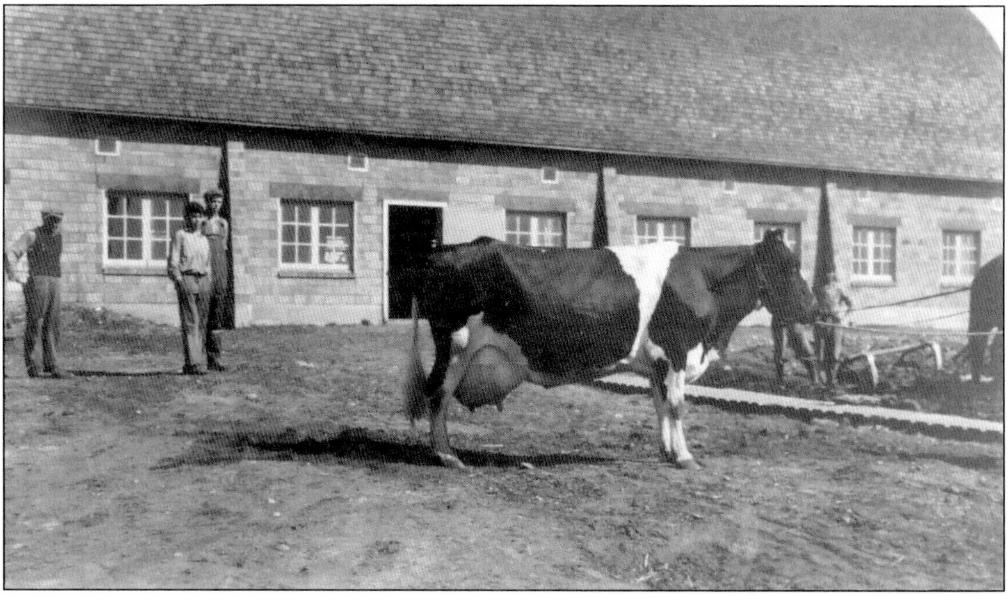

Julius Rosenwald also contributed to the school's herd of Holstein and Guernsey cows. A lovely lady posed for this photograph in May 1932. (Courtesy of the Glenwood School for Boys and Girls.)

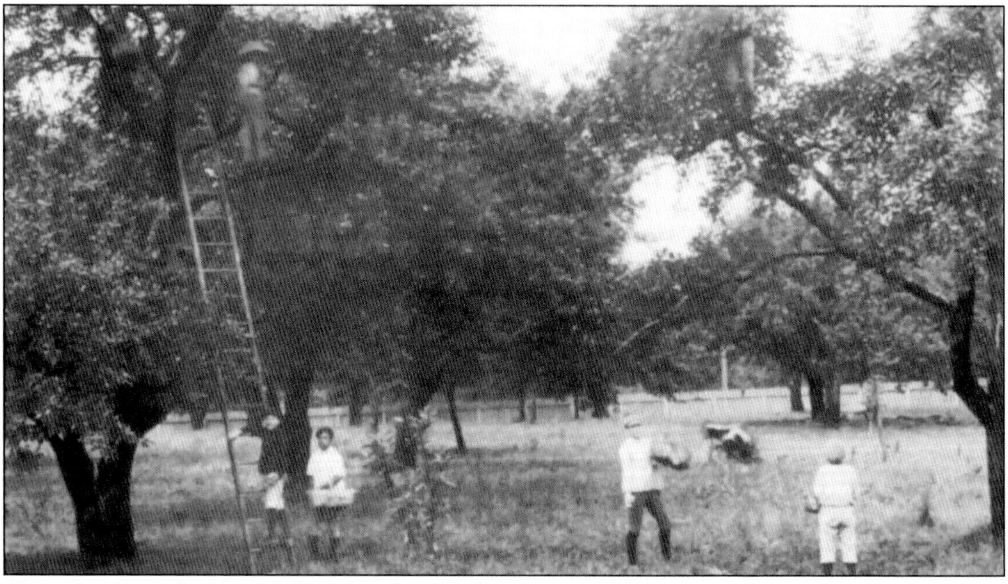

The school's orchard, with boys hard at work, is pictured here around 1890. (Courtesy of the Glenwood School for Boys and Girls.)

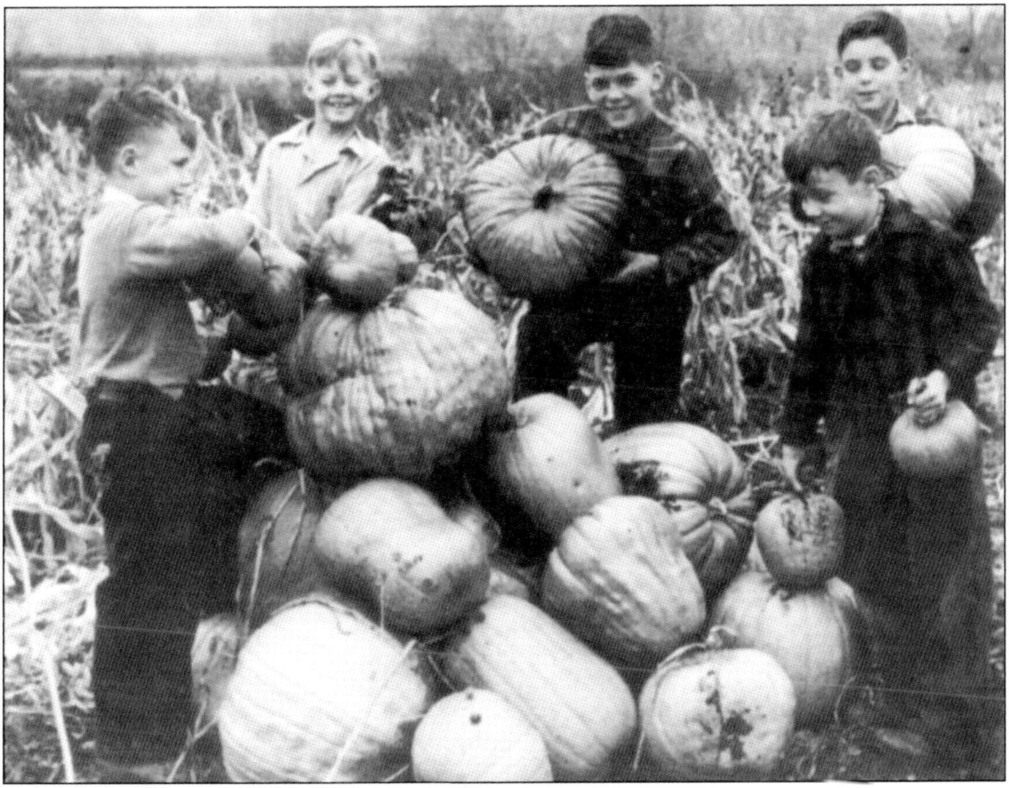

Where the Glenwood Plaza shopping center now stands was once home to pumpkin fields, among other crops. (Courtesy of the Glenwood School for Boys and Girls.)

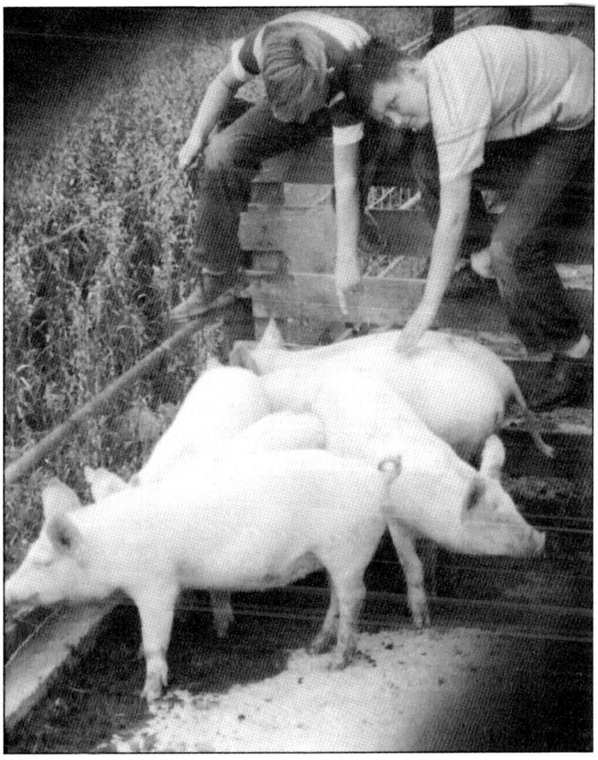

In 1950, the Glenwood School for Boys and its Yorkshire boars brought home several awards from the Illinois State Fair, including one for the grand champion Yorkshire boar. (Courtesy of the Glenwood School for Boys and Girls.)

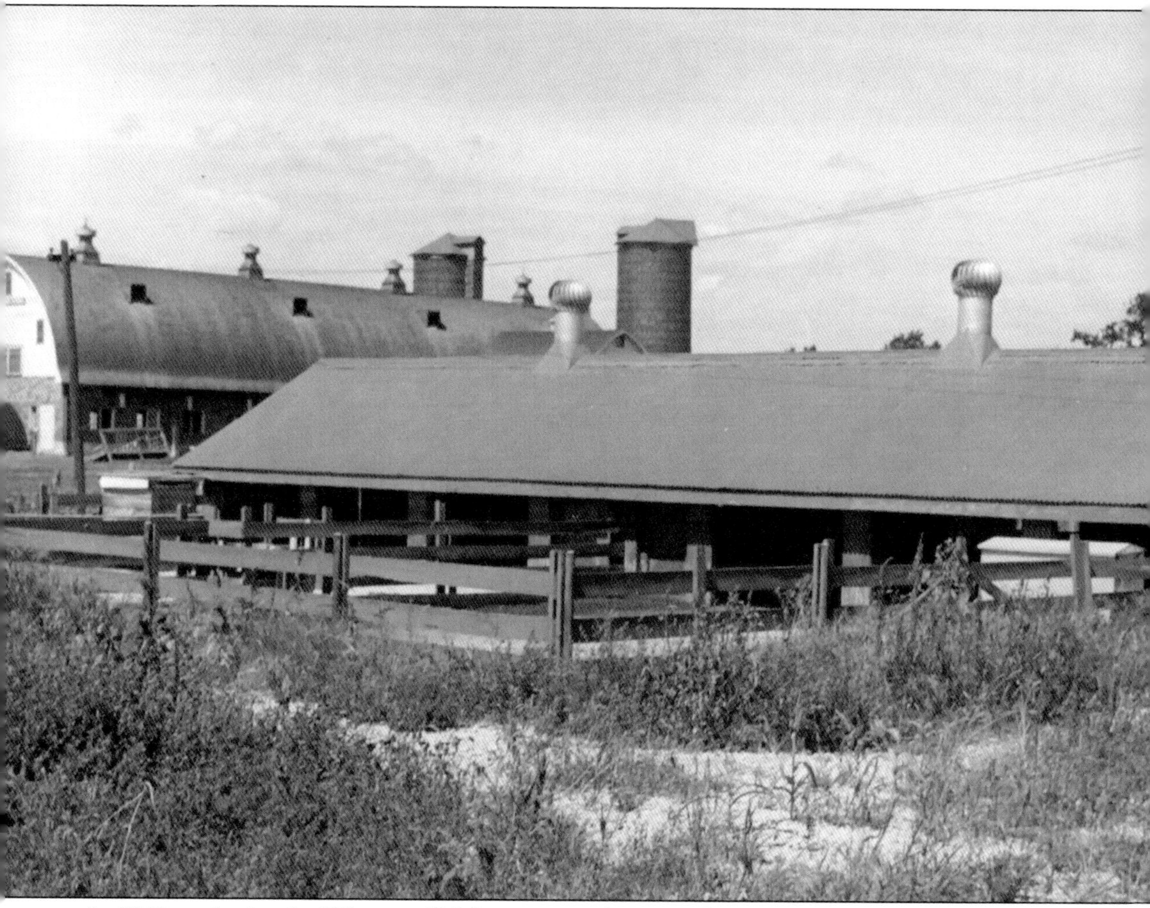

In 1949, twelve head of Glenwood Holsteins were shown at the Central State Fair in Crown Point, Indiana. They won 15 ribbons in various classes, including first place for the breeders' graded herd and a junior yearling heifer. (Courtesy of the Glenwood School for Boys and Girls.)

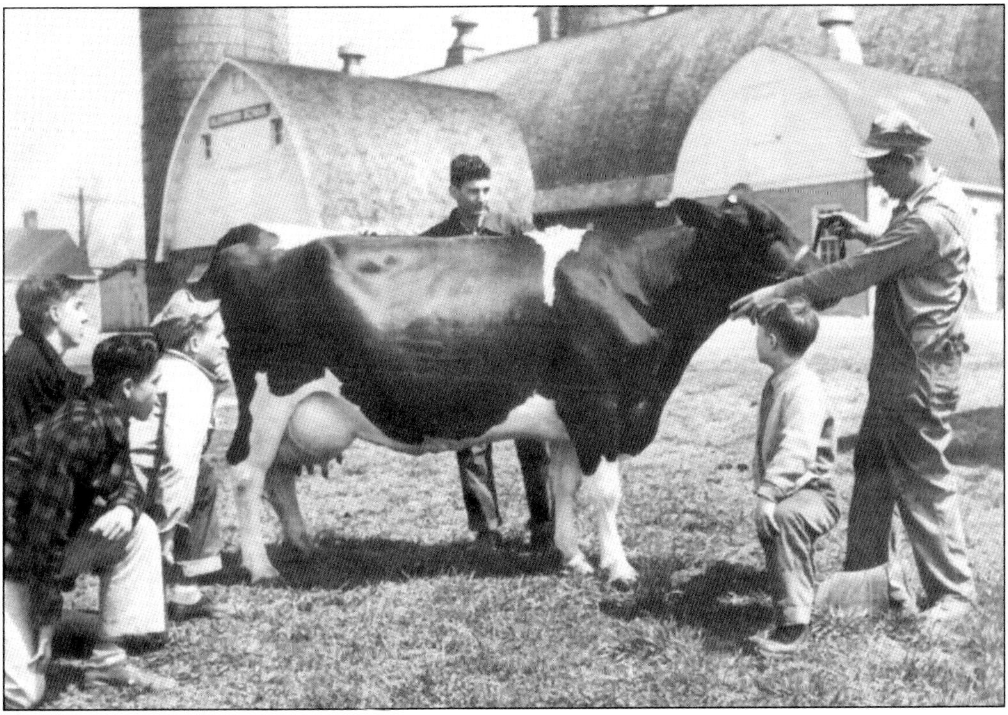

In the 1950s, the Glenwood School's Holstein cattle were capturing honors for milk production. One animal named Chieftain Annabel produced 422 pounds of butterfat and 12,505 pounds of milk on a twice-a-day milking for 365 days at the age of two years. (Courtesy of the Glenwood School for Boys and Girls.)

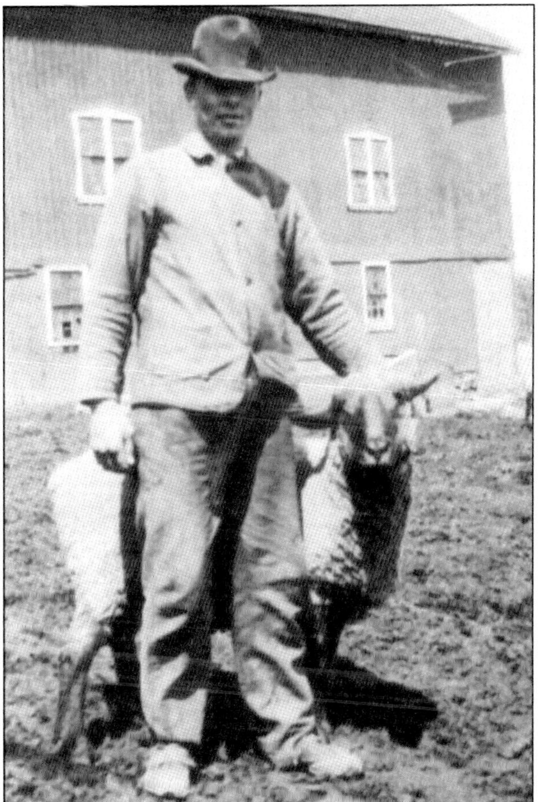

In 1912, students were asked what they expected to do when they left Glenwood. The majority of responders wanted to be farmers. (Courtesy of the Glenwood School for Boys and Girls.)

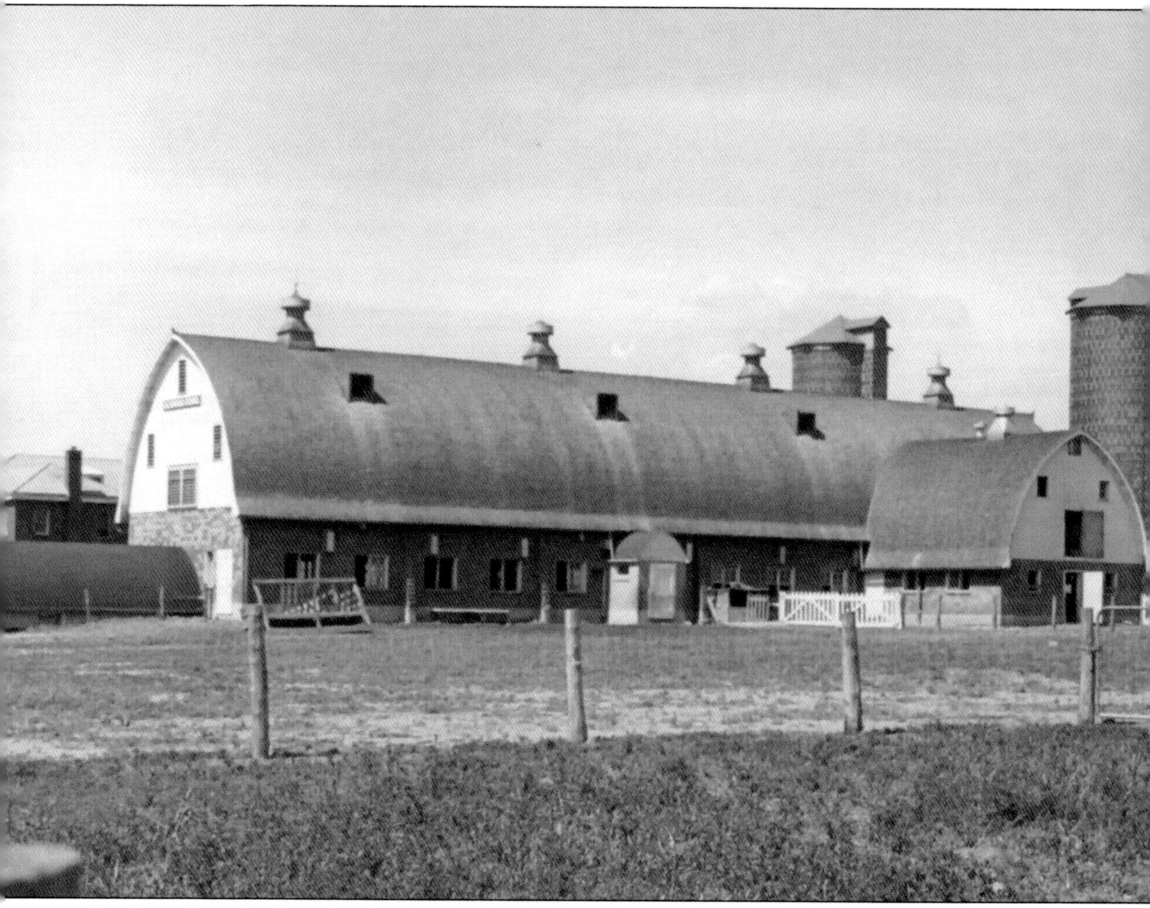

On June 7, 1957, the school's 92 Holsteins were sold one by one to local dairy farmers, bringing an end to an era. (Courtesy of the Glenwood School for Boys and Girls.)

In 1937, the school celebrated its 50th anniversary of helping boys become men. (Courtesy of the Glenwood School for Boys and Girls.)

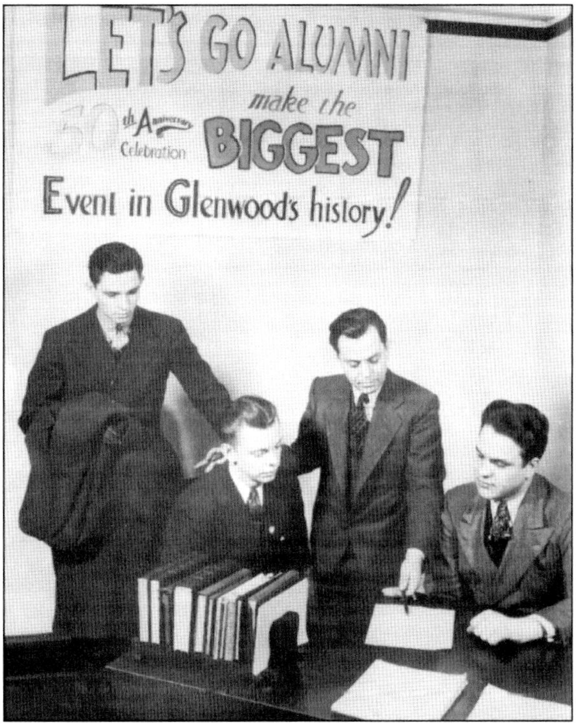

Mrs. Egan attends to an injured Alfred Rudd in October 1951. (Courtesy of the Glenwood School for Boys and Girls.)

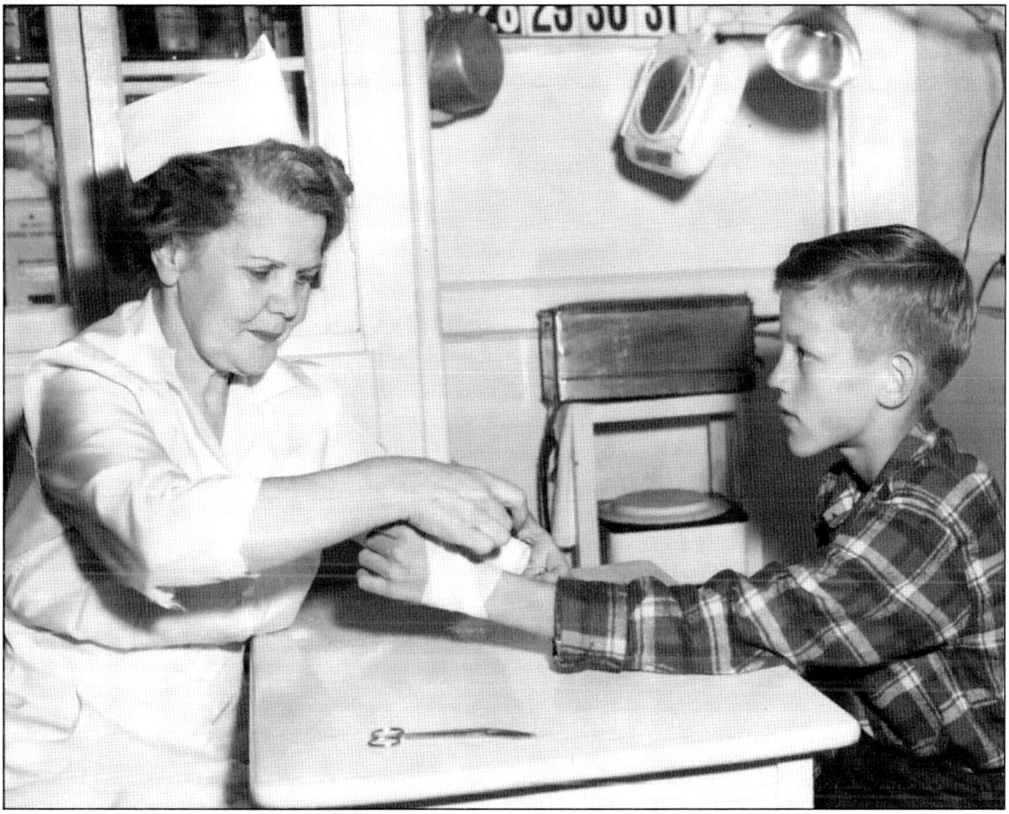

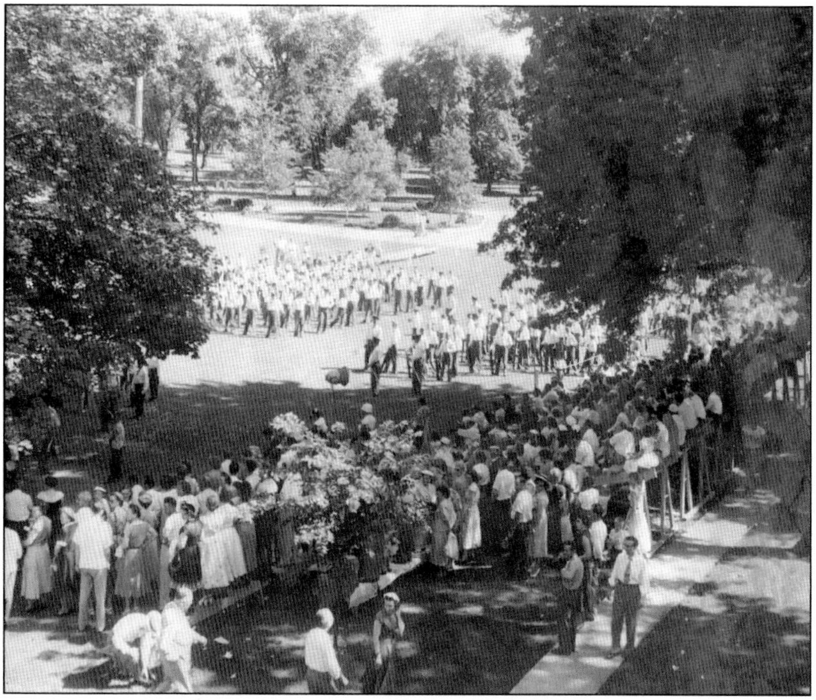

Pictured here is Flag Day on June 13, 1954. (Courtesy of the Glenwood School for Boys and Girls.)

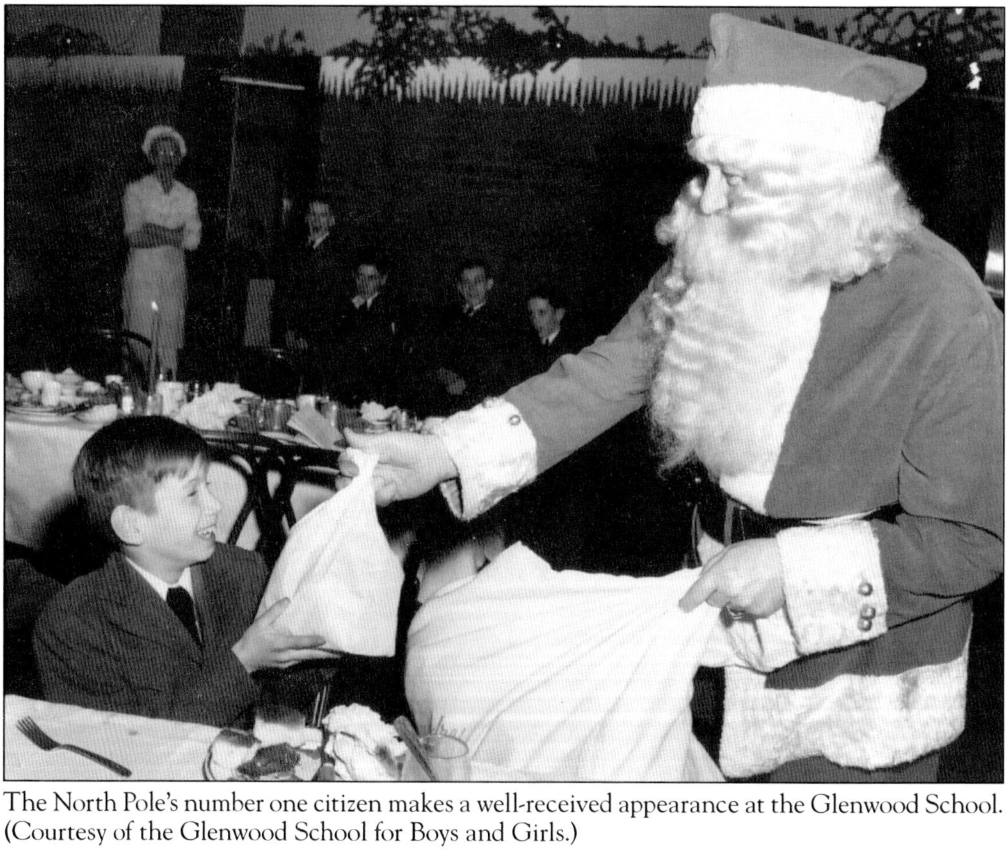

The North Pole's number one citizen makes a well-received appearance at the Glenwood School. (Courtesy of the Glenwood School for Boys and Girls.)

Choir was among the extracurricular activities available at the school. (Courtesy of the Glenwood School for Boys and Girls.)

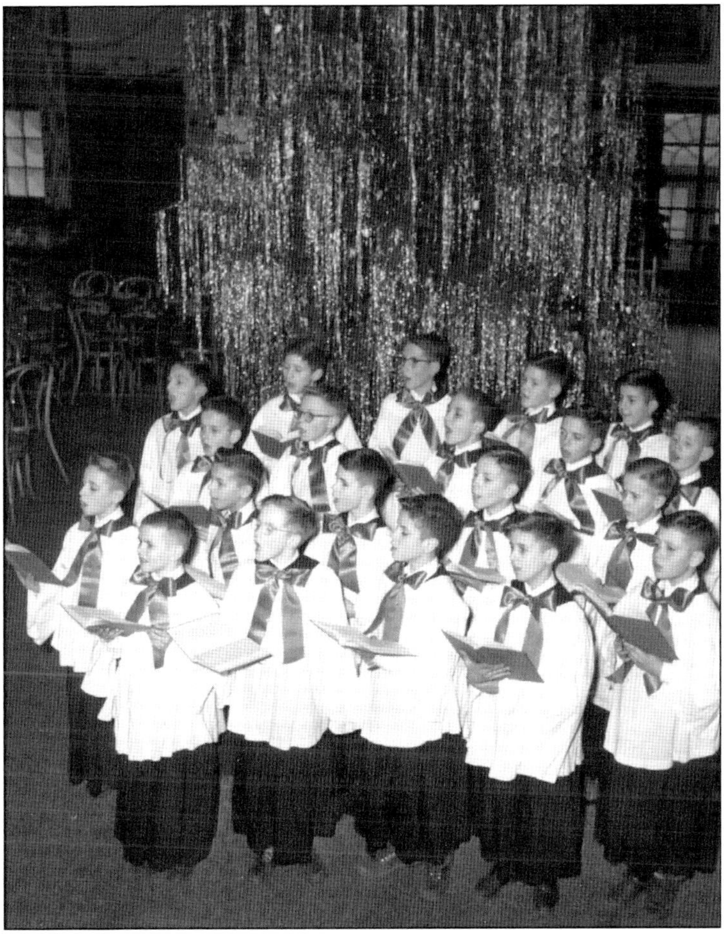

In 1962, the 39-piece marching band's instruments included five new fiberglass sousaphones. (Courtesy of the Glenwood School for Boys and Girls.)

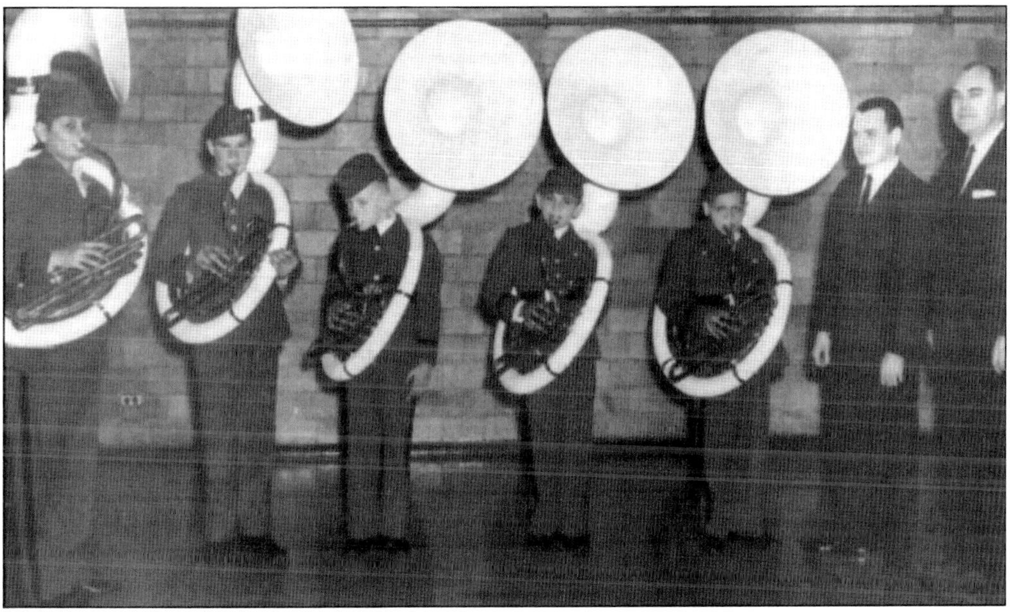

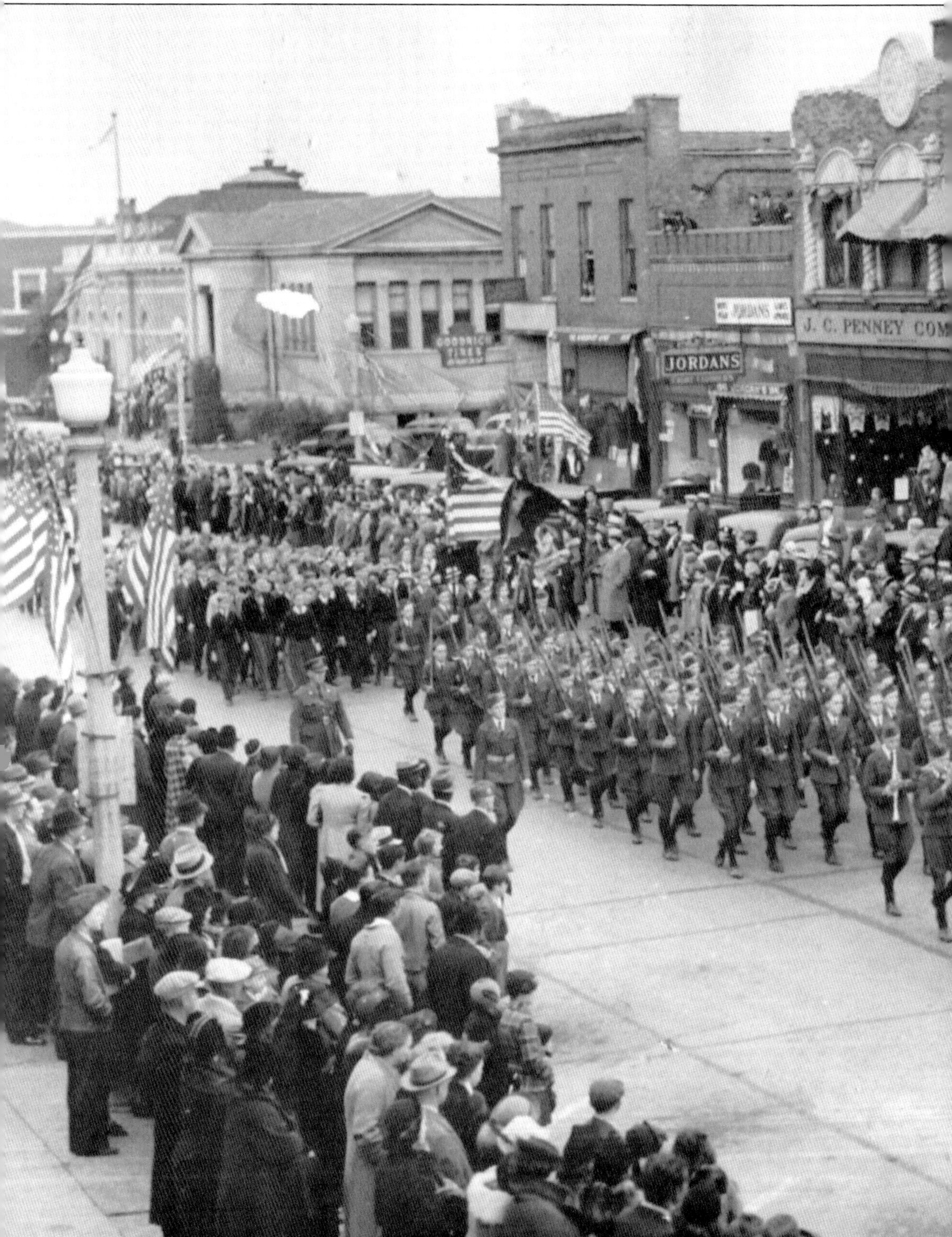
JORDANS
JORDANS
J. C. PENNEY COM

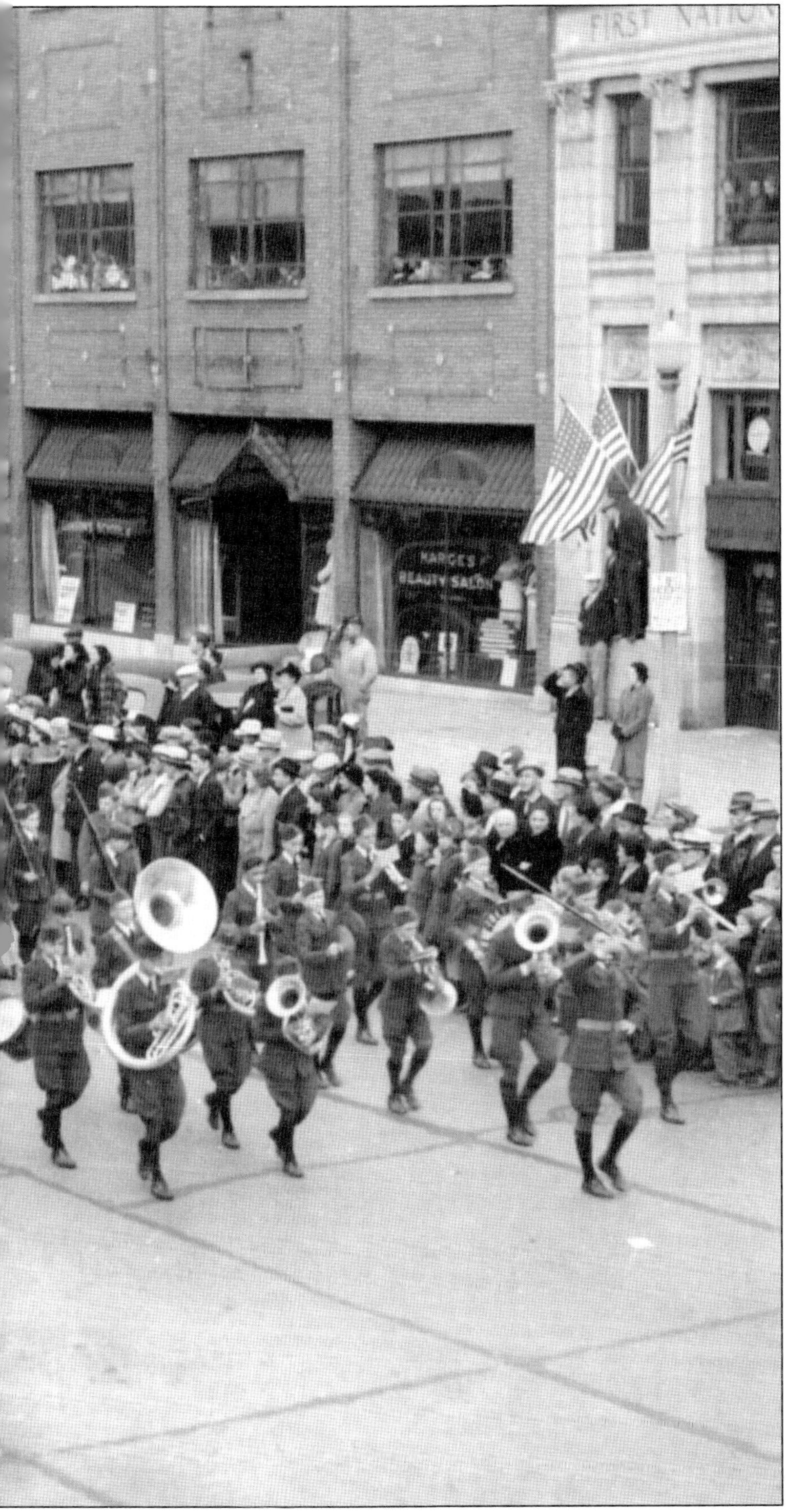

Capt. Haskell W. Harr (1894–1986), one-time musical and military director at the Glenwood School, brings the entire student body out for a Chicago Heights parade in 1935. Harr also developed drum instruction books that are still in use today. Before becoming a member of the faculty at the Glenwood School, Captain Harr had played xylophone accompaniment for Sally Rand during the 1933 World's Fair in Chicago. (Courtesy of the Glenwood School for Boys and Girls.)

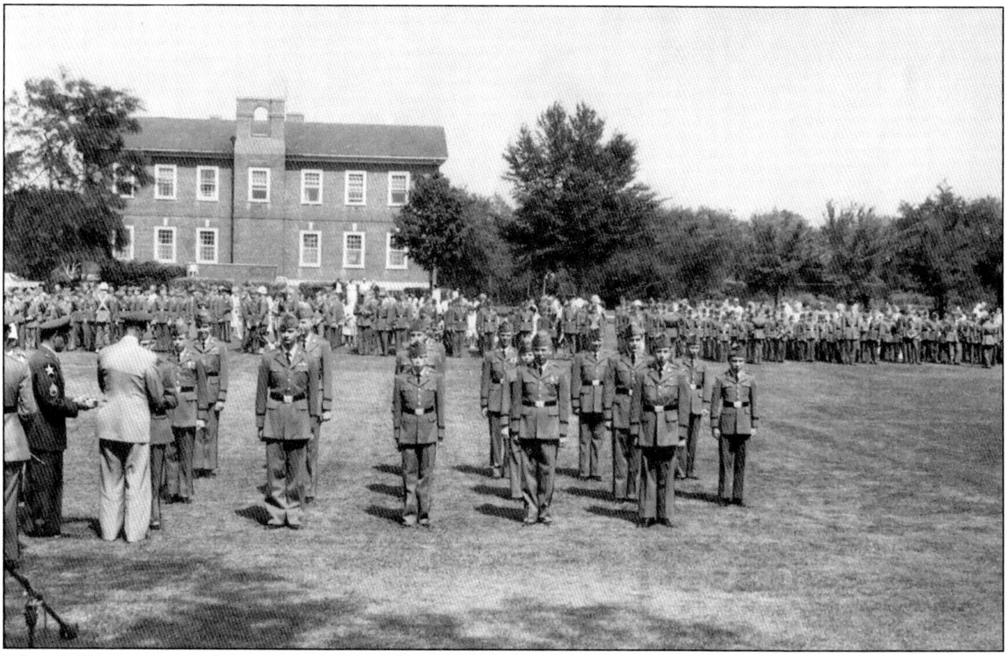

The cadets of Lincoln Cottage take the field on Flag Day in 1963. (Courtesy of the Glenwood School for Boys and Girls.)

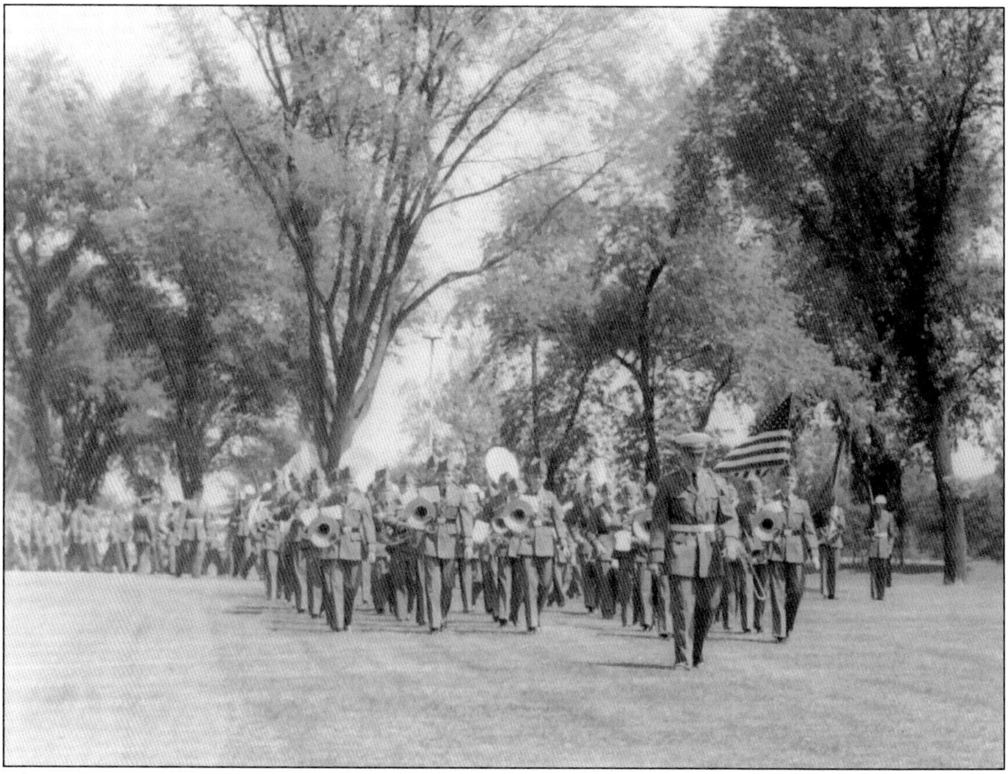

The military-style uniforms that were worn on special occasions, such as Memorial Day (pictured here in 1964), were phased out by 1986. (Courtesy of the Glenwood School for Boys and Girls.)

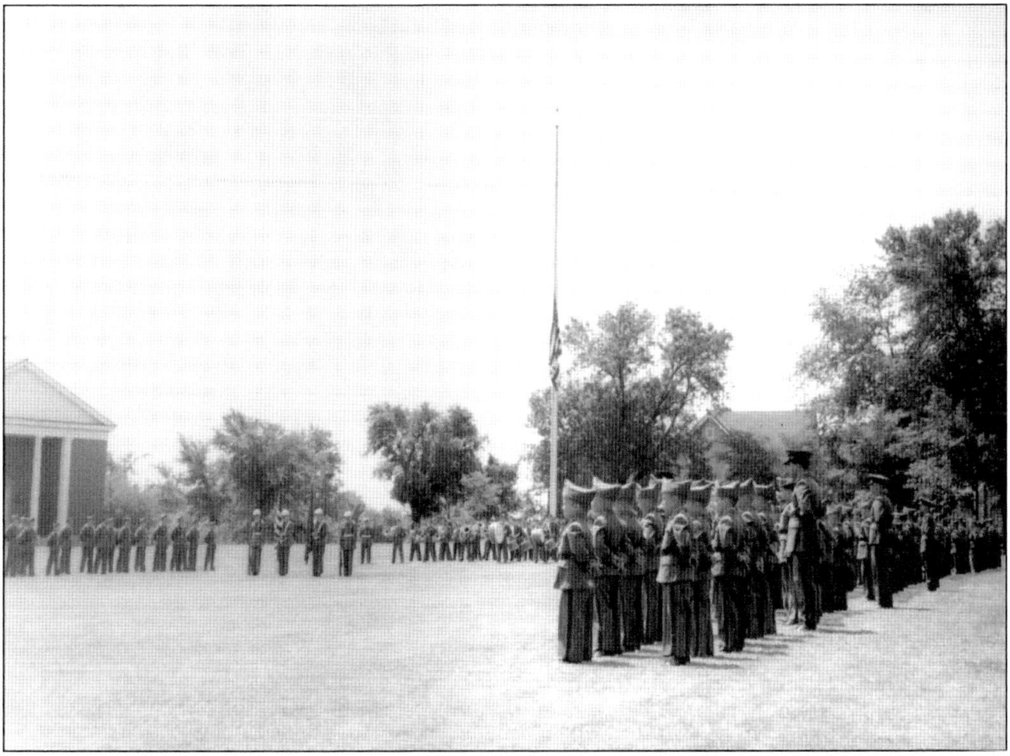

In 1964, the school held what was called the 68th Annual Competitive Military Drill. (Courtesy of the Glenwood School for Boys and Girls.)

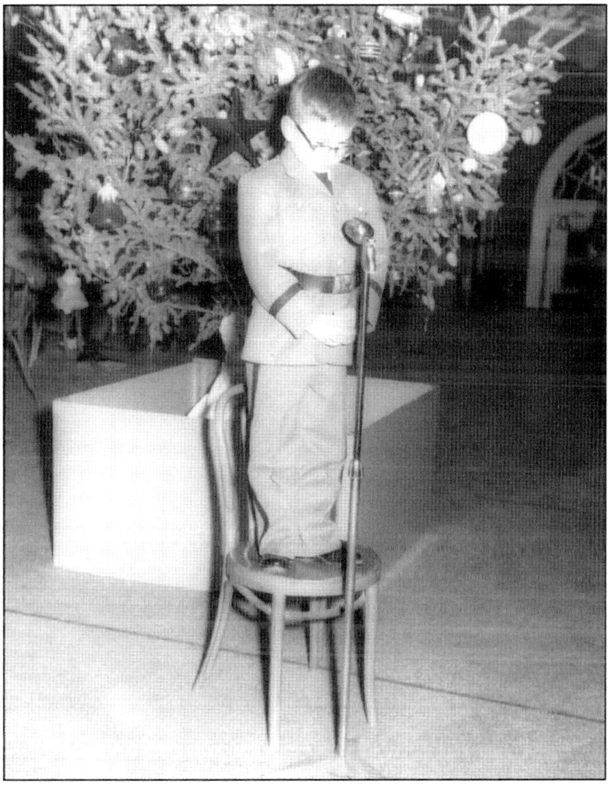

At the Christmas dinner in 1965, one little cadet finds out that it is lonely at the top. (Courtesy of the Glenwood School for Boys and Girls.)

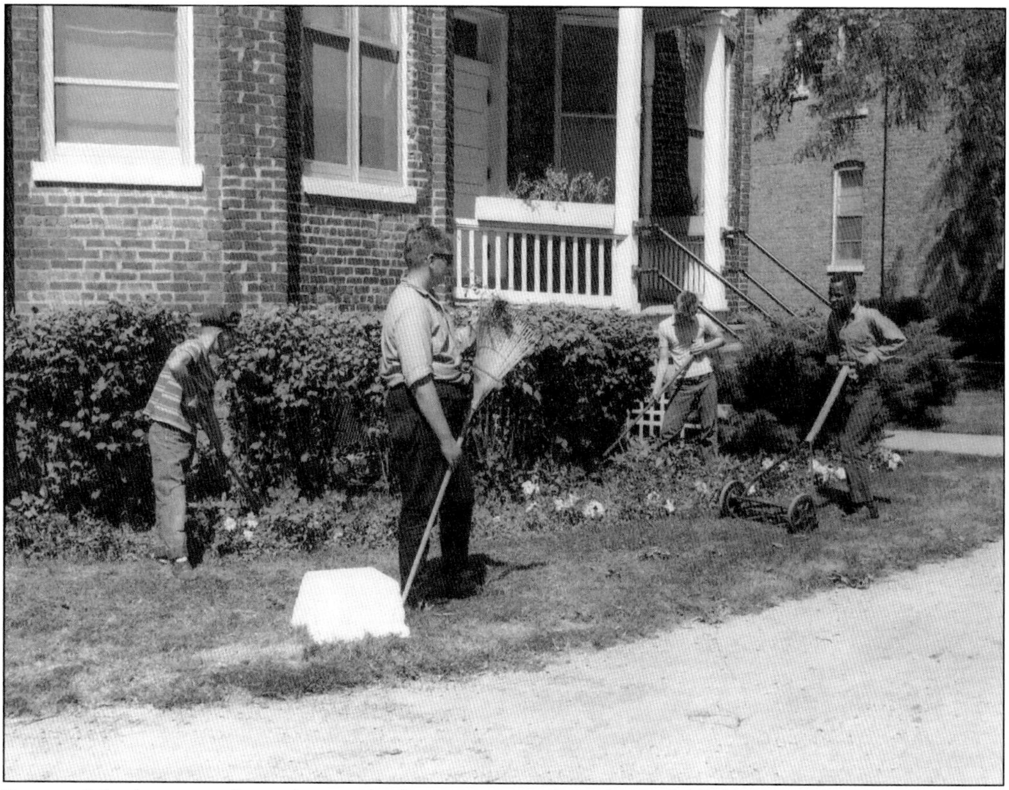

Some of the boys stay busy doing a little summer yard work in 1966. (Courtesy of the Glenwood School for Boys and Girls.)

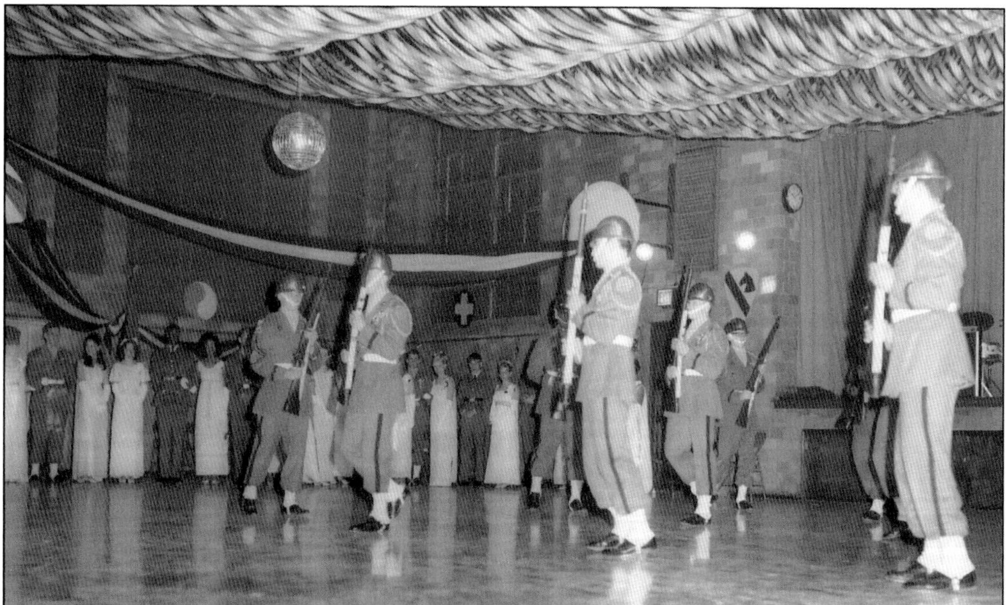

The 20th Annual Military Ball was held on May 6, 1967. (Courtesy of the Glenwood School for Boys and Girls.)

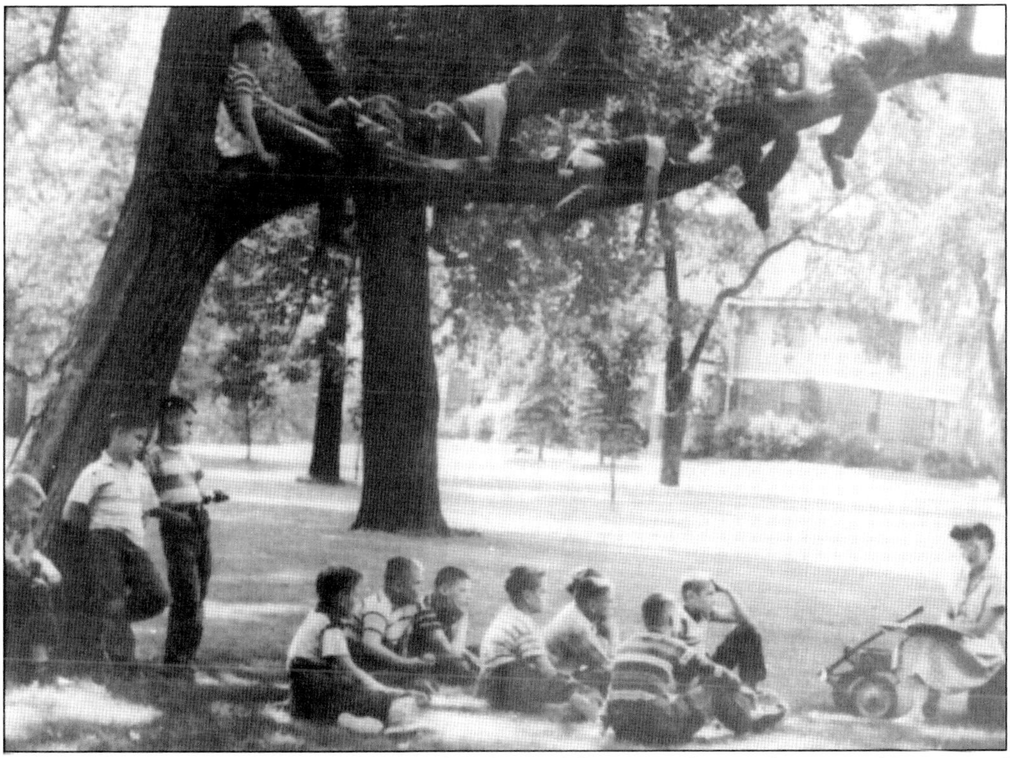

Some of the boys get a chance to enjoy their beautiful campus during class time. (Courtesy of the Glenwood School for Boys and Girls.)

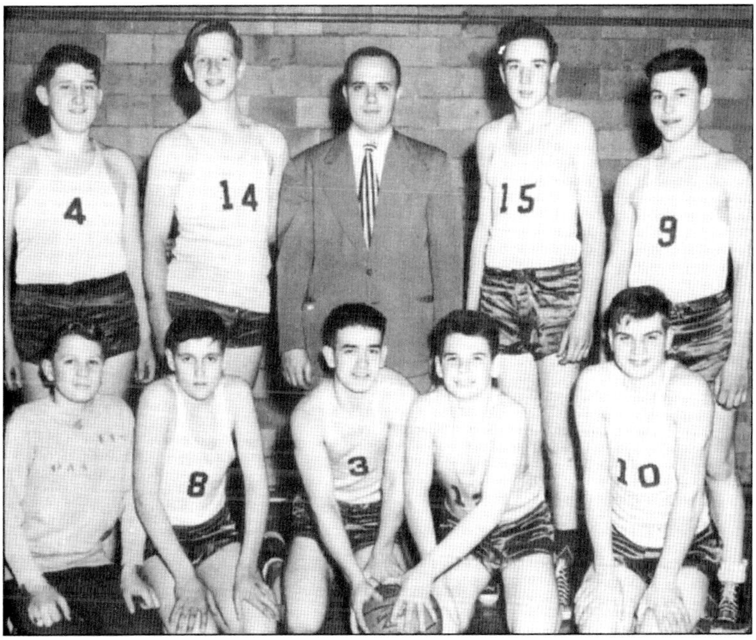

During the 1961 and 1962 season, the Glenwood Boys' basketball team went 0–20. They improved over the next six years, however, winning the school's first league basketball championship in 1967 with a 69–67, come-from-behind win. (Courtesy of the Glenwood School for Boys and Girls.)

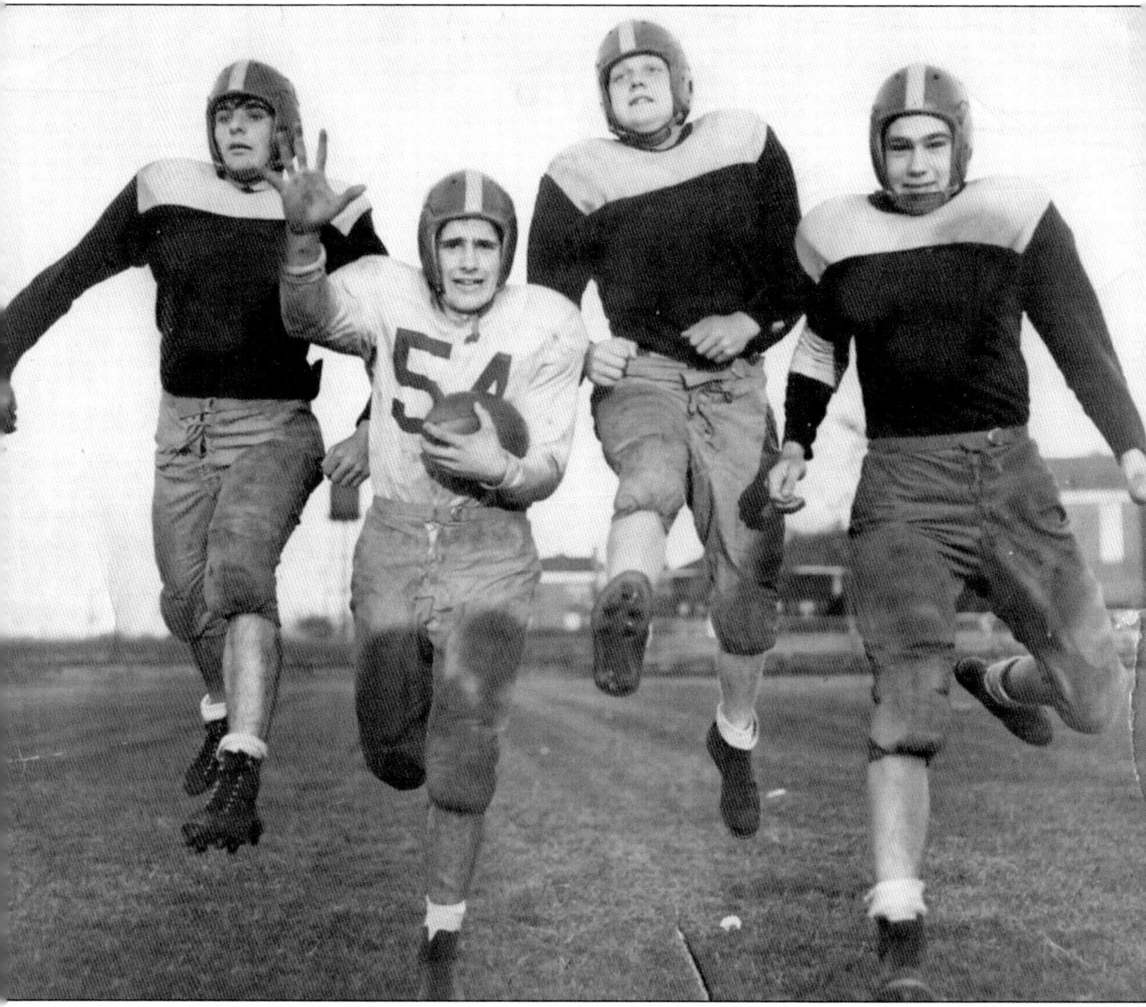

Playing football in 1950 are, from left to right, Frank Williams, Rich Carney, John Muza, and Art Scrowcroft. Art Scrowcroft was 1 of 25 soldiers killed when a C-46 transport plane crashed into the Sea of Japan on November 15, 1952. Art was a member of the 1092nd engineers. He had been serving in Korea since February 1952. (Courtesy of the Glenwood School for Boys and Girls.)

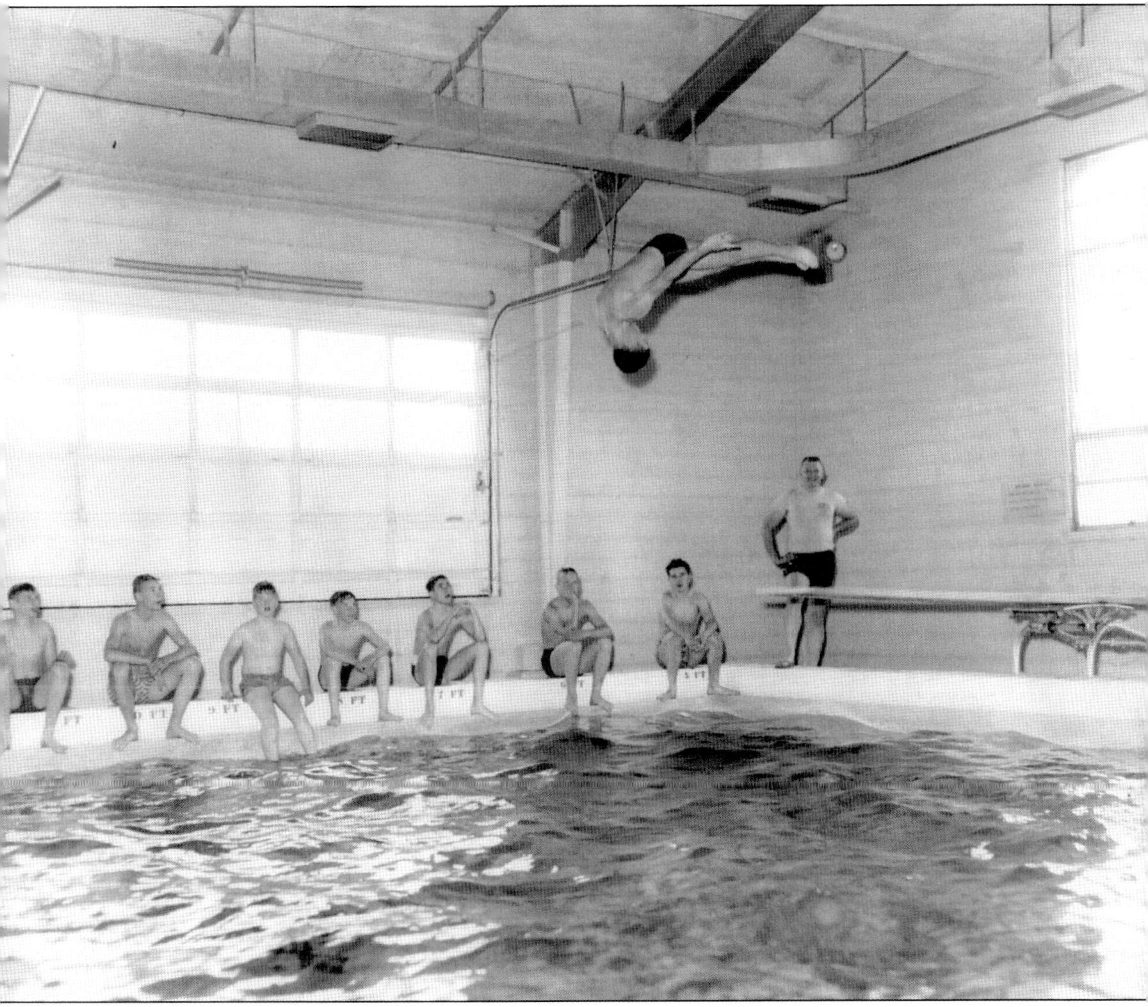

The first swimming pool was built through a gift from Mrs. Charles Morrison in 1921. On the day the pool was dedicated, Mrs. Morrison was unable to attend and, in her place, she sent her sister, who noticed that not very many boys were swimming and inquired as to why. She was informed that very few of the boys owned swimming attire. In addition to Mrs. Charles Morrison's donation that funded the pool, her sister wrote a check on the spot to see to it that every boy would be dressed to swim in the future. A new pool, shown here, opened inside the Dudley Gymnasium and Physical Education Center in 1941. (Courtesy of the Glenwood School for Boys and Girls.)

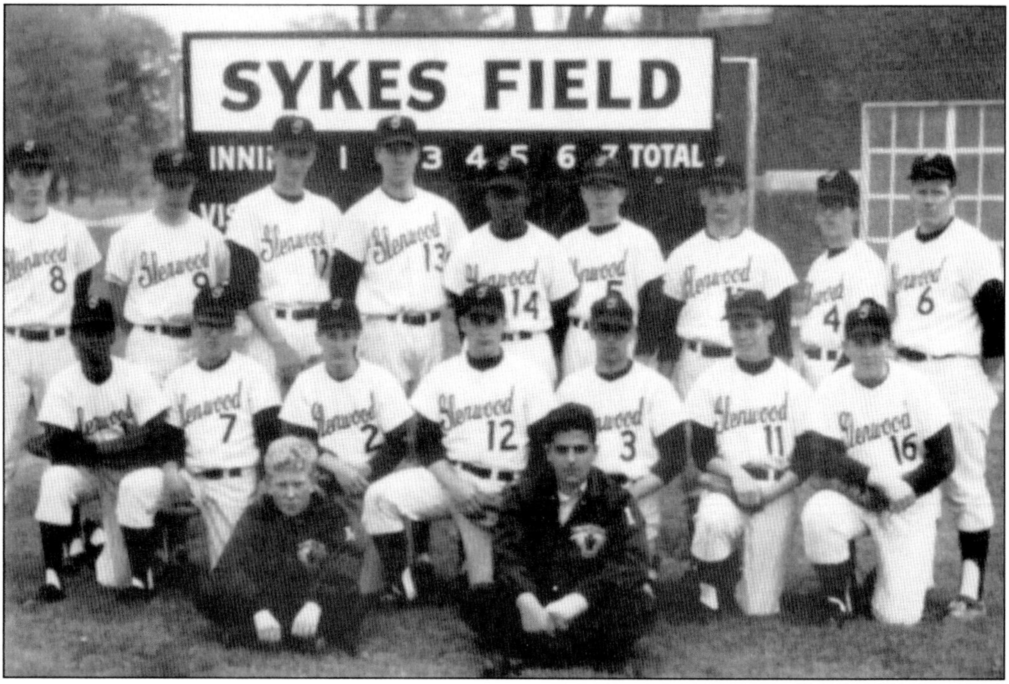

The Glenwood School baseball team played ball on the school property, but it was the sale of some of that property that allowed for Arquilla Field to be built. The new Little League field for the town of Glenwood was right across the street from the Glenwood School. (Courtesy of the Glenwood School for Boys and Girls.)

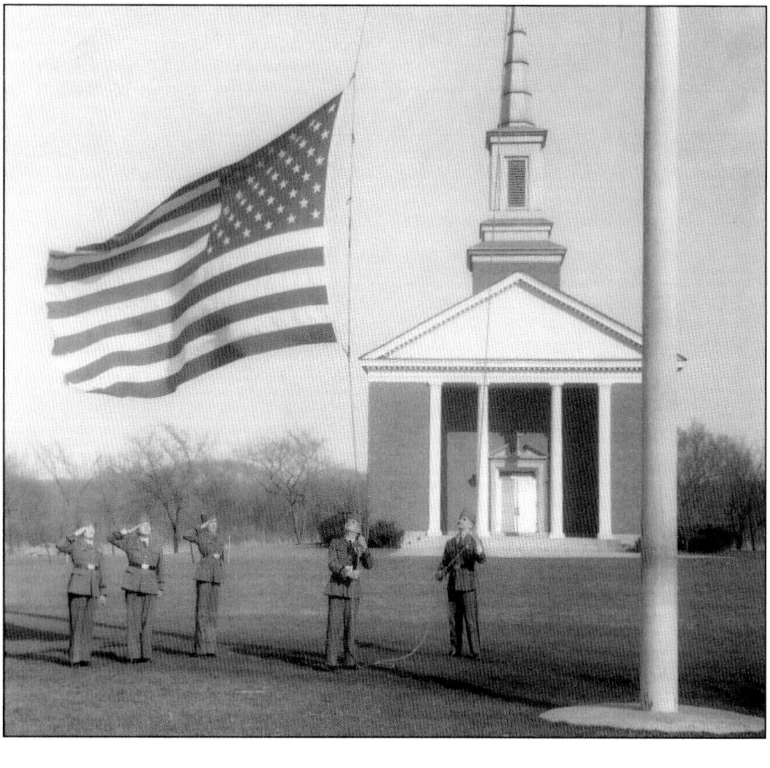

A group of cadets raise the flag in front of the Oliver M. Burton Memorial Chapel. For years, residents have gathered in the chapel the week before Christmas for the candlelight annual pledge service. At the service, gift pledges are made toward a worthy cause determined by a committee. (Courtesy of the Glenwood School for Boys and Girls.)

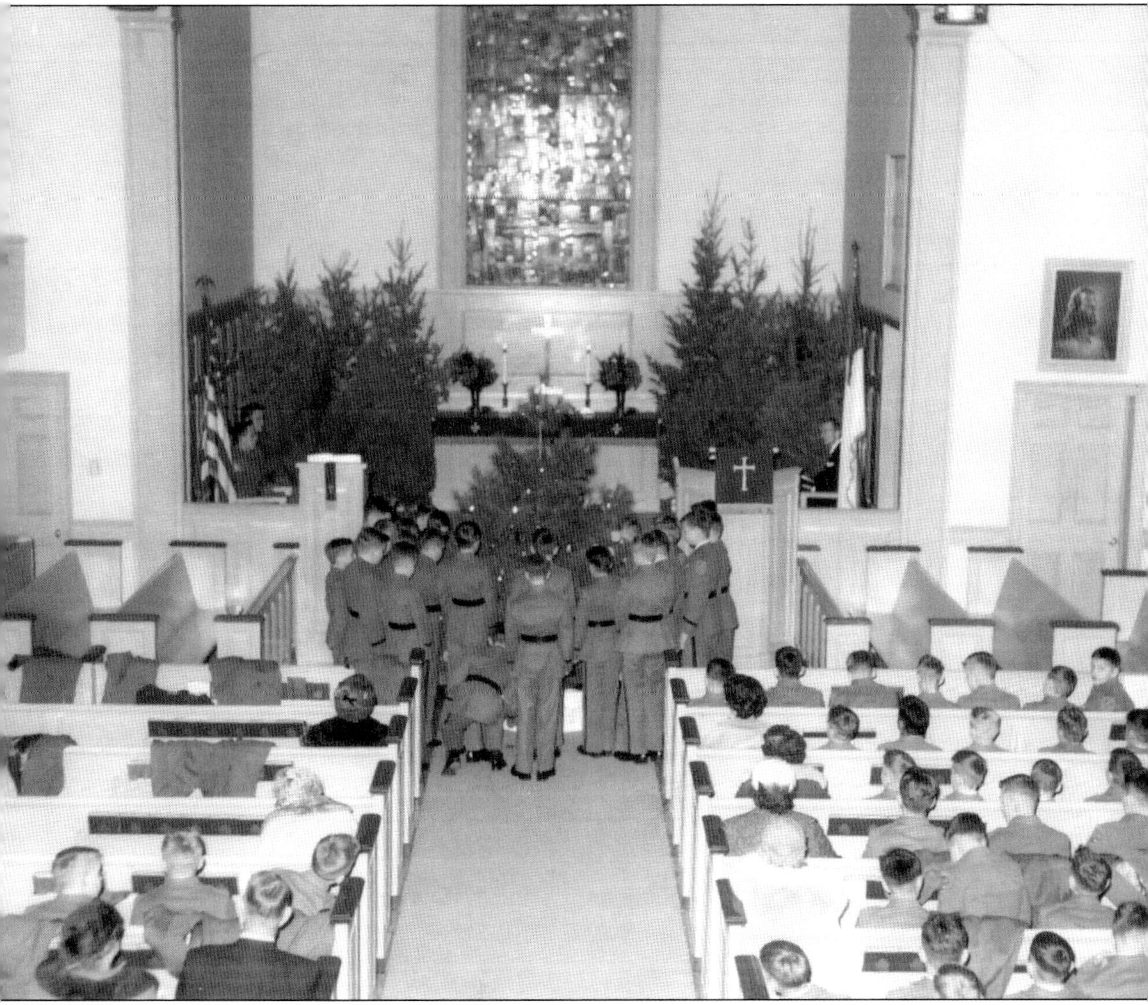

This is a view inside the Oliver M. Burton Memorial Chapel during the Christmas pledge service in 1963. (Courtesy of the Glenwood School for Boys and Girls.)

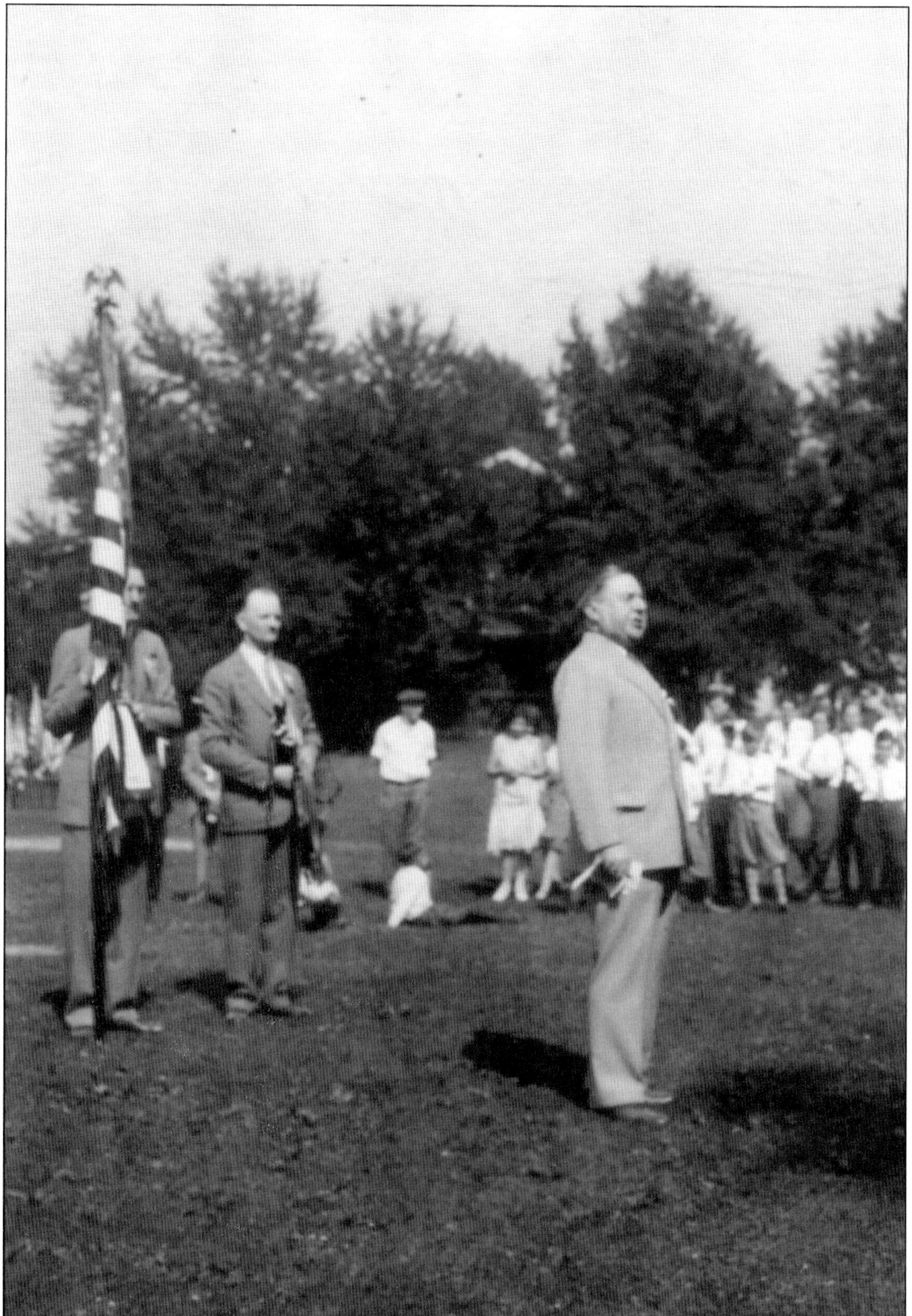

On May 24, 1932, Norman C. Mather gives the Anniversary Day address to the student body. (Courtesy of the Glenwood School for Boys and Girls.)

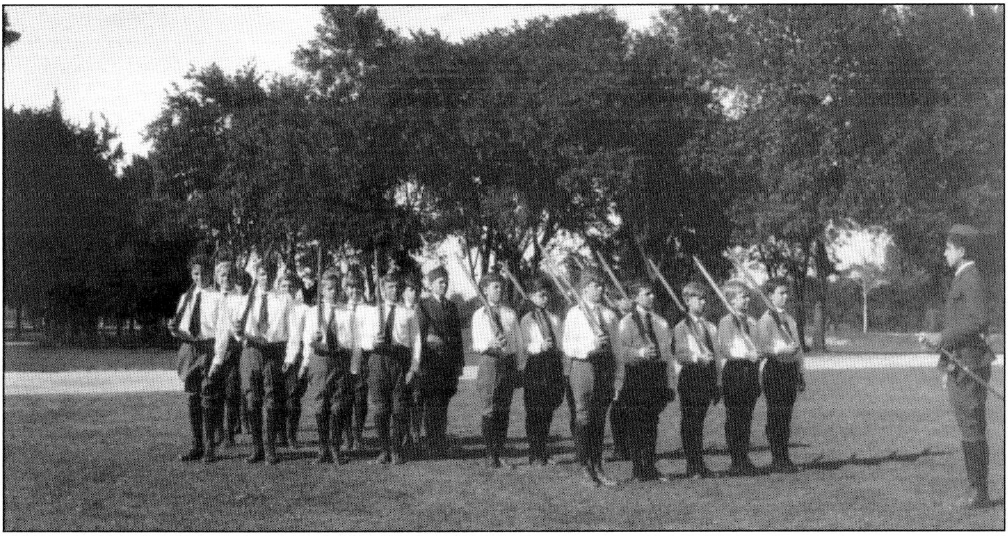

Military training began at the Glenwood School in 1892, with Francis Brady acting as drillmaster. Eventually, military contests were held between the different cottages. In 1927, Wallace Company won the day. (Courtesy of the Glenwood School for Boys and Girls.)

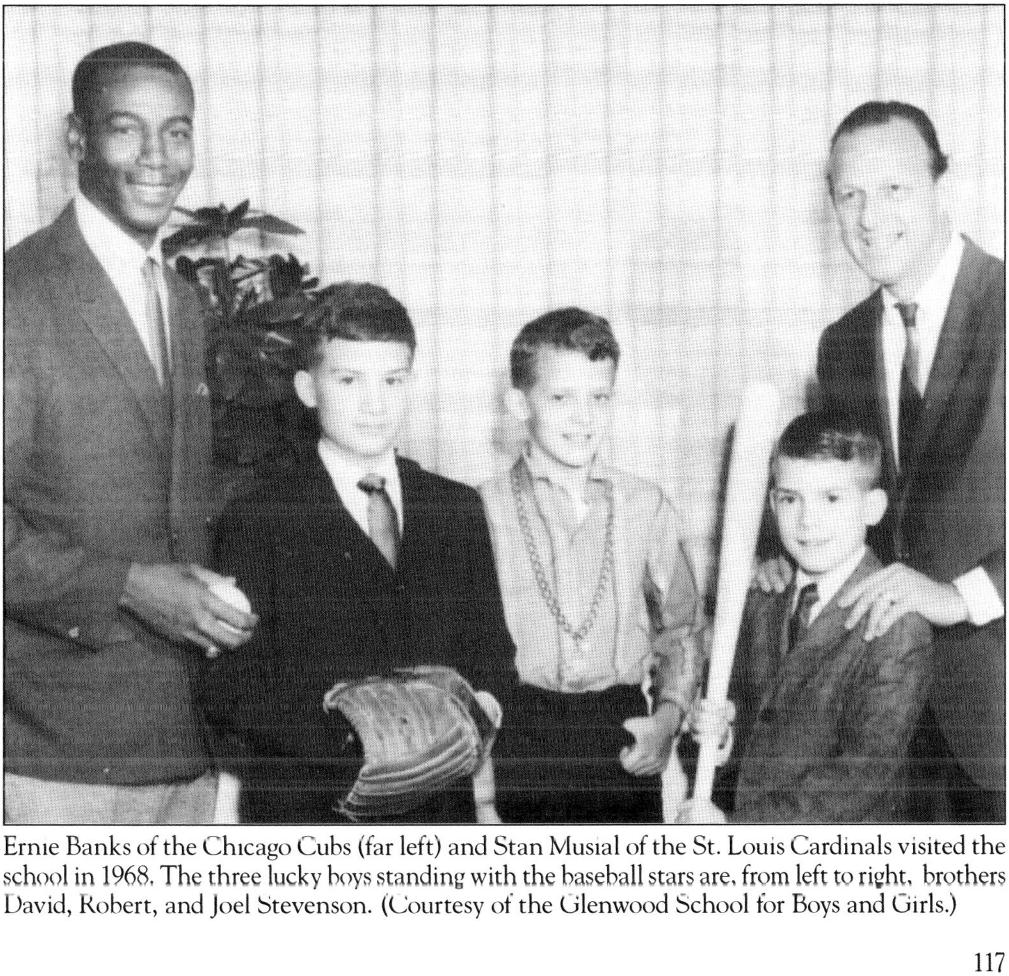

Ernie Banks of the Chicago Cubs (far left) and Stan Musial of the St. Louis Cardinals visited the school in 1968. The three lucky boys standing with the baseball stars are, from left to right, brothers David, Robert, and Joel Stevenson. (Courtesy of the Glenwood School for Boys and Girls.)

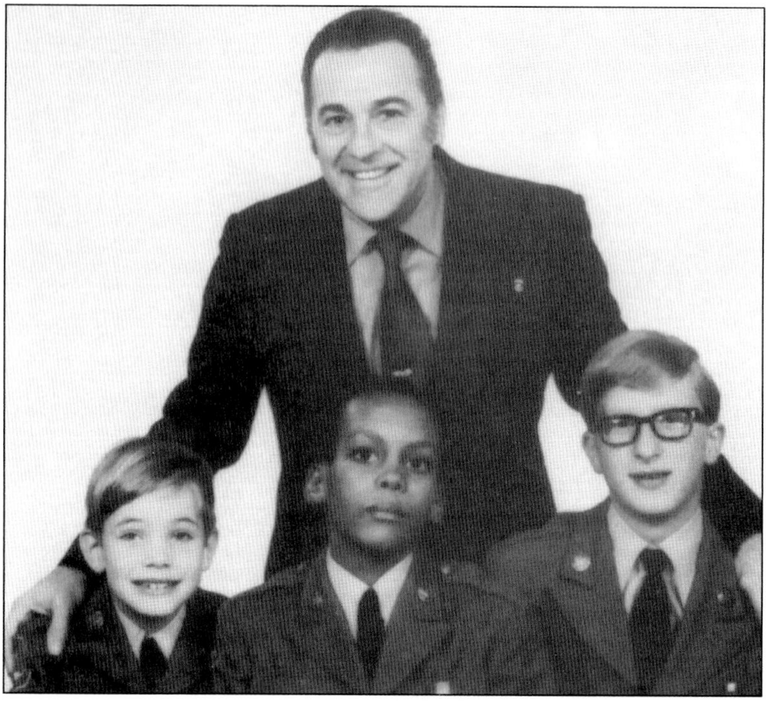

Local sports legend, Cubs broadcaster, and manager/shortstop of the 1948 World Series champion Cleveland Indians, Lou Boudreau was also an associate of Glenwood School for Boys. In 1973, he visited with, from left to right, James Evans, Billy Burke, and David Powell. (Courtesy of the Glenwood School for Boys and Girls.)

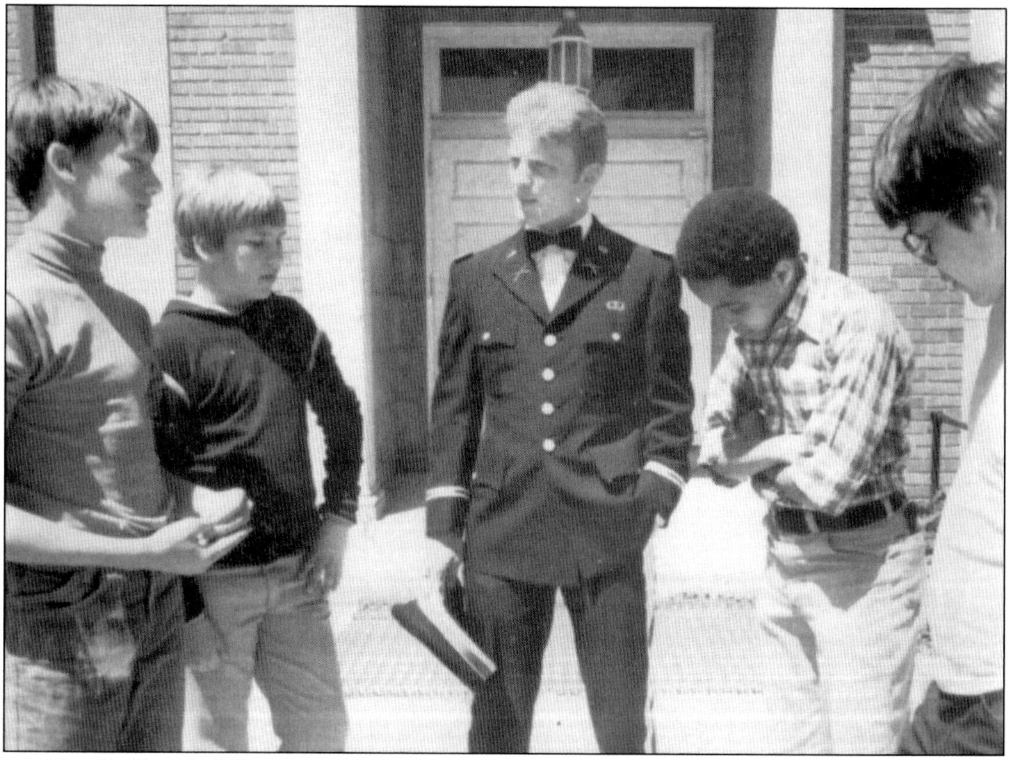

Lt. Alan Duff of the US Army talks with some Glenwood boys. Duff was the first Glenwood boy to be accepted to the United States Military Academy at West Point, New York. (Courtesy of the Glenwood School for Boys and Girls.)

Looking west, this is a bird's-eye view of the Glenwood School for Boys and Girls in 1983. (Courtesy of the Glenwood School for Boys and Girls.)

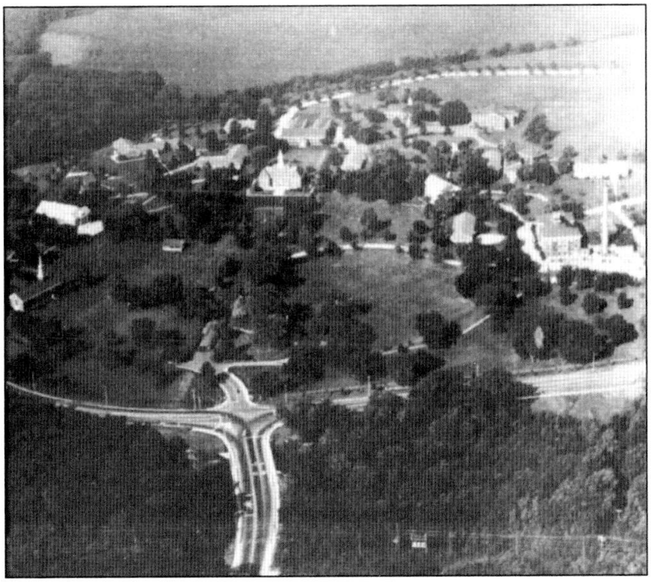

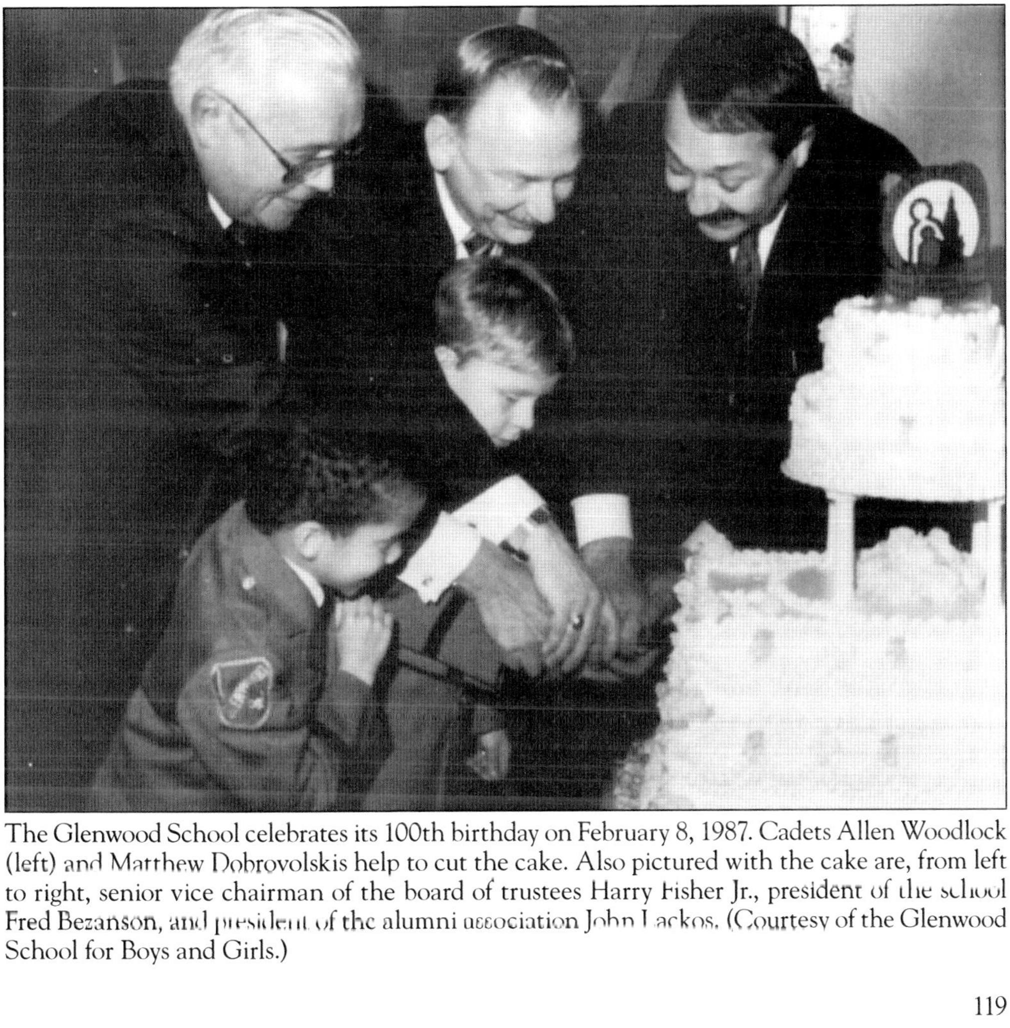

The Glenwood School celebrates its 100th birthday on February 8, 1987. Cadets Allen Woodlock (left) and Matthew Dobrovolskis help to cut the cake. Also pictured with the cake are, from left to right, senior vice chairman of the board of trustees Harry Fisher Jr., president of the school Fred Bezanson, and president of the alumni association John Lackos. (Courtesy of the Glenwood School for Boys and Girls.)

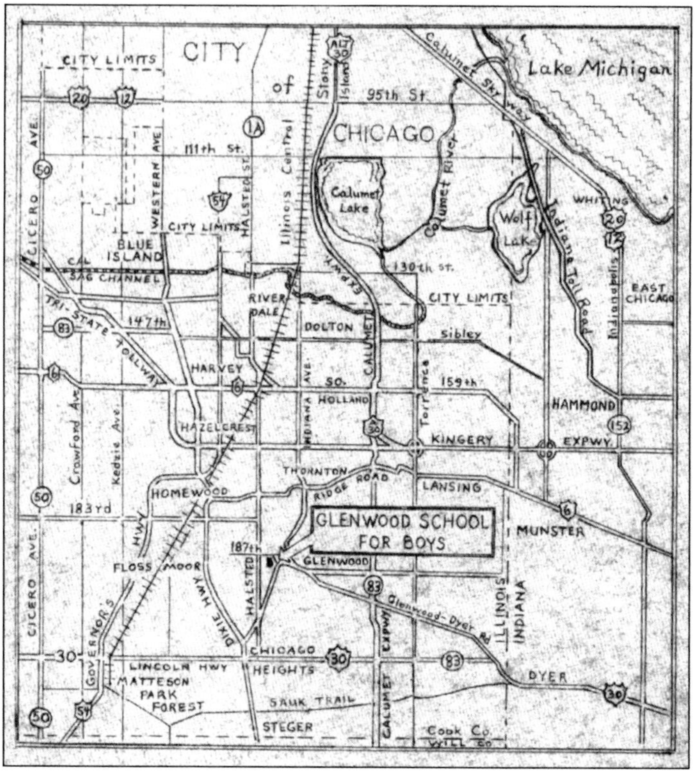

All roads lead to the Glenwood School for Boys (and now girls). (Courtesy of the Glenwood School for Boys and Girls.)

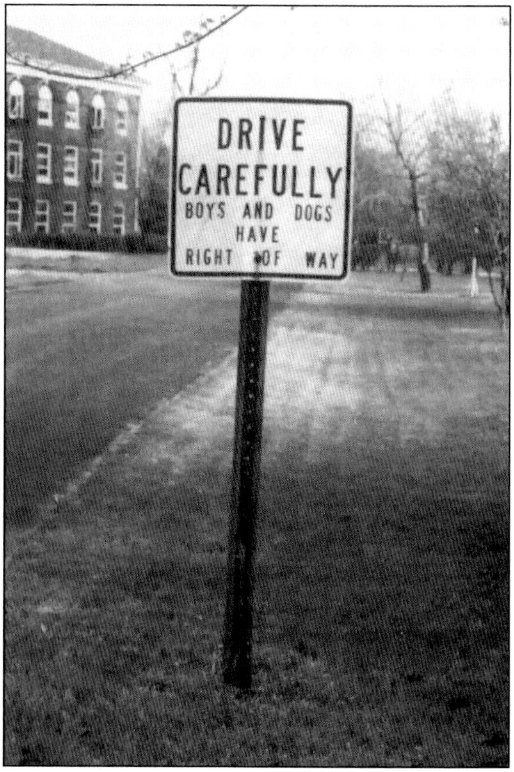

Pictured is an interesting traffic sign that once stood on the grounds of the Glenwood School. On June 10, 2003, Glenwood opened its first residential cottage for girls. (Courtesy of the Glenwood School for Boys and Girls.)

Four

Mount Glenwood Cemetery

Mount Glenwood Memory Gardens is located in the extreme northwestern part of the village of Glenwood at 18301 East Glenwood-Thornton Road. The story of the gardens begins in the summer of 1908. A man known as Mr. Patton—along with Dr. E.S. Miller, J.L. Parks, R.M. Leach, Jackson Gordon, and L.W. Dickerson—formed Mount Glenwood Memory Gardens. The *Chicago Defender* wrote on October 29, 1910, "The unrest and heavy heartedness of a washerwoman telling how she had to pay $50 for a grave and white people $25 stirred his very being. [Mr. Patton] decided to give them a chance the same as any other citizen." So, in a time not given to enlightenment, Mount Glenwood Memory Gardens became the first cemetery in the Chicago area where African Americans were buried.

"On Decoration Day, 300 people took a special C&EI train for Mount Glenwood Cemetery. The cemetery is a beautiful sight to behold. It is locked in, as it were, by the forest. At intervals, a train on the Chicago and Eastern Illinois Railway passes, making its appearance and disappearing as if on a stage," wrote the *Chicago Defender* in an article titled "Decoration Day at Mt. Glenwood" on June 4, 1910. At one time, trains would stop at Mount Glenwood Cemetery's gate. Weekend trains would bring families from Chicago to pay their respects to the dearly departed. Visitors would often make a day of it, and picnics at the cemetery were a common sight. A part of the train station entrance gate can still be seen at the back of the grounds. Several prominent African Americans are buried at Mount Glenwood, including Elijah Muhammed, who was once the leader of the Nation of Islam; Frederick Slater, who was Illinois' first African American circuit court judge and the first African American inducted in the NFL Hall of Fame; and Dr. Charles Gavin, the first African American to be admitted to the National College of Orthopedic Surgeons.

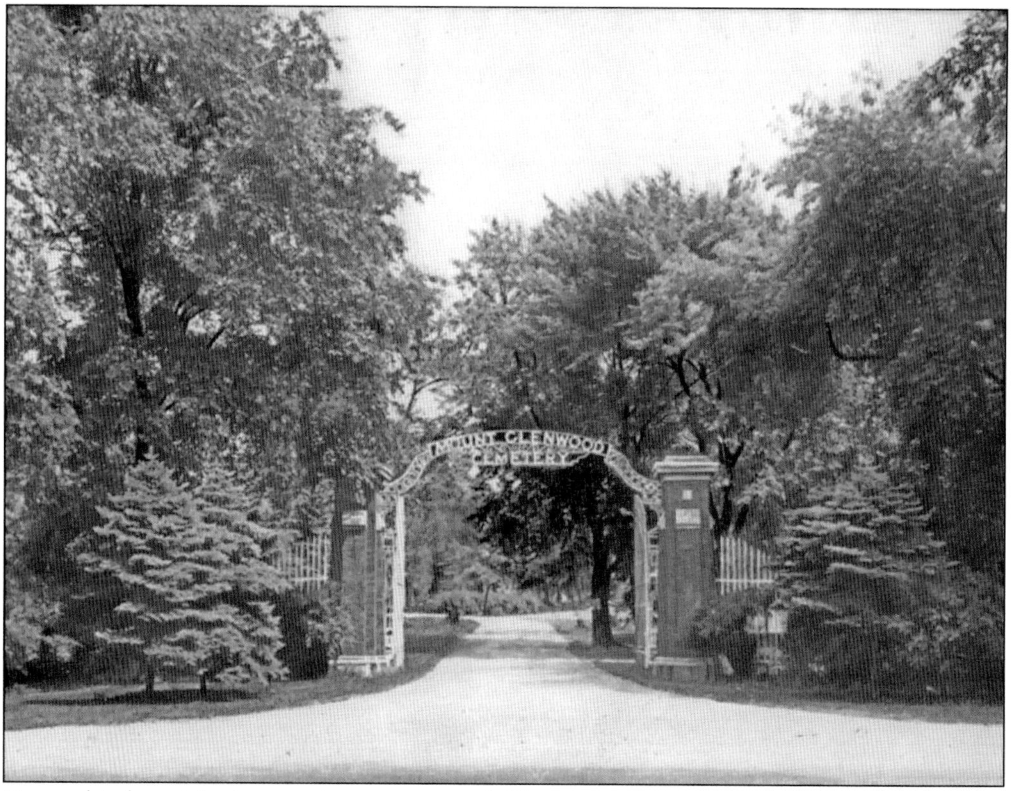

Pictured is the original gate as it once appeared. The entrance was located at the railroad tracks, at what is now the back of the cemetery. (Courtesy of Mount Glenwood Cemetery.)

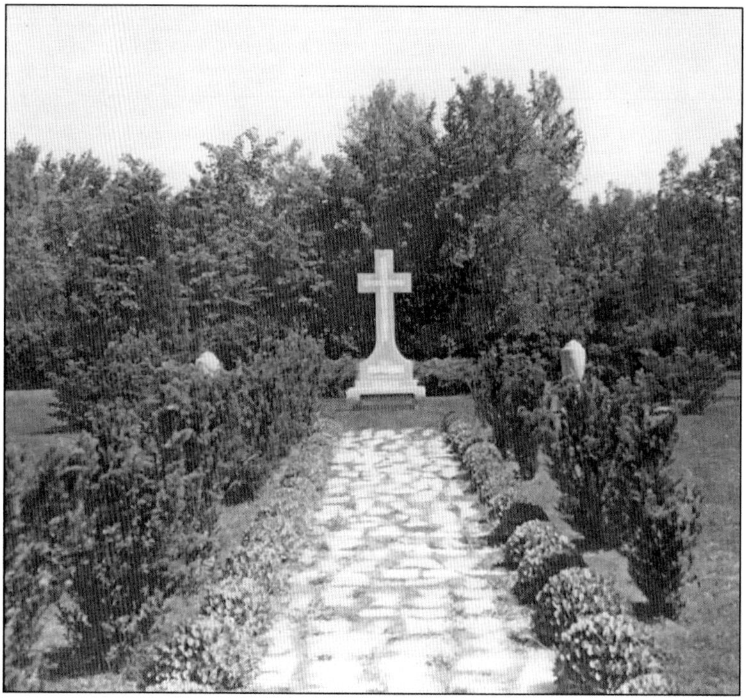

Mount Glenwood Memory Gardens founders were aware of the changing times and the need for equality in both life and death, thus, establishing one of the first racially integrated cemeteries. (Courtesy of Mount Glenwood Cemetery.)

Mount Glenwood Memory Gardens was the first cemetery in the Chicago area to serve African Americans. (Courtesy of Mount Glenwood Cemetery.)

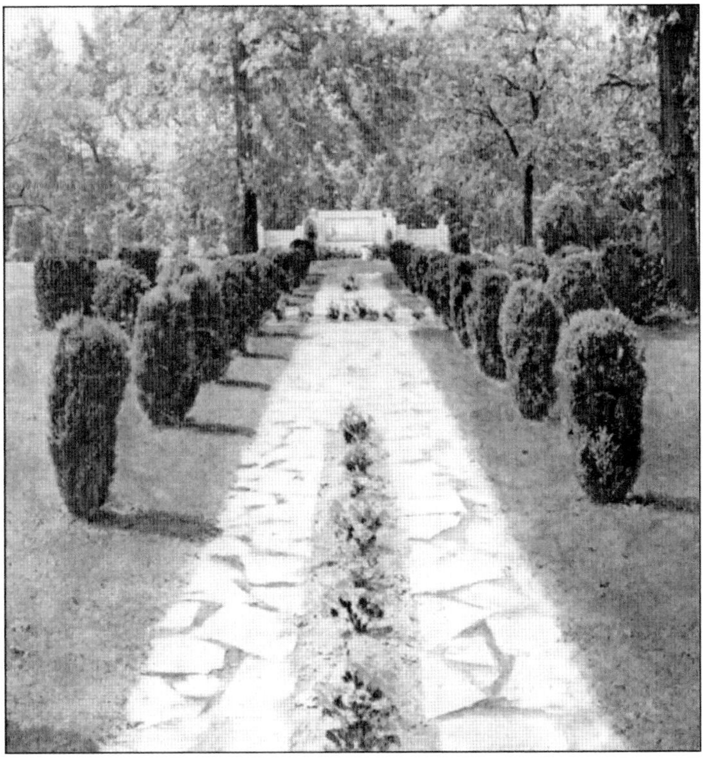

This is a pre-1950s photograph of Mount Glenwood Cemetery located at 18301 Glenwood-Thornton Road. (Courtesy of Mount Glenwood Cemetery.)

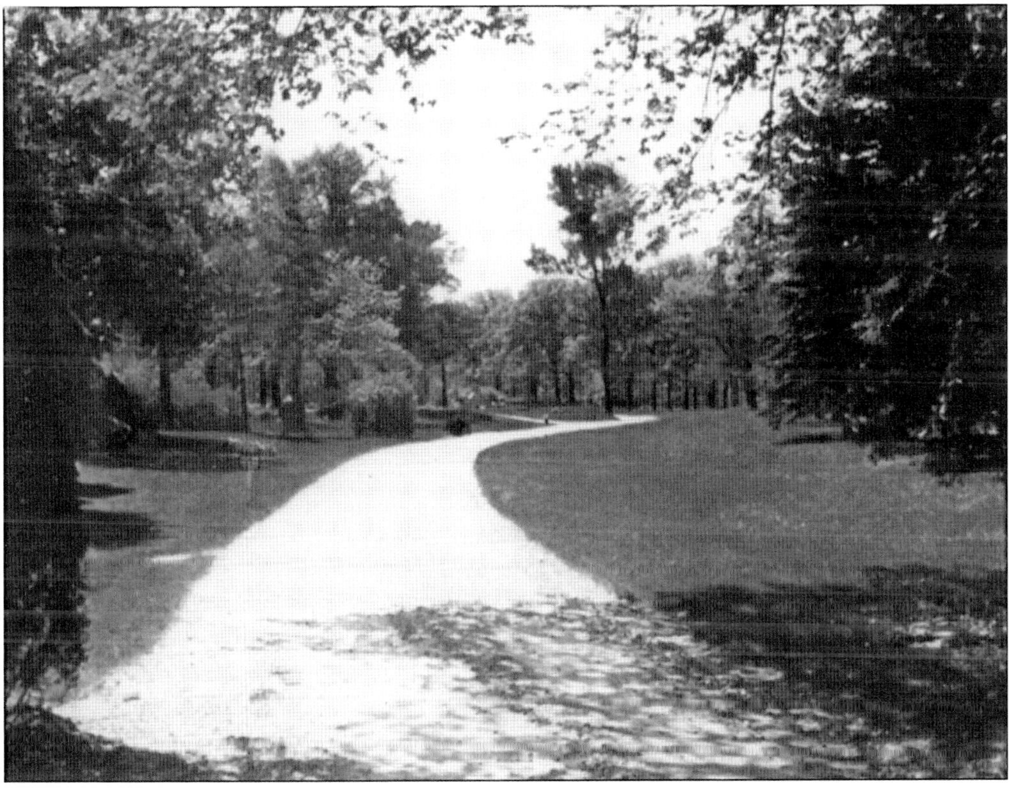

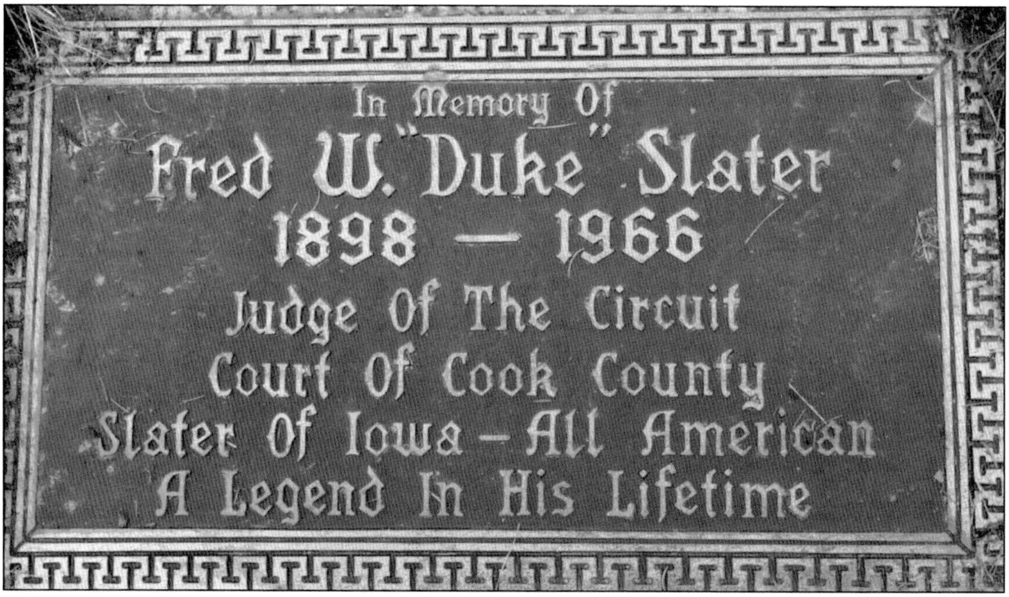

Frederick Wayman "Duke" Slater was Illinois's first African American circuit court judge and was also the first African American inducted in the NFL Hall of Fame. (Photograph by the author.)

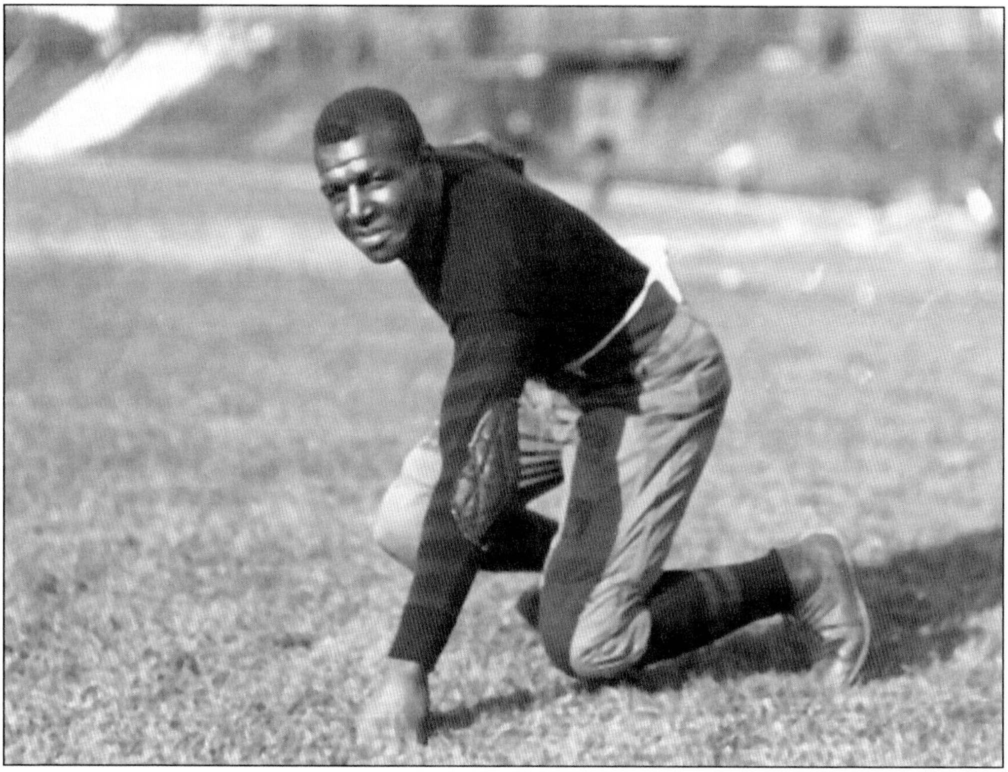

Duke Slater played for the University of Iowa. As a sophomore in 1919, Duke was an unanimous first-team All-Big Ten selection and a second-team All-American. During his senior year in 1921, he led Iowa to a perfect 7–0 record and its first Big Ten title in 21 years. Slater helped Iowa defeat Notre Dame 10–7 to snap a 20-game winning streak for the Irish. (Private collection.)

Marshall "Major" Taylor was born in Indiana on November 26, 1878. In the 1890s, he was said to be the world's fastest bicyclist. (Photograph by the author.)

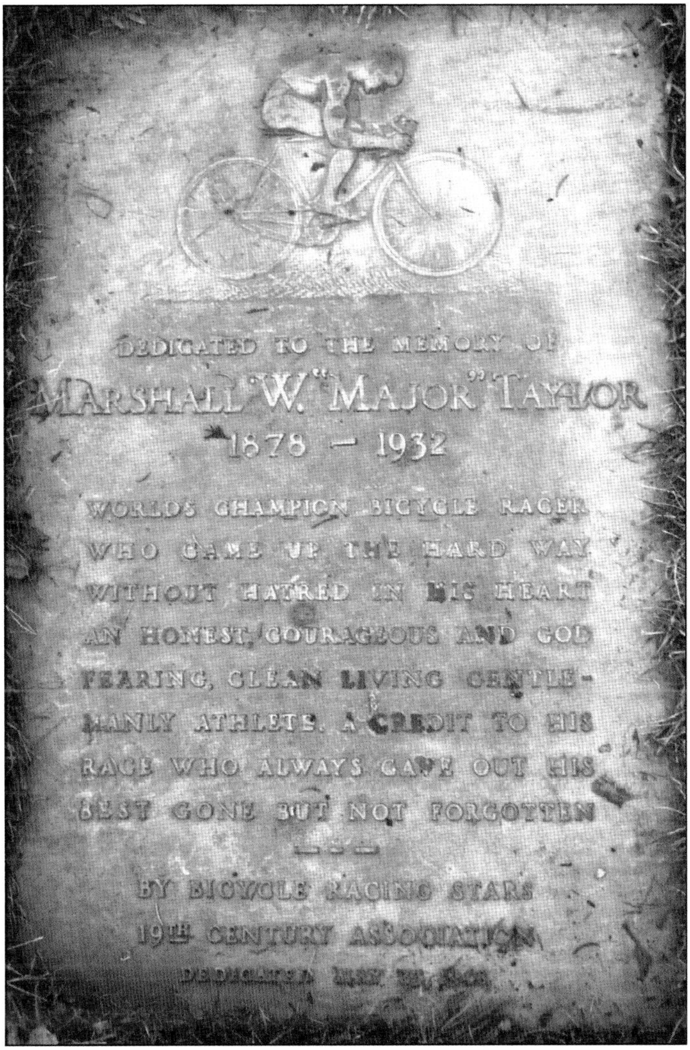

By 1898, Major Taylor was the holder of seven world records, including the one-mile paced standing start. He died on June 21, 1932, in the charity ward of Cook County Hospital in Chicago and was buried in an unmarked grave. In 1948, a group of former professional bike racers, with money donated by Schwinn Bicycle Company owner Frank Schwinn, had Taylor's remains exhumed and reburied in a more prominent part of Mount Glenwood Cemetery, near the grave of Duke Slater. (Courtesy of the Major Taylor Association.)

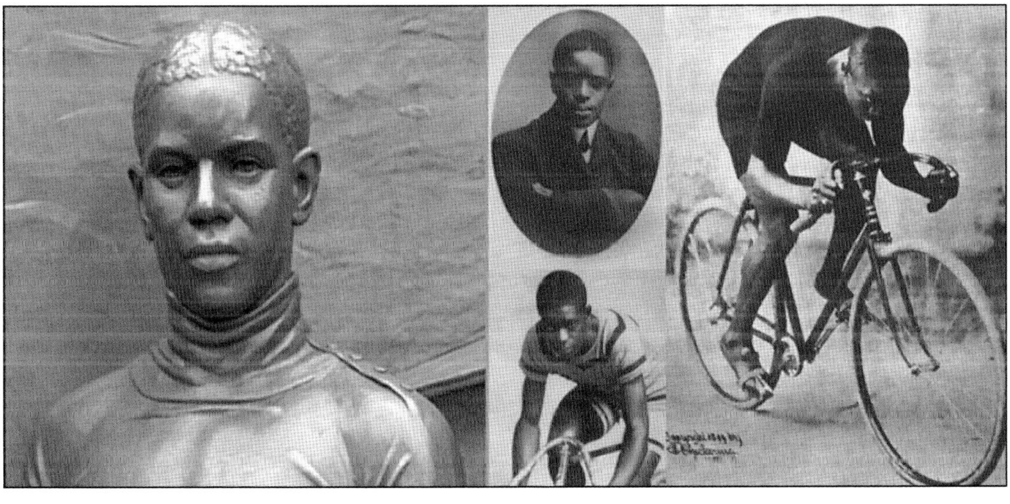

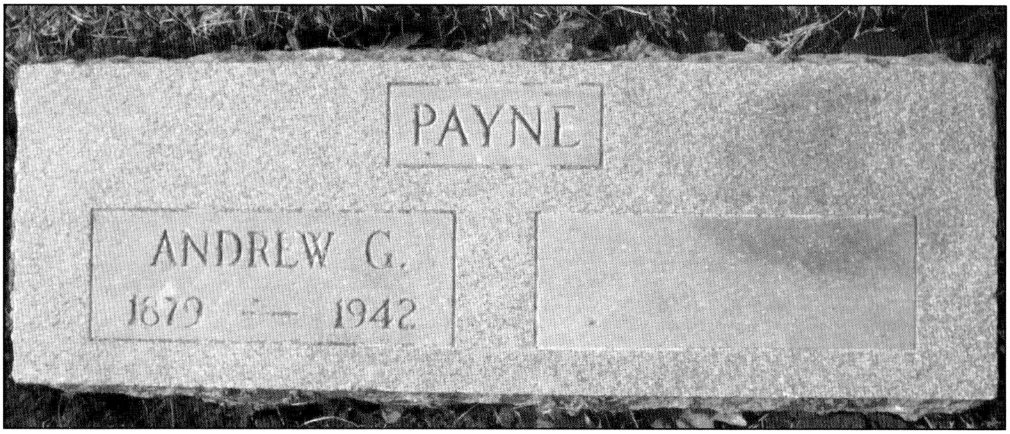

Andrew "Jap" Payne played in the Negro Baseball League. He was a member of the original Philadelphia Giants in 1902 and played both infield and outfield for various other teams until 1919. He is said to have been a good hitter with above average power. (Photograph by the author.)

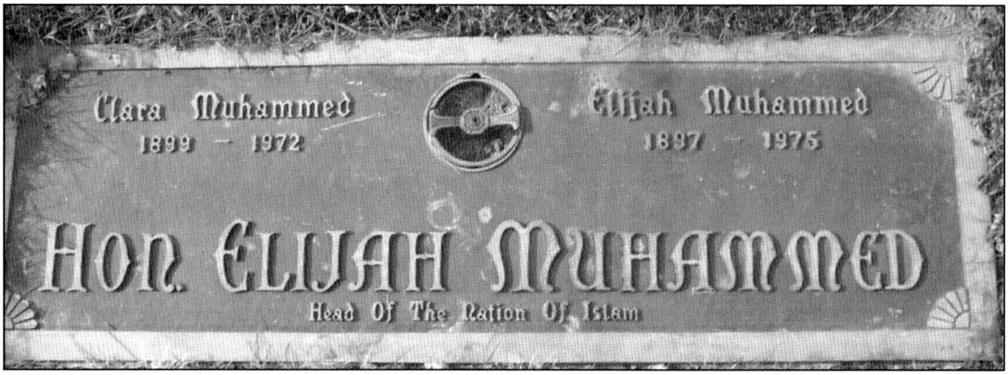

Elijah Muhammed was the leader of the Nation of Islam from 1934 until his death in 1975. He was born Elijah Robert Poole in Sandersville, Georgia, on October 7, 1897. On May 8, 1942, he was arrested for failure to register for the draft during World War II. He was found guilty and served four years at the federal correctional institution in Milan, Michigan. (Photograph by the author.)

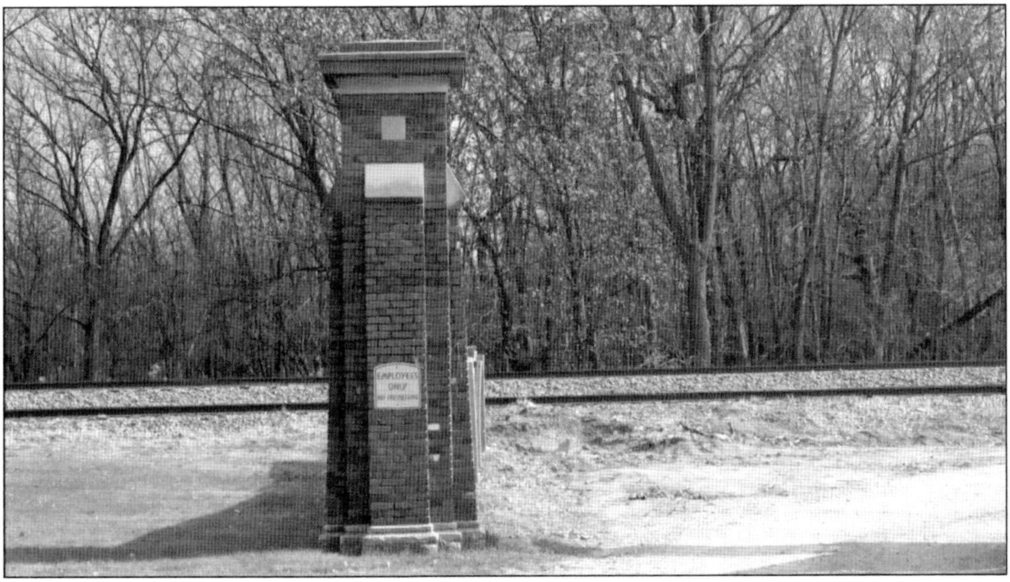

Part of the original gate is captured here as it appears today. Notice the railroad tracks that once brought visitors to the cemetery on the Chicago and Eastern Illinois Railway. (Photograph by the author.)

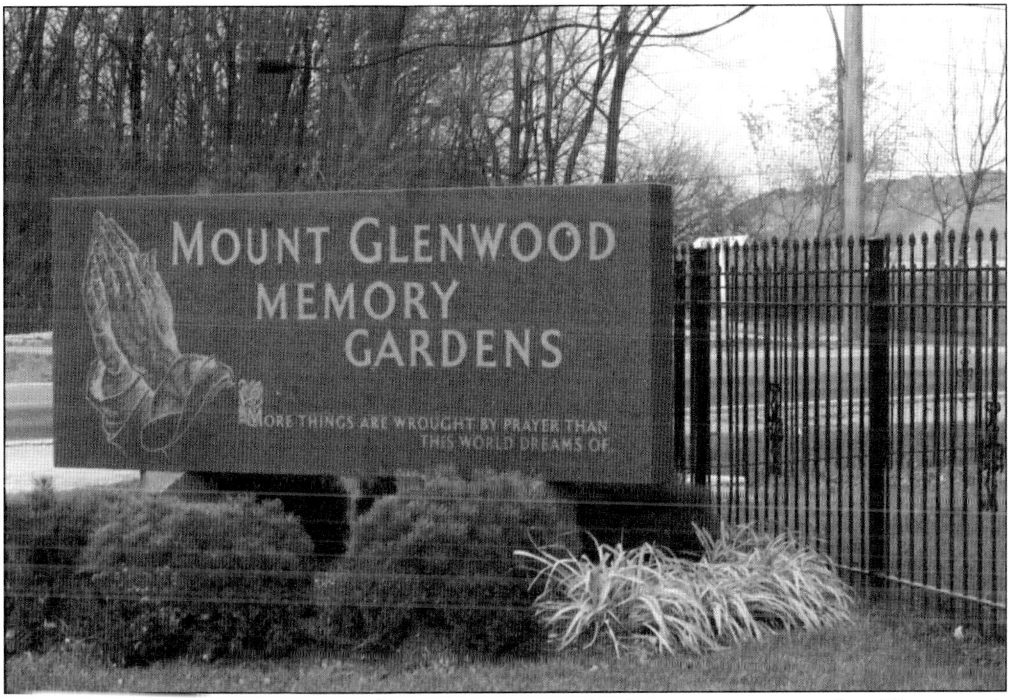

Pictured is the entrance to Mount Glenwood Memory Gardens as it appears today. (Photograph by the author.)